MW00643658

Introducing Emotional Concussions

What do I mean by an Emotional Concussion? What is it? An Emotional Concussion is an event or experience that has been disturbing or traumatic. The event or experience may have occurred at any time in your life, from birth to this precise moment. I prefer the term emotional concussion to trauma for the simple reason that it's easier to perceive and understand. A shift in perception leads to healing.

People have a visceral response to the word trauma. Individuals will respond to the word trauma based on their own personal experiences. Quite often I hear people excuse one of their own experiences as minor or trivial compared to someone else's event. Or, on the contrary, they tell me no one can understand the pain they have suffered. In my experiences it's all relative. Two people can share a similar event and one moves on with relative ease and the other watches their life fall apart. Why? Because our responses to these events are like making a soup from scratch. Look at it this way. Take a pot of hot water and every time someone has one of these events, we add an ingredient. For example, a disturbing event adds a pinch of pepper. A good experience, we add a vegetable, let's say a carrot. Each event adds another ingredient. Disturbing/traumatic events adds pepper or Cajun sauce and even turns up the heat a few degrees on the stove. Positive events add some spices and additional nutritious ingredients. Think of a nurturing home as mom or dad stirring the pot to keep the heat evenly distributed throughout. The more nurturing the more evenly the heat is distributed. So, doesn't it make sense why two people can share a similar experience and have a different reaction? Similar ingredients, different amounts, ratios and attention.

When I started using the term emotional concussion people seemed much more willing to accept this phrase to relate to their own experiences. Trauma sounds permanent, broken and damaged. A concussion can heal. A concussion is a temporary situation and we expect it to heal. The first thing I say to people when I meet with them is "there's nothing wrong with your mind", your mind has experienced some events and experiences that are having an effect on the way your mind is responding in the present. Our mind filters everything through these events and experiences before creating a response to what's happening now. Our subconscious mind is survival based and uses this technique to protect us from being hurt again. What do we know about this information being presented right now? Have we seen it, heard it, smelt it before? If so, what do we need to do based on what we know and have experienced.

As I explained in my first book, "You Must Be Out of Your Mind", some of these events have been recorded and stored in high resolution, high definition. The intensity of these pictures and sounds create an error message and the subconscious mind sees them in real time and creates a response in the present situation. Our subconscious mind believes there is something happening now and creates an emotion like fear or anger to create an action. The purpose of an emotion like fear is to escape a threat, the purpose of anger is to attack a threat. However, nothing is happening. It's an automatic response to protect you from something that isn't happening. That is a glitch, an error message. Make sense?

So now, if you've had a number of emotional concussions throughout your life this will affect how your mind responds in the present. These responses will have an effect on your success. This book discusses 10 things that successful people never do. If you do any of these then there's a reason why you do. An emotional concussion may be causing a particular behavior that may now be a habit. In the next ten chapters we'll examine ten such behaviors and help you develop an understanding of why you may be responding in this particular manner. What event created the emotional concussion? Let's start the healing!

Table of Contents

Tables and Figures

List of Tables

List of Figures

List of Abbreviations

FOMO	Fear of missing out
IPI	Inspired Performance Institute
TIPP	The Inspired Performance Program

Introducing the value of success

Let me ask you one question: *How do you define success?*

I know; it's a tough question to ask, more so a tougher question to answer. Ask that question to everyone you know, and you'll never know *what* or *how* they'll answer. Perhaps they will attempt to define with a sensible answer, only to come up short when they realize the way they've achieved success throughout their lives. Or the way they've defined success before is not the way that looks today—in other words, success is a fluid concept throughout their lives. Still, some believe that success shouldn't be the goal, but rather the journey towards the goal that matters. In essence, success as a term is subjective.

Like before, it's a tough question to ask, more so a tougher question to answer. For some, success means money—a mansion, a fleet of expensive cars, a corner office, and the lap of luxury. Or for a writer like Baker, as a child he believed that money meant respect and success (Baker D. , 2014). Others look at having the best gadgets and the most expensive trinkets that are fresh on the market. Smartphones, tablets, consoles and fashion accessories that will become obsolete in a week measure the (real or per-

1

ceived) influence of someone's success. Still, others believe success equals health, wellness, and spirituality, looking at becoming their best self through self-achievement and self-improvement. There's nothing wrong with finding ways to better ourselves, of course, but these can derail one's path to success if it loses direction and focus. How many people have wasted time, money, and resources trying to be successful, only to see all they've worked for fall apart? In essence, success is unmeasurable by any objective fashion.

Defining Success

But if success is neither definable or measurable, then why bother to try and seek a proper definition of success? Because, dear reader, "defining what success means to you is an important part of defining yourself as an individual" (White A., 2017). You'll have a deeper grasp of your identity without any pressure from others or yourself to keep up in the rat race. When you learn to define success in your terms, you won't' allow others to impose their vision of success on you (Baker D.C. 2014). You'll gain a deeper sense of satisfaction when you achieve success on your terms without succumbing to expectations imposed by others a tricky thing to pull off masterfully. Don't feel afraid nor pressured to look at how others define or measure success—not everything in the world is dependent on fame, wealth, or power. In fact, Gallegos (2017) defined success as "doing anything well, exceeding at something and that might be a lot of different activity" and "Success is being happy. Success is being fruitful."

Etymologically speaking, the word "success" comes from the Latin *sucesus*, meaning "an advance, a coming up; a good result [and] a happy outcome" ("Success"). This word is closely related to the Latin word for fortune, "fortuna," only differing on the word's perception: "'Success' is the result of an activity, and the 'fortuna' [is] a passive meditative expectation of the gain that will be granted" (Petryshyn). For Gitlin (2016), "success is following" a proposed goal, but he chided the fact that following blindly towards a goal is unappealing and uninspiring. I beg to differ: looking towards success can be an immensely rewarding and enriching experience, so long as you are prepared for the (very) bumpy ride ahead.

The Merriam-Webster dictionary defines success as a "favorable or desired outcome" or "the attainment of wealth, favor, or eminence", while the Oxford Living Dictionary looks at success as "the accomplishment of an aim or purpose" and "the attainment of fame, wealth, or social status" (Merriam-Webster; Oxford). Even if these definitions offer broad descriptions of what many consider to be *materially* successful, both definitions are severely limited in their scope and don't account for the many other ways people feel successful in life beyond fame, wealth, and power. These definitions aren't wrong in and of themselves; however, these are another reason to suggest that *you* must be the one responsible for defining success for yourself. Without it, you'll be in danger of exposing yourself to much undue resentment and frustration.

Paul Jun (2017) suggested that "the purpose of defining your own success is to start living a life based on your own expectations and terms" (par. 10). To define success, look at those things that make you feel happy and not necessarily wealthy or powerful. Maybe opening several businesses or achieving sales targets are out of your reach; something as simple as finishing a book draft, learning how to play an instrument like the piano or the guitar, or volunteering weekly at a local charitable organization are also valid markers of personal success. In fact, even making small steps towards a bigger goal, like saving a certain amount of money or investing, serve as important realistic steps for your success.

A State of Mind

If you ask me, I'll tell you that success is *a state of mind.* You see, I believe you can be a roaring success in many aspects of your life and miserable in others. Why? Because, to some, it would absolutely be true: for instance, I've known people who have had incredible financial fortunes, yet their home life is a mess. A friend of mine built a multi-million-dollar business, flew around in his private jet, and vacationed all around the world. However, the pressures of building his business led him to act out severe dysfunction through functional alcoholism (he was a happy drunk, the life of the party), generosity by being taken advantage of by his so-called friends, and anger outbursts to his family. How could he maintain this type of control in one situation and lose it in another? Quite simple—*survival*. You see, this man had to maintain control around his business life, even if his inner circle would face the wrath at times, yet they had no choice but to tolerate it. His family and career subordinates were hostages that had to suffer through his moods: When it was good it was great, and when it was bad it was worse. Then the charmer would arrive and smooth everyone's feathers. Knowing these circumstances, would you define this person as *successful*? There is no right or wrong answer; success is a matter of perspective. Some people would take his life in a heartbeat and others would want him to be broke and happy. In the end, it doesn't matter how successful you think he is since the grass is (not) always greener—what *does* matter is the attitude you take towards people's success.

At Home and At Work

A very wise man once told me, "The hardest line to walk is the line between success at home and success at work." I was thirty years old at the time and had a pretty good idea what he was talking about: I had three children, a beautiful wife, and a growing business. I traveled across the country working many long and late hours. I took note of his advice and made conscious attempts at walking the fine line. Travel plans were arranged around the kids' sports and school activities. Extending a trip to avoid making another one later was on par for the course. Since I was the boss, everyone accommodated my schedule towards my needs; if I had worked for someone else, that could've been impossible to accomplish.

Even executives I know who are making huge salaries don't have that kind of flexibility; for instance, I know of an associate who works for a billionaire that would be told to get on a plane at a moment's notice and meet his boss on his yacht in Dubai, with no idea how long or how much time he'd wait for his boss to show up for the meeting. Did I mention he was very well compensated? His children attended private schools. His wife drove any car she wanted. They lived on a lake. Would you define this person as successful? Or would you probably need more information before making a judgment? Or, perhaps, that's all you need to know: Financial success is more than enough, and the family can deal with the consequences as they see fit. I believe he's successful because, despite his erratic and unpredictable schedule, coupled with traveling halfway around the world at a moment's notice, he balances both his business and family life successfully. His only son loves spending time building things with him, and his wife is happy and successful in her career.

But let me ask you another question: How do you manage success? How do you keep building on your success when you've already achieved it?

How Success Affects You

Understanding how success affects you is crucial for your wellbeing. As Cardone (2011) said about the virtues of success,

> Success provides confidence, security, a sense of
> well-being, the ability to contribute at a greater
> level, hope, and leadership. Without success, you,
> the group, your company, your goals, dreams, and
> even entire civilizations cease to exist (par. 4).

Equating the lack of success and the destruction of civilization sounds extreme and far-fetched at first glance, but the value of success in our lives is undeniable. By understanding the role of success and the exposed reality within, you'll feel free to achieve your dreams and strive towards peak performance. Success shouldn't be completely focused on materialism, wealth, or unrestrained ambition, for these are self-defeating, disingenuous, and ephemeral at best. Instead, true success values wholeness in every dimension, including the physical, the spiritual, and the psychological (Herriot).

Another unorthodox measure of success is culture, as proposed by Lehmann (2015); in his perspective, admiring the arts, literature, mysticism, and spirituality created in the world are "moments that are very special and that touch the soul", enriching one's life beyond one's bank account" (par. 10). Connors (2016) offered a similar approach to success: "Success is an attitude. Success requires maximum effort. It is peace of mind" (par. 4). In Connor's case, the author's "positive attitude," life enjoyment, family, and fulfilling dreams served as proof of his success (2016, par. 14). As you see, there's no one aim of success—it's on you to figure out what's appropriate.

Is Happiness Success?

So, can someone be broke, and happy, *and* successful? Absolutely—because success is a matter of perspective. In 2010, I made a business trip to Colombia and saw something that made a lasting impression on me. As I drove back to the airport, I saw miles and miles of disintegrating houses that by most definitions would seem uninhabitable. You could describe them as shacks or huts that would be falling apart to my very own eyes. I wondered what kind of life could this be for the people who live in these conditions. And then I saw it, women at their front doors, sweeping outside the entrance, cleaning the dirt in the front of what I considered was a porch. I thought to myself, *what possessed these women to do this?* Amazing! The one thing that was obvious is they had not given up, maybe they were happy. Maybe they wanted to feel a sense of pride in taking care of their children. They never dwelled on their poverty. They were happy with what they have achieved. If they never had more, then they might see themselves as successful because they could feed their children and provide a clean home.

I also remembered a story that Donald Trump said when he was severely indebted due to his real estate holdings. As he exited the building with his wife, he turned to her and said something to the fact, as he pointed to a janitor, "That guy is richer than me if he has ten bucks in his wallet:" His liabilities exceeded his assets, and if you measured success only by money, the janitor was definitely more successful. As we now know, time—and a healthy perspective can change everything.

Schuster, Fösterlung, and Weiner (1989) conducted a study to determine the causal dimensions that determine success and failure, and determined four: the *locus*, or the location of an

9

internal or external cause; the *stable*, or the causes as constant or variable over time; the *controllability*, or personal responsibility with or without subjection to "volitional influence", and *globality*, or cross-cultural generality. In this study, these causal dimensions were determined to change drastically according to culture; as a result, even among cultures, there are wildly different definitions of success. For instance, "An American might perceive aptitude as an *internal* [emphasis added] cause of success, whereas in Eastern culture high aptitude might be considered a divine art and thus perceived as an *external* [emphasis added] cause" (p. 197).

Figure 1: Causal Determinants of Success.

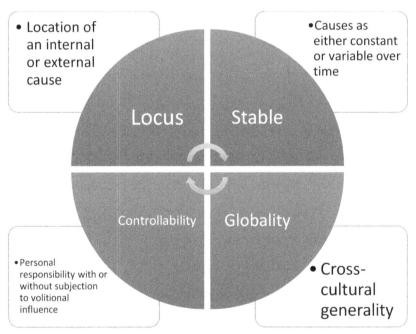

Note: Adapted from "Perceiving the causes of success and failure: A cross-cultural examination of attributional concepts," by B. Shuster, F. Fösterlung, & B. Weiner, 1989, *Harvard Business Review*, p. 191-213.

Likewise, Torres (2009) analyzed various traits held by acculturated first- or second-generation Latinos to reveal that successful Latinos have "effective cultural navigators when they establish realistic goals, a plan to accomplish the goals, and a desire to overcome potentially difficult circumstances" (p. 586). In another study comparing visions of success between people with East Asian and European American heritage, European Americans would favor "being a big fish in a small pond"—a relation to our individualistic culture—, while the Chinese prefer being a small fish in a bigger, albeit more impressive, pond, emphasizing China's collectivist culture (Werber, 2017; Seaton, Marsh, and Craven, 2009).

You see, there's not just one definition of success that you're forced to abide by Some make their lists and stick to it as time goes on. Others prefer a more spontaneous approach. However, you prefer to reach your goals and succeed in whatever enterprise you desire, the Inspired Performance Program (TIPP) is here to lead the way. We don't coach, nor do we attempt to tell you what or how to be successful in a very unrealistic amount of time. Instead, we want to clear the glitches and error messages you may have carried from your past. These negative events have created many self-imposed expectations that only hinder your peak performance today. You don't need experiences that only hold you back—it's time to empower yourself and lead to succeed!

The Values of Success

Today, there's a shift in the values that define personal success—and that's a very good prospect of culture. In a 2014 survey undertaken through a collaboration between Ipsos and Strayer University, 67% of respondents believed success was possible through "achieving personal goals"; 66% said "good relationships with friends and family"; 60% said "loving what you do for a living", and only one in five equated money with success (Smith, 2014). With this shift in priorities, Dr. Michael Platter, president of Strayer University, believed that Americans are "finding that multiple paths of success do exist" beyond monetary means and are also learning how to develop other priorities besides material wealth (Smith, 2014).

Shana Lebowitz authored an article in Business Insider in March of 2017 where she highlighted what success meant to 12 highly successful people. For example, Richard Branson, who has a net worth of 5 billion dollars says, *"Too many people measure how successful they are by how much money they make or the people that they associate with,"* he wrote on LinkedIn. *"In my opinion, true success should be measured by how happy you are."* Are you like me? When I read something like that, I think if I had 5 billion dollars I'd be pretty happy too. However, what I do know is that money truly can't buy happiness and that is exactly Richard's point. You need to feel fulfilled. That is not because of money, but rather what you do with the money. See the difference? If you just accumulate money and do nothing but buy things, chances are you will not feel fulfilled and that would result in a feeling of dissatisfaction. (Branson, 2016, par. 2).

From the same article, Maya Angelou's take on success is among the best: *"Success is liking yourself, liking what you do, and liking how you do it."*

Likewise, Bill Gates believes success is about building relationships and leaving behind a legacy by adding something valuable to contribute to making a difference in the world by "inventing something or raising kids or helping people in need" (Clifford, 2017). Bill Gates is a very wealthy man with a net worth of about $86 billion dollars. The inventor Thomas Edison defined success as 1% inspiration and 99% perspiration. Mr. Edison held over 1,000 patents and was a tireless worker. Billionaire Mark Cuban stated in an interview with Steiner Sports, *"to me the definition of success is waking up in the morning with a smile on your face, knowing it's going to be a great day. I was happy and felt like I was successful when I was poor, living six guys in a three-bedroom apartment, sleeping on the floor."* So, as you can see, there are many different ways to measure success and also look at what the definition of success means to you. It is a personal choice; no one else can define what success is for you. You set the terms and limits, and once you figure that out, you can then focus on your goals.

So, is the opposite of success failure? A little later in this book we will examine how successful people deal with it. One thing I can definitely tell you is that success is not an accident. This book was written to highlight not what successful people do, but rather the things that they don't do. They have specific processes, habits, philosophies, and behaviors. To be successful, you need to understand how and why successful people do what they do and how they are defined by their actions and how they live their life.

Leading a Successful Life

There are some basics involved in leading a successful life, and you don't need to possess all of these, but certainly need to have some of these basics:

- First, it helps if you have some purpose and meaning, spiritual health, having a positive impact on other people's lives.

- Second, having social health, with relationships that are positive, interacting with friends and people that you love and trust. Social interaction is very important, and it would be difficult to achieve success without having some measure of social wellbeing.

- Third, having emotional health, feeling good about yourself and having a good, positive self-image.

- Also, physical health is important, but not mandatory. Being physically healthy makes life easier, at least a baseline of health.

- Being mentally fit is beneficial, reading books keeping your mind sharp. Taking action by putting your ideas to work, setting clear and defined goals and then reaching those goals.

- And of course, what most people assume goes hand in hand with success, material wealth at some level. Anybody who defines themselves as successful has at least one or more of these common traits.

Figure 2: Values of Health.

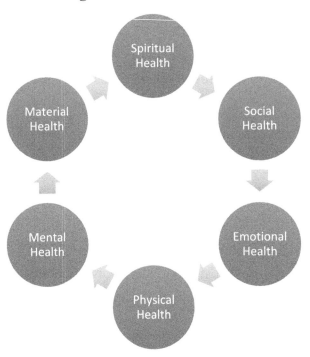

That being said, one must properly evaluate how the "emotional conflicts" on the road to career success, such as "questioning the value" and the price you pay for belonging to your company, is worth the success you're accruing today (LaBier, 2012). For this reason, it's important to evaluate how successful you are in your career against your perceptions. If not, as a high achiever you will be suffering in "well-paid silence" while sacrificing your dreams (Anderson & Baron, 2015).

Even while searching for ways to achieve career success, or "the real or perceived achievements individuals have accumulated as a result of their work experiences," can become invaluable tools to measure one's satisfaction (Judge et al., 1999). Career success can be *extrinsic*, where any measures are objective and observable, like pay rates and promotions; or *intrinsic*, where subjective reactions to career are present, like job satisfaction or achieving a work-life balance (Judge et al., 1999). In order to address success, one must first engage in proactive behavior which, according to Grant, "tak[es] initiative" and "challenge[s] the status quo" by making the best of their circumstances (quoted, in Seibert, Kraimer, & Crant, 2001). More so, a proactive personality involves influences "unconstrained" by such circumstances and, in turn, transform their actions into career success (p. 847). For instance, a study on student achievement revealed that "pupils tended to attribute success mainly to external causes and failure mainly to internal causes" (Bar-Tal & Darom, 1979). That being said, what does personal success and career success have in common?

For psychologist Angela Duckworth, successful characters share two important traits: *grit*, or "the tendency to stick with long-term goals"; and *self-control*, or the ability to "defer gratification and plan for the future" (Reeves, Venator, & Howard, 2014). In a Brookings Institute report on character traits, these measures were

17

evaluated as *drive* and *prudence* (p. 5,6). People with drive are industrious and resilient, and prudent people know how to "plan for the future" and achieve their goals with purpose (p. 6). As a result, people with a strong sense of drive are more likely to complete a degree despite growing college enrollment and have a greater chance of income mobility, while people who are able to successfully delay gratification have higher school achievement and exhibit healthier behavior (pp. 6-8). In the end, the ability for both drive and prudence to contribute to success is undeniable, as developing these traits "contribute to higher earnings, more education, better health outcomes and less criminal behavior" (p. 9).

Success even differs within genders—while "women highlight the importance of balance and relationships," men attribute their value to "material success" (Dyke & Murphy, 2006). In addition, women care for "professional achievement and personal relationships" as men "compartmentalize corners," oftentimes choosing one over the sake of the other (p. 366, 377). However, perceptions of success between genders are much more nuanced and often erroneous. For instance, Bentley University's Preparedness Study has revealed that seven in ten respondents and 63% of women believe that "men are better suited to succeed in business" even if 9 in 10 women who pursue business careers are seen as "generally successful" and 80% believe women "could be more prepared to 'have it all'" (Schlitzer). In the grand scheme of things, gender barely matters: research undertaken by Vanderbilt University on the future prospects of gifted children revealed that both men and women "have gone on to generate creative contributions, become leaders in their profession, earn high incomes, and be pleased with the quality of their lives (Kiesel, 2015).

In the study, gifted men would become CEOS or work as STEM (science, technology, engineering, math) employees, while women would work in education, healthcare, or become homemakers; at the same time, men would work in high-level careers that often required 50 or more weekly hours"—and were willing to work even more if it would further their careers—, women valued more flexibility through part-time work (Kiesel, 2015). In reality, how men and women define success barely differs from one another, and are only secondary to the true value of success: "Instead of being impressed by how much money or power we have in our professional life, we should focus on whether our work is an expression of kindness and justice" (Akhavan, 2015/2016). For this reason, success can't be measured by material things, but by how many lives were impacted because of your actions (Mueller, S. 2017). Successful people leave an important legacy in their wake.

It goes without saying that happy people are successful. Lyubumorsky, King, and Diener (2005) revealed that individuals experiencing "a positive mood or emotion" have greater opportunities to improve their relationships, build their skills, and enjoy greater levels of relaxation after "expending more high levels of effort than others" (p. 804). Likewise, positivity correlates with "resources and characteristics that parallel success and thinking" (p. 846). More so, Stahl (2016) attributed five important traits of successful people: risk-taking; hard work; willingness to admit their wrongs; adaptability; and delegation. You'll read of these traits later, but for now, it's important to know there are many ways to guarantee success. Look at this example (Praveen, 2017):

> Success is when you are able to act as per your views and beliefs. It is when your heart and mind are in coordination. It is when you do what you love and love what you do. Success is not a magical status, but rather an act of living peacefully and successfully.

In other terms, when your mind is free from glitches and error messages, you can replace your negative thoughts with positive ones, and you invite optimism into your personal and professional life, you'll enjoy unparalleled levels of success. Even if a positive outcome isn't guaranteed, successful people recognize that any attempt to achieve success is "worth the effort" regardless of the outcome (Hurd, 2014). That is why simple things such as remembering your proudest achievements (not the ones society attributes to) and creating small objectives that would reform your goals are very important to determine the value of success (Frost, n.d.). As Lanthier (2016) stated, "be sure to remember that we all have our strengths and gifts in your life. Your purpose is to give it away […] You want to be in that tiny space where passion, vocation, and profession meet" (p. 14)—and those are the values that will guide you towards ultimate success.

#1. Procrastinate

Time is more valuable than money. Successful people know this, and make decisions clearly and quickly.

Putting Things Off

Do you put things off for later when they could be done today? Sometimes you genuinely forget about washing the dirty dishes or taking out the trash. It happens to everybody—it's something that you shouldn't worry about. However, if you *deliberately* and *repeatedly* avoid things because they feel unpleasant to do or you feel afraid that anything could go wrong, then you may be struggling with procrastination. You see, when you procrastinate, you sacrifice your time and effort for your convenience and productivity. However, procrastination is not an emotion, but rather the consequences of something (you believe) needs to be avoided. So, how do you avoid procrastination in order to become successful?

Conventional wisdom on procrastination often goes like this: "Don't procrastinate!" Such advice is short, sweet, and to the point, but there are many problems with this advice: first, you can't tell someone how *not* to procrastinate *without* giving them the proper tools to bring about change. Second, people won't commit to an action when commanded or to—unless they're facing a life-or-death situation. Telling a procrastinator not to procrastinate renders the same effect as if you told a baker not to bake a cake or a writer not to write—none. People choose to commit to change out of their own volition, and in order to take advantage of it, you must allow them to make a choice. In the case of procrastination, do you choose to complete a portion of a project now when you have ample time to freely revise any portion of it, or later when the deadline is fast approaching and you are pressed for both time and opportunity? Finally, and most importantly, the subconscious mind cannot understand negation.

In order to understand this concept, allow me to relate this thought about procrastination: "[…] procrastination, in psychological terms, is when the value of doing *something else* [emphasis added] outweighs the value of working *now* [emphasis added]" (Berkman, 2015, par. 6). Thus, forcing yourself to *not* procrastinate without a direction to focus on is meaningless. There are many variables to consider when making a decision such as eliminating procrastination; for instance, what are the benefits of procrastinating now against the consequences of procrastinating later? The subconscious mind's lack of understanding negation does not mean that it readily ignores the "negative desire statements"; instead, it attempts to focus on a feeling to create its visual imagery (Yates, n.d., par. 21). The subconscious does not care for any type of positive or negative loaded language; for the subconscious, "language is merely a series of signals" that only come to your attention when necessary (La Vertu, 2017). For this reason, conventional yet vacuous strategies to address procrastination won't work.

The Purpose of Procrastination

Believe it or not, procrastination is serving a purpose, even if it isn't beneficial. However, your subconscious mind is most likely trying to protect you from something. There may have been an event or experience at some time in your life that created the use of procrastination. Your mind is reviewing the old data about the event and distracting you from experiencing the same or similar result. It's an error message, and the Inspired Performance Program (tIPP) process can help correct this error message for you. As you go through the program, you may not remember the event, but, believe me, there's a reason for the procrastination.

At times, everyone puts things off until the last minute. However, chronic procrastinators are avoiding difficult tasks and deliberately looking for distractions. In most cases, this reflects a struggle with self-control. How often have you heard a procrastinator say that they perform better under pressure? Once you look at it, it's simply a way to rationalize their behavior. The pursuit of perfection is very common among procrastinators. Why? Because psychologically, it's more acceptable never to do

24

something than to face the possibility of falling short and not performing at your best. So, you see, procrastination has a purpose in this scenario. Chances are there have been experiences that created this strive for perfection. Perhaps a demanding parent or teacher. Now, I have to add a disclaimer here. It's not always the parent's fault. Here's what I mean. A young child may misinterpret what a parent's intentions are. For example, the parent, with all the best of intentions, says to a child, "I know you can do better, bring that B up to an A." Seems pretty innocuous, right? Not to the mind of a young child trying to be accepted and loved. The child's mind will perceive that they need to make it better and where does that stop. A child doesn't have enough life experience to interpret or understand the nuances of their parent's intentions. So now, if they continue to meet with this at other times in their life, they might develop a fear of not performing up to the standards. So, what is the answer, avoidance? That way no one will notice that they may have possibly failed. This belief is formed in the subconscious survival mind. In order to perform at your highest level, this error message needs to be updated. That is exactly what the Inspired Performance Program does.

What is procrastination?

Lay (1986) defined procrastination as "the tendency to postpone that which is necessary to reach some goal" (p. 442). This concept makes procrastination look like a self-imposed roadblock of sorts hindering the way towards a goal. On the other hand, Steel (2007) argued that "to procrastinate is to voluntarily delay an intended course of action despite expecting to be worse off for the delay" (p. 66). According to this definition, a procrastinator knows that the action is not beneficial to them in the long run, but continues to do so out of fear or habit. As Fisman (2008). Stated, "We tend to put too much weight on the here and now when evaluating the costs and benefits of action (or inaction), and this seamlessly flows into other aspects of life (p. 2). Still, Chu and Choi (2005) have defined procrastination as "the lack or absence of self-regulated performance and the behavioral tendency to postpone what is necessary to reach a goal" (p. 245). The authors' study also considered the societal implications of procrastination by looking at how procrastinators are stereotyped and socially depicted as "lazy and self-indulgent individuals who are unable to self-regulate". While procrastination is "associated with high efficiency, productivity, and superior performance" for "organized and highly motivated individuals" (p. 245). Naturally, comparing procrastinators to more industrious individuals does no favors, and only entrenches procrastinators' behavior. But, at the same time, these scholarly definitions serve as important benchmarks over what is valued in industriousness against procrastination.

Etymologically speaking, procrastination entered the English language lexicon in the 1490s and was derived from the Middle French word *procrastination*, itself derived from the Latin *procrastinationem*, meaning "a putting off from day to day"; the word itself is derived in two: the prefix *pro*, meaning "forward", and *crastinus*, or "belonging to tomorrow" (Harper, 2017). In essence, to procrastinate is to delay or defer an action for tomorrow—which makes it conscious and within our control. This attitude is much what the Greeks called *akrasia*, or "the state of acting against your better judgment [...] when you do one thing even though you know should do something else" (Clear, 2017, par. 6). Also known as "weakness of will," *akrasia* has less to do with our inherent ability to perform or commit to a project, but rather with our ability to honor that commitment against other influences that hamper our decision-making. In a 2008 study, an example of *akrasia* exhibited the following structure: "You hold a certain judgment about what you think is worthwhile doing, but ultimately you do something else or nothing at all" (Kalis, Mojzisch, Schweizer, & Kaiser, 2008, p. 402). Procrastination isn't simply about the ignorance of the expected time needed to complete a task and the actual amount needed to complete it. This is known as the "planning fallacy," where individuals underestimate a task's duration and are often "simplified" when working in teams (Moss, 2016). In many cases, individuals disregard the necessary amount of time to complete a task, refuse to consider "alternative possibilities" that may complicate the task's delivery, or fail to manage time properly, among many other considerations for the planning fallacy (par. 8). This is why Galef (2016) considered how "our intuitions aren't very good at thinking about compound probabilities"—for instance, the larger or more commonplace the task is, the greater the opportunity of one stem taking much more time and, thusly, would delay the task.

Table 1: Underpinning mechanisms of the planning fallacy.

Mechanism	Characteristics
Focal bias	Estimates of the duration are needed to complete the task are inaccurate
Anchoring and adjustment	Individuals do not sufficiently adjust their expectations and biases to the future
Motivation	Incentives often make people underestimate the time needed to complete a task (e.g., money, discounts, freebies)

Note: Adapted from "The planning fallacy," by Dr. Simon Moss (2016).

Kalis, Mojzisch, Schweizer, and Kaiser (2008) determined that "weakness of will" suggested that since our will tends to be "the general power that leads us to action," our wills are too weak to "translate our values into action" (p. 402). To determine the extent of akrasia, two questions need to be answered: First, is it possible to act against your best interest? Second, how should you "explain" or "define" the value of your choices? (p. 403). Think of a task that has a missing deadline; even if the deadline is (mostly) static and unmovable, you attempt to plan to make steps towards the future, but continue to make choices towards the present simultaneously. In other words, you wish to complete the *future* deadline, while your present self-continues to dutifully delay the task; as Clear (2017) stated, "Your brain values long-term benefits when they are in the future, but it values instant gratification when it comes to the present moment" (par. 10).

Buehler, Griffin, and Ross (1994) established how prediction—and, in a sense, procrastination—is an example of its "focus on the future" that oftentimes hinders future-oriented individuals to attach and "incorporate" past experiences into their predictions (p. 367). Even though predictions are normal, setting predictions only limit your actions towards a goal, suggesting that "procrastinators are self-handicappers: rather than failure, they prefer to create conditions that make success impossible, a reflex that of course creates a vicious cycle" (Surowiecki, 2010, par. 2).

Procrastination comes at a premium for business and personal finance. A 2007 study by business research firm Barex revealed that "information overload" from business professionals' "unnecessary interruptions cost productivity an estimated \$650 billion [or about \$757.4 billion, adjusted for inflation in 2016]" (Lohr, 2007, par. 2). One in five people suffers from procrastination to the point that "their careers, relationships, and health are threatened" (Holland, 2008, par. 2; Day, 2008, par. 1). In 2013, consumers paid \$12 billion in credit card fees and by 2014 was expected to rise to numbers between \$13 billion to \$14 billion in 2014, whereas the share of procrastination has quintupled from 5% to 26% in 2008 (Voigt, 2014, par. 5, 6). Even in business, procrastination is the most dangerous and "expensive invisible cost": a 2012 study on employee productivity revealed that workers wasted about 2.09 hours daily due to "non-job-related activities," wasting employers \$10,396 per employee yearly (Vaden, 2012, par. 1). You see, procrastination is completely avoidable *and* very costly if you're not careful with your business or personal finances.

The Irrationality of Procrastination

When someone procrastinates, it's amazing to look at the things they can do rather than what they should be doing. They may rationalize by thinking, "I need to get these other things done first so I can concentrate on what I need to do. Let's first answer some emails, maybe do some cleaning or have lunch first." This rationalization is a result of the subconscious mind trying to protect you. The conscious mind uses reason and logic, but it will be easily overridden if there's a perceived threat to your safety.

Allow me to illustrate it this way: A young man at a high school dance sees a pretty girl across the room he wants to dance with. In order to dance with her, he needs to walk across the room and approach her. The conscious part of his mind is thinking, "I hope she doesn't laugh at me or reject me." The subconscious survival brain says, "is she a lion, a lion that could kill us?" Halfway across the floor, he sees his best friend and thinks, "I should talk to him first. Phew! Safe again!"

Even if this example is a funny exaggeration of a common event, it serves to describe how our conscious and subconscious minds sometimes miscommunicate a perceived threat: His conscious mind knew he wanted to dance with the girl, but to the subconscious mind it was a risk not worth taking. You see, our primitive survival brain is still operating as it did when our ancestors were in constant danger just a few thousand years ago. The young man's subconscious mind wanted to avoid being exposed by rejection, standing out alone and an easy target for the lion. The subconscious part of our mind sees the benefit of staying safe and being part of the tribe. Don't do anything that could make us vulnerable to attack, left alone. And if someone experiences this multiple times throughout their life, it reinforces the need to avoid perceived threats, and the use of procrastination is reinforced.

There is nothing wrong with your mind: it's a glitch, an error message that needs to be updated and performance improves when the need for procrastination is eliminated. Your mind couldn't have done it any other way. Your mind is using faulty intelligence, and that's why things have not gone the way you planned. If you were taught that one plus one equals three, can you see why this would create an issue when this formula came up in an equation? You would be wondering how everyone else seemed to come up with a different answer than you and yet you seemed so sure you had the answer. Through the Inspired Performance Program (tIPP), you'll learn how to fix the error message, and the system is back online, producing at peak performance.

Procrastinators suffer from many irrational beliefs; namely, they "are frequently unsure of their ability to complete a task," and are not consciously aware of what can be considered "an adequately accomplished task" (Ferrari, Johnson, & McCown, 1995, p. 35). Because the procrastinator believes the task is, by its nature, impossible to accomplish satisfactorily, delaying a task and engaging in avoidant behavior serves to protect their egos from the fear of failure. In other words, some procrastinatory behavior may represent a form of rebellion to those in authority"

(Lay, 1986, p. 475)—in this case, procrastinating on a task serves as an implicit defiance to the task-giver. However, oftentimes procrastinators fail to see failure as "a prelude to many successes" and cannot recognize that failure cannot define them—even if setbacks are inevitable (Knaus, 2017, par. 7).

Procrastination = Fear

Fear is at the root of procrastination, which will only grow stronger if one cannot face the fear and begin working at *something* towards the set goal (Warrell, 2013, par. 3, 4). Another motive for procrastination is a deep-seated fear of rejection, where procrastinators are unwilling to act on unpleasant or difficult tasks for fear of facing rejection by others. Whereas the fear of failure springs from an internal motivation, the fear of rejection is externally motivated—and both are irrational reactions. Langens and Schüler (2005) emphasized that "individuals high in fear of rejection typically report low levels of *perceived* [emphasis added] social support and are more vulnerable to stressful experiences" (p. 819). Without (any perceived) social support, people are less likely to succeed on their own—and that includes procrastinators, more so by doubting their personal value (p. 819). Fear of rejection and procrastination can feed a self-sustaining cycle; for instance, Kumar and Kaushal (2017) stated that last-minute delays on work necessary for others could harbor resentment, itself triggering a fear of rejection (p. 4222).

Ironically, procrastination can also be borne from an irrational fear of success. Lay (1986) acknowledged how "success increases anxiety and leads to procrastination, particularly in mixed reinforcement situations in which painful consequences are associated with pleasurable events" (p. 475). Ogilvie (1968) referred how success brings new forms of stress, including social "and emotional isolation"; "guilt feelings about self-aversion or overt suggestion; rationalization; unconscious resentment; and fear of old traditions or old idols" (p. 35-36). Like most fears, fear of success is unconscious—success, when it should be an important motivator, is also dangerous to procrastinators since they have a "greater tendency to delay a commitment if the individual lacks a motive or the drive to accomplish it" (Rozental & Carlbring, 2014, p. 1492).

The pursuit of perfection is significantly common among procrastinators because, psychologically, it's more acceptable never to do something than face the possibility of falling short and not performing at your best. In a sense, procrastination serves as a form of personal *self-protection* from suffering any type of pain, and there may have been experiences that created this striving for perfection. For example, a demanding parent or teacher may have held a student to an unrealistic performance standard, to which the student internalized to the degree that it's impossible to separate work performance from perfection. Or that student could've learned that perfection was necessary in order to survive all by themselves, say if constantly criticized by others because of their weight, job prospects, or even social status.

That being said, it's not always the parent's fault A young child is prone to misinterpret a parent's intentions. If a parent, with the best of his or her intentions, says to a child, " I know you can do better, bring that B up to an A," to the child's young mind that reflects a disapproval of his or her performance, and will either overcompensate or rebel against such perceptions because a child has no life experience to interpret or understand the nuances of their parent's intentions. If they continue to meet with this at other times in their life, they might develop a fear of not performing up to those unrealistic standards. As a result, they employ avoidance techniques, formed out of the subconscious survival mind; that way, no one will notice that they *may* have possibly failed. To perform at peak performance, this error message needs to be updated and swept away, learning how to handle *manageable*— yet *challenging*—expectations.

How Procrastinators Function

Successful People Don't...

Many procrastinators suffer from impulsivity issues, which can be considered "a failure of our self-control mechanisms; as Konnikova suggested, both negative habits are conversely related to another—for example, an impulsive person would say, "We should wait, but instead we act now." A procrastinator internally reacts to oneself, "We shouldn't wait, but instead we wait" (Konikova, 2014, par. 8). As a regulatory failure, procrastination can also be considered a form of self-harm–by purposely failing to "achieve one's goals [...] in a transgression against the self", since intentionally delaying any financial or health matters can snowball into catastrophic consequences (Wohl, Pychyl, & Bennett, 2010, p. 803). As Steel (2011) reported, low self-confidence and task aversion are important triggers to procrastination; by delaying difficult or boring tasks like filing for taxes and setting up medical appointments, impulsivity also "makes small and immediate temptations [...] much more attractive" (par. 3, 4, 9). What's the point of filing taxes online when you can check your e-mail or read the daily horoscope?

Because, neuropsychologically, "procrastination can be described as a problem with the executive function, which is the skill set that allows us to plan, prioritize, and carry out tasks" (Aranda, 2016), it can also be viewed as "a stress-like attempt to avoid feelings" (2016). Sudler (2014) noted that students' lack of self-regulation compromised the value and orientation of the tasks at work (p. 4). Executive functioning research undertaken by Laura Rabin in 2011 established that "procrastination may emerge as a result of a dysfunction of the executive function producing systems of the brain," including the amygdala, the part of the brain that regulates "fear, memory, emotion, and decision-making" (Abbey-Vital, 2014, par. 3, 4). As de Botton and Morris (2017) stated, "The perfect distance for doing nothing is when you have the constant chance to do something."

Figure 3: Consequences of poor executive functioning due to procrastination.

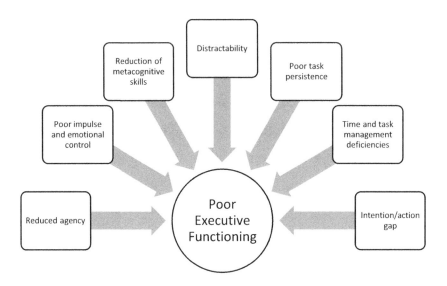

Note: Adapted from "The science of procrastination," by I. Abbey-Vital, 2014, *The Brain Bank North West*, https://thebrain-bank.scienceblog.com/2014/05/13/the-science-of-procrastination/; "Why do we procrastinate? [Video]," by M. Aranda, 2016, *YouTube*, https://www.youtube.com/watch?v=pKyHX0zqynk; and "Academic procrastination as mediated by executive functioning, perfectionism, and frustration intolerance in college students," by E.L. Sudler, 2014, Doctoral dissertation.

Tice and Baumeister (1999), not only noted in their research how procrastination is a "self-defeating behavior," but also recognized the costs and benefits of procrastination in stress, illness, and performance (p. 454). Regarding stress and illness, while procrastination is significantly correlated with depression, irrational beliefs, low self-esteem, anxiety, and poor study habits, procrastination's effects on last-minute suffering since the stress is condensed in a shorter period even if there are extremely high levels of anxiety due to pressure (p. 454). Regarding performance, while some stress improves performance, postponing tasks until the deadline makes no difference, even if procrastinators suffer less effort on the task (p. 455). Tice and Baumeister also reported that "procrastinators appear to benefit from the carefree situation they create for themselves early in the project phase," but "procrastinators end up producing inferior work" (p. 454).

Types of Procrastinators

We used to believe that procrastination is stereotyped as a one-size-fits-all approach, where procrastinators are lazy and refuse to do their work. That being said, there are many types of procrastination; for instance, research noted "most creative professionals tend to play around with a difficult problem before they try to resolve it" (Pajaron, 2012, par. 6). Chu and Choi (2005) also established two different types of procrastinators: *active procrastinators*, who deliberately delay their actions to the last minute, even though they can actively perform in a timely manner;

and *passive* or *traditional* procrastinators, who postpone tasks because they are paralyzed by quick decision-making (p. 247). Whereas active procrastinators "prefer to work under pressure", oftentimes for thrill-seeking or self-imposed challenges and their actions are perceived as positive, passive procrastinators are derided for their inactivity, more so today when the advent of technology has made distractions much more accessible *and* acceptable (Martini, 2013, p. 7, 8).

In another variant of active procrastination, *decisional procrastination* occurs when people make a "purpose[ful] delay in making decisions within some specific timeframe," who in many cases cannot "weigh alternatives" under stress or duress, and exhibit a forgetful or absentminded character (Ferrari, 1992, p. 673). However, unlike active or passive procrastination, decisional procrastination tends to be limited to major decisions only. Moreover, behavioral procrastination observes people delaying tasks to protect a vulnerable self-esteem situation. In this case, behavioral procrastinators measure their self-worth solely on task ability and delaying the (perceived) negative task only feeds the procrastinator's inability (p. 674). Unfortunately, this type of behavior is the one that leaves people without the means or the will to "accomplish personal goals" (Orellana-Damacela, Tindale, & Suarez-Balcazar, 2000, p. 225). Finally, these are the non-procrastinators, who complete their tasks promptly and are generally not subject to the negative consequences of procrastination (Martini, 2013, p. 3).

Table 2: Summary of types of procrastinators and their characteristics.

Type of Procrastinator	Characteristics
Active	Prefers to work under pressure, making deliberate decisions to procrastinate
Passive	Are paralyzed by their indecision to act and fail to complete tasks in a timely manner
Decisional	Purposely delay in making decisions within a specific time frame
Behavioral	Delay tasks to protect their self-esteem
Non-procrastinator	Prefers to complete tasks in a timely manner

Note: Adapted from "Rethinking procrastination: Positive effects of 'active' procrastination behavior on attitudes and performance." by A.H.C. Chu, & J.N. Choi, 2005, *The Journal of Social Psychology*, 245-264; "Dysfunctional procrastination and its relationship with self-esteem, interpersonal dependency, and self-defeating behaviors," by J.R. Ferrari, 1994, *Personality and Individual Differences*, 673-679; "*The influence of active procrastination and passive procrastination on university students' education and success in college*," by F.S. Martini, 2013, Published Master's thesis; and *Academic procrastination as mediated by executive functioning, perfectionism, and frustration intolerance in college students*, by Sudler, E.L., 2014, Doctoral dissertation.

It's important to analyze the many distinctions and factors that affect procrastinators, such as:

- **Time use and perception:** Whereas passive procrastinators "drift aimlessly from one activity to another", active procrastinators exhibit better "time structure" and "sense of purpose", allowing them to deliberately prioritize their time and actions "on the basis of urgency and priority" (Chu & Choi, 2005, p. 248).

- **Self-efficacy:** Essentially, this aspect refers to the belief that reliable "task performance is important for successful goal achievement;" as a result, a combination of "ability and motivation" predict how active a person's self-efficacy will be (p. 248).

- **Motivation:** People can be moved to do something by intrinsic (or internal) or extrinsic (or external) means (Chu & Choi, 2005, p. 248; Ryan & Deci, 2000, p. 54). Intrinsic motivations act upon internal satisfaction, "fun or challenge," while extrinsic motivations are offered for any "instrumental value" (Ryan & Deci, 2000, p. 56, 60). Research has shown that even if external motivation would help fight against "task delay," people who are internally motivated were "more devoted to their projects" than others who were externally motivated through other means (Chu & Choi, 2005, p. 249).

- **Stress:** Drawing from self-efficacy, coping with stress brought on by procrastination will determine if it will be task-oriented (focused on immediate problems), emotion-oriented (focused on diminishing emotional distress), or avoidance-oriented (focused on ignoring and/or distancing oneself from the problem (Chu & Choi, 2005, p. 250). Kisburn and Whitlock (n.d.) also considered that coping could be meaning-oriented, which involves "searching for meaning in adversity and drawing on values, beliefs, and goals to modify the meaning given to and personal response to a stressful situation."

- **Personal outcome:** Due to the snowballing effects of chronic procrastination, this can lead to "higher levels of stress and anxiety, weak impulse control, lack of persistence, lack of work discipline, lack of time management skills, and the inability to work methodically" (Ferrari, Johnson, & McCown, 1995, p. 8).

Procrastinators' Self-Judgment

We've explained how procrastination is seen by others; now, how are they seen by themselves? Not very favorably, as noted by Ferrari (1992)—in this case, procrastinators attempt to "save face" and "gain social approval by creating and maintaining "harsh, stern, [and] inflexible treatment" to other perceived procrastinators, believing that this is the treatment they should receive to themselves (p. 318). Sirois and Pychyl (2016) referred to the "negative and punitive thoughts directed at the self" like self-blame and self-judgment as part of the causes that perpetuate procrastination (p. 7). Because "self-doubt and fear" lie at the root of procrastination, the subconscious mind wants "to protect and keep us safe" at the expense of furthering our accomplishments (Field, 2014).

Instead, research by Wohl, Pychyl, and Bennett (2010) has revealed that self-forgiveness is the way to go to reduce the extent and damage of procrastination. "Forgiving oneself has the beneficial effect of reducing subsequent procrastination by reducing the effect of the outcome of an explanation" (p. 806). In the research, three conditions must be present in order for self-forgiveness to exhibit a long-term effect: first, one must acknowledge the commission of a transgression and accept responsibility; second, experience guilt and regret; and finally, overcome feelings of guilt and experience a motivational change away from self-punishment to self-acceptance (p. 806). Golpour, Mohammad Amini, Kasraie, & Senobar (2015) addressed the role of self-compassion in procrastination, stating that negative values of self-compassion like "self-judgment, isolation, and sympathy" have a "positive correlation with depression," and positive values like self-kindness and mindfulness could predict the onset or absence of depression (p. 208). Likewise, Sirois (2014) confirmed that lower levels of self-compassion relate to higher levels of stress, and a policy promoting self-compassion as a healthier alternative to procrastination as "a quality that can enhance self-regulation through reducing negative self-evaluations such as self-blame" (p. 39).

This is where the Inspired Performance Institute can help you jump-start your career and improve your business. Through the Inspired Performance Program, you can develop the skills to clear past glitches that induce procrastination in your business life. Procrastination is both dangerous, toxic, and contagious for any organization, and that is why learning and uprooting the causes of procrastination is critical to attaining peak performance levels. Be it from fear, despair, or thrill-seeking; it's important to evaluate clearly and objectively why this frustration is consuming your lifestyle. By clearing your subconscious mind from past influences and anchoring your successes, you will grow to become successful and lead your business to the next level!

#2. Worry

Don't worry if people tell you if you have a "bad idea" —look between the cracks and seize the opportunity!

Don't Worry About What Other People Think

Successful people don't worry about what other people think of their ideas. That doesn't mean they don't listen to good advice. When a successful person has a great idea, something they wholeheartedly believe in, they will continue to pursue it in spite of people telling them that it will never work. Throughout history, there are many incredible examples of how this process has led to some of the greatest products ever invented. So, if you're an entrepreneur and find yourself worrying too much about what people think of you, or think of your idea, there is a good reason why. You see, it's in our nature to want to be liked, to fit in and this thought process goes back to a time when if you were not accepted and ultimately rejected, you could die. So, it makes sense why someone would be worried about not being liked because the primitive mind is trying to survive.

Can Stress Be Valuable?

Most people understand that stress is not good for you if it becomes a persistent issue. That form of stress is referred to as chronic stress. Chronic stress can be a killer, and that is something we address with the Inspired Performance Program. There is a reason for stress; it does have a purpose. Stress about something that is currently happening makes sense; it is an unavoidable part of modern life. That is referred to as acute stress. That is the response to a current or immediate threat. This is more commonly known as fight, flight or freeze response. The purpose is your mind is requesting an action, do something about the threat. Once the threat or danger has been handled, the response is turned off. Acute stress prepares your brain for peak performance. It is our natural response to a situation that requires our attention. I refer to this as our Emergency Management System. The alarm sets off a physiological response in the body, stress hormones are released to make the body alert, stronger, and motivated.

Most people think of the word stress as a negative. That's because it is linked to heart attacks, ulcers, hair loss, and many other conditions. However, stress does have some benefits in the appropriate situations. It allows the mind to become alert, motivated and strong, sometimes giving you the energy that you need to become more focused. Think about the people who would be considered adrenaline junkies who will get the emotional high by doing dangerous sports. Or the rush we get when we ride a roller coaster. That adrenaline rush will create a surge of energy that will actually begin to start your immune system to work. So, there are some benefits to stress, but not when it becomes chronic. When there is a threat of any kind in a situation that requires your attention, stress can actually be beneficial by bringing awareness and focus on the situation. It is your own body's natural defense system and operating protocol.

So, let's look at some specific ways that stress can actually be beneficial. During times of stress, we actually activate our immune system because it activates the adrenal glands that balance immunity. The adrenal glands will release cortisol, which is your fight/flight response. The hormone will act as an inflammatory response during the initial stress reaction and then also serve as an anti-inflammatory as the central nervous system begins to calm down when the situation is resolved. The primitive part of the brain that is responding to the flight/fight request is actually preparing the body for the release of those immune cells into the bloodstream. These immune cells will help if there's an injury to the body. So, stress can actually improve health under the right circumstances and balance.

If you're already participating in the Inspired Performance Program (tIPP), you'll hear about our gratitude audio series. In the gratitude series of audios you'll hear about the hormone called oxytocin, and this hormone is referred to as the bonding hormone. Oxytocin will head off the production of the stress hormones such as adrenaline and reduce blood pressure by dilating the arteries to help prevent the body from the more negative effects of anxiety. Oxytocin is released when we hug or become intimate with a partner. A mother and her baby will feel the effects of this hormone during breastfeeding. Being grateful you survived a threat or reconnecting with loved ones releases oxytocin and all the positive effects that come after the initial stress is successfully handled.

Now, I'm not advocating that stress is a great situation to find yourself in very often, in fact, the opposite is true. If you experience some events in your life that have been disturbing, you will build up some resiliency to handling stress later in life. If you've never experienced any or very little stress throughout your life, life has always been pretty easy, then when you do get into a stressful situation, your body is really not experienced with it and may tend to overreact. If you read my book "You Must Be Out of Your Mind" I discuss that I grew up in a generation where most parents believed in the school of hard knocks. And there is some truth to the fact that some tough times can be beneficial to build up the resiliency. That generation lived through two world wars and the Great Depression; resiliency was a key tool for survival. The issue we deal with at the Inspired Performance Institute is the problem created by memory and when memories are creating stress through what I call error messages.

The Age of Anxiety

Anxiety and worry have become the illness of the 21st century—and everybody you know is probably worrying about something, right at this moment! Some people worry about the economy. Others worry about the weather and how it will affect their future plans. Still, others worry about terrorism, crime, and their safety. Some people attempt to self-medicate or compulsively out-think their worry, while others fully embrace it and, perhaps unintentionally, find ways upon which they can further their worry. Even the most level-headed of us are suffering the effects of overzealous worrying. The question, thus, should not be if we are afraid—we should ask ourselves *what* are we afraid of.

According to the third Chapman University Survey of American Fears in 2016, the top five fears of Americans include: corrupt government officials (60.6%); a terrorist attack (41%); "having enough money for the future" (39.9%); terrorism and gun control (tied at 38.5%) (Bowerman, 2016; Wilkinson College, 2016). In fact, financial worries and an ever-diminishing sense of job security are the major causes of psychological and emotional distress, which can be alleviated through proper budgeting and financial planning and improving communication with bosses and employers (Pomlett, 2016); this way, the worry is lessened due to a realistic measure. Conversely, Dunn (2017) acknowledged that people worried about money due to engaging in a cycle of bad money-related decisions, which he terms *financial stress-eating*: "I worry about money because I've made poor decisions. I make poor decisions because I'm worried about money" (par. 8).

Anxiety is a common experience in our modern society—and it also hinders any chances to be successful if you allow it to invade your life. Today, the experience of anxiety is fraught with many contradictions, from the "digitally connected" aspect of communication that more often than not becomes insulating, to the basic need of being socially accepted or facing the fear of missing out (FOMO), to growing and dealing with the aftermath of the recession (Chunn, 2016, par. 9). The number of those reported suffering common symptoms of anxiety has skyrocketed, not because of increasing numbers, but because people today are more willing to admit "they are suffering from a mental health condition" (Twenge, 2014, par. 2). The author also proposed three theories that may answer this growing trend: weaker community ties; a greater focus on materialistic goals, such as fame and fortune; and excessively high expectation (par. 1).

Conceptualizing Anxiety

Anxiety can be conceptualized as "a state of distress and/or physiological arousal in reaction to stimuli, including novel situations and the potential for undesirable outcomes" (Brooks & Schweitzer, 2011, p. 44); in this case, anxiety happens when the person is exposed to an unfamiliar environment where there is an uncertain (but is perceived to tilt towards the negative) outcome that may or may not be unfavorable. Negotiation, bargaining, or even an action can trigger distress. Two outcomes can occur to resolve the anxiety: either "terminate" negotiation early, or quickly resolve the situation on potentially less than favorable terms (p. 44). In both cases, anxiety can also be described as "fear, frustration, stress, worry, apprehension, and nervousness," all emotions with negative connotations (p. 44).

On the other hand, Leal, Goes, Ferreira, and Teixeira-Silva (2017) conceptualized anxiety as "an organic response, characterized by apprehension and increased surveillance in situations of uncertain danger or potential threats to the organism" (p. 2). In this case, anxiety is not defined solely by the potential discomfort of a course of action, but instead, the threat and any attributed value to it, be it real or imaginary. It also involves realizing what steps, even if unnecessary, are needed to stop the threat at its root. An example is the threat of bodily harm: from adaptive methods like taking self-defense classes and owning a gun for protection, to maladaptive ones like carrying too many weapons or ruminating about potential events, anxiety can lead to both proactive and reactive behaviors to alleviate the threat. Additionally, (Reiss, Peterson, Gursky, & McNally (1986) established an important difference between *anxiety expectancy*, an "associative learning process in which the individual has learned that a given stimulus arouses anxiety [and/or] fear," and *anxiety sensitivity*, where the individual believes the "expense of anxiety [and/or] fear causes illness, embarrassment, or additional anxiety" (p. 1, 2). Both processes are not mutually exclusive: for instance, someone can be *expectant* of anxiety during an anxiety-provoking moment, but not necessarily *sensitive* to it constantly.

The Value of Valence

Not that anxiety, in and of itself, is a negative emotion. Psychologists use the term *valence* to describe the "positive" and "negative character" of an emotion and/or its aspects (Colombetti, 2006). This means that a typically "negative" emotion like anxiety, in reality, covers many more aspects of emotion than expected, depending on context. For instance, anxiety can be positively valenced as excitement or arousal, while negatively valenced aspects of anxiety include dread and apprehension. That being said, Barrett (2006) related that common emotions like fear and happiness cannot be determined by a "clear biological or behavior," but rather by "experience" in a "category that is constructed by the human mind" (p. 36). In another aspect of valence, emotions can be treated as "the forces that attract individuals to desirable objects and repel them from undesirable ones" (Schuman, Sander, & Scherer, 2013, p. 1). For instance, anxiety has a negative valence, which makes the emotion undesirable to experience, whereas excitement is seen as something with a positive, desirable valence. But negative states of anxiety, even if their valence is inherently neutral, can be detrimental to decision-making in three ways: by distorting people's thoughts into negativity; by altering the decision-making process through short-circuiting the person's internal judgment; and by shifting motives and concerns into other moods (Ragunathan & Pham, 1999).

There are also two different ways to look at anxiety: *state anxiety*, where "the psychological and physiological transient reactions [are] directly related to adverse events" (Leal, Goes, Ferreira, & Teixeira-Silva, 2017, p. 2); and *trait anxiety*, where people "experience more intense degrees of state anxiety to specific situations than most people do and experience anxiety toward a broader range of situations than most people" (Hatfield, 2017, par. 3). The things that can be anxiety-provoking for you are not the same anxiety-provoking things to me. To point the distraction out, let us look at the anxiety people feel when negotiating: people with state anxiety might feel apprehension before and during the negotiation process, but may subside immediately after the negotiations, while people with trait anxiety feel apprehensive. not only at negotiating, but also at specific aspects of negotiation, such as bargaining, or exposing the terms and conditions upon which to negotiate. For this reason, anxiety is often defined as "a trait, a state, a stimulus, a response, a drive, and as a motive" (Endler & Kocovski, 2011, p. 232).

Needless to say, living with and furthering anxiety over the long term is not without its problems. Brooks (2014) noted in her research into reformulating anxiety, it "drains working memory capacity, decreases self-confidence, and harms performance" (p. 1). This correlates with the negative variance of anxiety as "a negative [and] aversive emotion" (p. 1). Likewise, a 2000 study on athletes and anxiety revealed that athletes with a greater predisposition to trait anxiety amplify the perceived threats to their performance and, thus, overreact and attempt to overcompensate for its performance (Baker, Côte, & Hawes, 2000, p. 11). In addition, a study on anxious behavior in mice discovered a link to short-term memory loss, autoimmune inflammation, and even faced extinction and isolation from the group (Swan, 2017). These circumstances are serious and we, as business leaders, must take active steps to protect clients, employees, and contractors regarding anxiety.

In a more specific glance, worry seems to be an overwhelming part of our entrepreneurial society. To wit, successful entrepreneurs are recognized for exhibiting seven common traits (Ngah & Salleh, 2015): tolerance of ambiguity; autonomy; nonconformity; aloofness and adroitness; risk-taking; adaptability to change; and low need for support. Every entrepreneur with adequate amounts of emotional intelligence (EI) potrays these qualities in some way, shape, or form. But anxiety, if left unchecked, can dampen the entrepreneurs' value and business performance regardless of the value offered to the market. Nearly half of surveyed entrepreneurs in a study reported suffering from mental health conditions—more than that of the general population, when at least a third of Americans "are living with extreme stress" and 48% believe that "their stress increased over the past five years" (American Psychological Association, 2007, par. 1). And, in the midst of the ups and downs of entrepreneurship, anxiety can creep in and cut short any strides entrepreneurs have collaborated with in the past; this is why Mello (2017) explained, "There are incredibly smart people out there who never make it: They are simply too afraid of what achieving success requires of them" (par. 15).

The Anxious State of Mind

Here is an interesting thought: Not everyone who is anxious worries. But everyone who worries has been anxious.

You see, anxiety is both damaging and detrimental to your personal and professional success. However, what about reframing your anxiety to excitement and enjoy the thrill of success as a challenge? Brooks (2014) reported in a study regarding the role of excitement as "arousal contingent" (p. 1), meaning that "minimal actions between the anxiety-provoking stimulus can trigger excitement to a subject." This transforms anxiety from a negative valence to a positive one, eliminating the pressure to hide or resolve the dread. You see, anxiety lowers self-confidence, limits mental processes because sufferers are constantly ruminating, and are more likely to engage in reassurance-seeking behaviors to (temporarily) stem the tide of anxiety. Try reframing that sleepless bout of insomnia as an opportunity to catch up on a side project for a few minutes. Or try looking at those butterflies in your stomach as a great chance to make a positive first impression. You'll see the difference!

Why the weird dichotomy? If you've noticed, anxiety is a state of personality rather than a state of mind as in worry. Kingston (2013) defined worry as "a chain of thoughts and images, negatively affect-laden and relatively uncontrollable [...]

an attempt to engage in mental problem-solving on an issue whose outcome is certain but contains the possibility of one or more negative outcomes" (p. 74). A key aspect of worry is the certainty of a possible outcome with a chance of negative expectations, most often unpleasant and unnecessary, that does not correspond with reality. It is considered an aversive emotional experience that arises alongside repetitive thoughts about the future (Sweeny & Dooley, 2017, p. 1), which makes worry in and of itself negatively valenced. But, even if worry is often seen as bad—which oftentimes it is—, does it actually serve any positive purpose?

Studies have shown worrying in moderate doses can improve trauma and depressive symptoms, maintain an increase of "uptake of health-seeking behaviors," succeed at problem-solving, work performance, graduate school, and on stressful life events (Romm, 2017, par. 3; Watkins, 2008). Reframed in a positive light, worry can become useful when it is "objective, controllable, and brief" by mentally prioritizing information, maintaining awareness of "potential unresolved threats," and preparing for any "adaptive behaviors" (Watkins, 2008, p. 234). Worrying is also related to "verbal intelligence" as a predictor of anxiety, worry, depression, and rumination (Dahl, 2014; Penney, Miedema, & Mazmanian, 2015).

But what motivates—and maintains—worry? Five factors are discovered to further and entrench worry:

- **Superstitious avoidance of worry:** In many cases, worrying about an event before it happens means that the event is less likely to occur or is eliminated. This lies at the root of most superstitions, as "wanting more control or certainty is the driving force behind most superstitions" (Albert, 2004, par. 8). While rituals and superstitions help maintain a sense of community, these often involve avoiding an undesirable action by pushing it away mentally (Risen & Nussbaum, 2013).

- **Actual avoidance of catastrophe:** Worriers believe their actions help with problem—solving and prevention of a negative event. Breazeale (2011) referred to this as *catastrophic thinking*, or "ruminating about irrational worst-case outcomes" (par. 1), which maintains high levels of anxiety and forces people into a state of paralysis when action should be the most important and sensitive outcome. Because catastrophic thinking is often automatic—more so since worriers believe that it avoids thinking about emotional, complex, or unpleasant topics (Loehr, 2008, p. 81), they also cannot acknowledge worry as a tool for "detecting and managing" risk through under-or over-estimation (Leahy, 2010, p. 243). In fact, this catastrophic worry is at the heart of generalized anxiety disorder (GAD).

- **Avoidance of deeper emotional topics:** Worry is considered a way to deflect attention and thoughts away from emotional topics as a form of emotional dysregulation. In a sense, "worry is a form of emotional avoidance—that we *worry* [emphasis added] rather than *feel* [emphasis added]" (Leahy, 2009, par. 2) with the goal to "master problems with emotional dysregulation and to feel more in control" (Newman, Llera, Erickson, Przeworski, & Castonguay, 2013, p. 5). Its verbal-linguistic basis also furthers avoidance, even if a "heightened intensity" exists (McLaughlin, Menin, & Farach, 2007, p. 1736).

- **Coping preparation:** Barlow (2004) referred to research on worry as "an attempted coping mechanism that actually serves to avoid the threatening emotional core of anxiety" (p. 99) which, however, is "nonfunctional" to the point "concentration and ongoing activities are disrupted" (p. 99). A form of "magical thinking" (Martini, 2013, par. 7), worrying as a coping mechanism frames worry in a positive, helpful force when, in reality, does nothing to *actively* change the circumstances.

- **Motivating device**: Even if worry by nature does nothing to change the circumstances, others believe its unpleasant stimulus encourages individuals to complete tasks

(Borkovec, 1994). If there is an actual positive accomplishment with the worry, then it is referred and implied to improve performance. That being said, Sweeny & Dooley (2017) revealed worriers could *moderately* prepare their expectations should there be a negative event (Rosenfeld, 2017).

Figure 4: Graphical description of factors exacerbating worry.

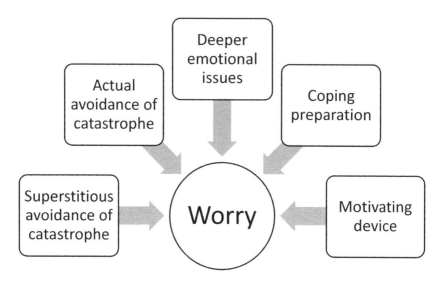

Note: Adapted from "The influence of active procrastination and passive procrastination on university students' education and success in college," by F.S. Martini, 2013, Published Master's thesis.

Worry is Useless

Nevid (2017) described worry as a "useless emotion" because it is the only one "that remains after all reasonable measures are taken to safeguard your family and personal interests" (par. 16). While worry may be warranted in times of significant stress or trauma, it is never necessary when facing life's stresses—hence, worry has "no positive payoff" to enjoy whatsoever (Block, 2012). Beyond control, Sofield (2015) argued worry is a form of selfishness by focusing worriers to suffer "the busyness of nothing" (par. 5). As a result, Nevid referred to an important relationship between worry and guilt:

> Worry and guilt are opposite sides of a wooden nickel—two useless emotions facing different directions. Worry looks ahead, seeing threat and disaster at every turn. Guilt looks behind, imposing self-blame for perceived misfortunes and disappointments (Nevid, 2017, par. 1).

Perfectionism and Rumination

There are people that believe success means perfection; as a result, they strive towards it—but, despite having achieved so much, they're not happy with themselves. Perfection is impossible. The most successful people make mistakes and have to deal with many setbacks on their journey through life. And that's okay as far as I'm concerned: Perfection is an illusion. If you believe perfection is part of success, then you will never see yourself as successful.

Having a healthy amount of pride and standards for your work is important. This demonstrates that you are willing to maintain healthy boundaries and strive towards excellence. However, if your standard of performance is excessively high, unreachable, unrealistic, and overly critical of yourself, then you may be suffering from perfectionism (Stöeber, Otto, Pescheck, Becker, & Stoll, 2003, p. 960). Perfectionism is thrice conceptualized as a "concern over mistakes and doubts about actions;" parental criticism and the need for approval; and "excessively high personal standards" (Stöber & Joorman, 2001, p. 50). Sassaroli & Ruggiero (2005) described an important construct of perfectionism: their compulsive need to avoid *any* mistake for fear of a catastrophic (and ultimately irrational) failure forces their actions to be "accompanied by feelings of self-criticism and a sense of ineffectiveness" (p. 135). On the other hand, "Worriers do not want to be the best, they are just afraid of making mistakes" (Stöeber & Joorman, 2001, p. 51), which renders commonplace advice to lower their expectations moot and useless. This is why, for example, workaholism may be validated through perfectionism and job satisfaction, among others (Burke, Davis, & Flett, 2008, p. 32).

Bieling, Israeli, & Anthony (2004) referred to scales of perfectionism by differentiating between "normal" or "adaptive" and "neurotic" or maladaptive "perfectionism". Whereas a healthy level of perfectionism reflects the "achievement of high standards" and is not psychologically distressing, maladaptive perfectionism is negatively reinforcing and self-defeating (1374, 1375). This ties to Spence and Robbins' definition of a workaholic as someone "highly work-involved, feels compelled or driven to work because of inner processes and is low in engagement at work" (as cited in Burke, Davis, & Flett, 2008, p. 32). In fact, perfectionism is not only about striving for achieving "perfect goals" or organization; rather, perfectionism of this type is mostly concerned with "concern or preoccupation over mistakes, doubts that one is doing the right thing, and a history of others having high expectations that have been internalized" Bieling, Israeli, & Anthony, 2004, p. 1383).

Which is why Pozin (2014) remarked on the role of perfectionism in entrepreneurship. Every entrepreneur wants their venture to be perfect, but real progress is often made out of messy beginnings" (par. 1). Robinson (2016) explained that, should perfectionism ravage entrepreneurs, these will render them:

- Paralyzed with unrealistic expectations;
- Stressful;
- Lacking creativity;
- Suffering from damaged health;
- Wasteful;
- Unable to cope with failure;
- Rigid and inflexible;
- Risk-averse;
- Isolated;
- Unhappy;

In addition, perfectionists are prone to *concealment,* or "the need to hide mistakes and failures," and *contingent self-worth,* or "the extent to which self-esteem was based on others' approval, physical appearance, success and competition, academic competence, and participation in activities" (Goldberg, 2009, par. 21; Burguess & DiPaolo, 2015, p. 190). Because of this, you must part with the glitches that have accompanied you for years in order to be fully successful.

Rumination is another insidious aspect of worry, one where your mind keeps chewing and chewing some thought or event in the past, present, and future. Rumination is "a class of conscious thoughts that revolve around a common instrumental theme that recurs in the absence of immediate environmental demands requiring the thoughts" (qtd. in Kingston, 2013, p. 22);

that is to say, the human penchant for self-reflection has taken a very dark turn. Like worry, rumination in both depression and anxiety is considered negatively valenced (Nolen-Hoeksema, Wisco, & Lyubimorsky, 2008, p. 400), self-focused and self-reflected, "repetitive and passive" (Treynor, Gonzalez, & Nolen-Hoeksema, 2003, p. 243); and may "contribute to a sense of hopelessness about the future" (Nolen-Hoeksema, 2000, p. 504). From the Latin word for chewing the cud (Harper, 2017), rumination may be appropriate for a cow, but it only causes problems and misery for sufferers (Murray Law, 2005).

Treynor, Gonzalez, & Nolen-Hoeksema, (2003) developed a "two-factor model for rumination" that factored in a continuum between *reflection*, or "an introspective turn to alleviate depression," and *brooding*, or "a passive comparison of one's current situation with some unachieved standard" (p. 256). In addition, ruminators believe their actions gain them insight, share a history of emotional concussions, suffer (or believe they suffer) "chronic, uncontrollable stressors," and exhibit perfectionistic, neurotic, or relational personalities (Murray Law, 2005, par. 20). This is why worry and rumination "share an abstract, over-general thinking style" and are "associated with cognitive inflexibility and difficulty in switching attention from negative stimuli," and "exacerbate depression and anxiety" (Nolen-Hoeksema, Wisco, & Lyubimorsky, 2008, p. 406).

Because rumination is mostly developed by parent modelling and/or maladaptive environments or reinforcements by insightfulness and avoidance (Kingston, 2013, p. 38), the response styles theory predicts that rumination "maintains and exacerbates depression by enhancing negative thinking, imposing problem-solving, interfering with instrumental behavior, and eroding social support (Nolen-Hoeksema, Wisco, & Lyubimorsky, 2008, p. 401). Do keep in mind, however, that why we ruminate is unclear, researchers believe it is "an unsuitable strategy adopted to try and cope with [negative] emotions" (Coxen, 2011, p. 71). Additionally, ruminators are more likely to develop major depression, show more severe symptoms of post-traumatic stress disorder (PTSD) and depression, face greater levels of isolation, hold on to longer and unnecessary grudges, and hurts problem-solving (Chand, 2016). Rumination is also "a huge barrier to insight" (Eurich, 2017, par. 2), more so when rumination points out areas where we experience a personal inadequacy (par. 4). Rumination amplifies a depressed mood, which triggers past traumatic memories and distractions have no more effect on reducing pessimistic or negative thinking (Lyubomirsky, Tucker, Caldwell, & Berg, 1999, p. 1042).

This is why a program like the Inspired Performance Program sponsors self-compassion to remove your glitches and succeed in business. Self-compassion is important because it raises "psychological well-being" and helps "emotional resilience" (Raes, 2010, p. 757). Through the program, we will show you how to quickly do away with past glitches so you can be free to enjoy your past successes on your way to your personal success. Self-kindness, common humanity and mindfulness (p. 757) are values that promote thoughts that regulate catastrophizing or "repetitive thinking" (p. 758, 760). Despite neurotic people having a greater probability to "detect threats in their environments" (Baer, 2014, par. 3), those with the self-discipline to disengage those worries make contact with their personal symbol and their business towards success!

#3. Conform

Think out-of-the-box whenever you launch upon your idea for success. Don't conform to anybody's expectation of success; instead, make (or break) your own!

Pressure to Conform

Have you ever felt pressured to conform to something you don't agree with? Have you ever followed a vague, boring, or downright outrageous or unethical request out of fear or need? All around you, people have always tried to conform their worldview and expectations if only to fit in, draw attention to themselves for fame (or infamy!), or even mangle and injure their bodies in order to achieve a very unrealistic standard. Conforming looks simple, but it is not: many people have lost relationships, careers, and even lives just by pursuing something that was always out of their reach. And in such an individualistic, market-driven society like the United States, negatively and mindlessly conforming to people's expectations without knowing the consequences can be very disastrous.

For teenagers, the pressure to conform poses a greater risk to their sense of identity due to peer pressure which, should these external influences not be kept in check, can force the teenagers to pay a very high price in the future. Brown (1986) defined peer pressure as "when people your age encourage you to do something or to keep from doing something else, no matter if you personally want to or not" (as cited in Santor, Messervey, & Kusumakar, 2000, p. 165). To explain, if a teenager's self-esteem is not fully developed or his or her atmospheric conditions are not strong enough to resist peer pressure, there is a greater susceptibility to suffer from negative consequences with the group. Adriani and Sonderegger (2016) noted that joining one group over another signals one's social status or perception of identity——as an example, people who have graduated from "elite" schools are expected to succeed due to their alma mater's prestigious status (p. 2). Positively, peer pressure can promote group harmony, accountability, and a healthy coexistence within a group—we *are* social creatures, after all. However, peer pressure's negative consequences can include risk-taking behavior, sexual promiscuity, and substance abuse, among other perils (Santor, Messervey, & Kusumakar, 2000, p. 164).

As it happens to teenagers, conformity also happens to working adults. In fact, the pressure to conform is one of the greatest challenges leaders, employees, and managers face today. Bregman (2015) stated how conformity becomes entangled in business culture: "If your colleagues take sick days, then you'll start taking them too. If your colleagues are messy, you'll become messier too" (par. 7). From dress codes to shady business transactions and outright illegality for fear of losing your job, the pressure to conform to business expectations can be disastrous for any company looking to become successful. Not that conformity is necessarily wrong for a company—some standardized rules and expectations must be maintained to keep harmony and a company culture. But conformity should never stymie growth at the expense of the status quo: "If staff members under-perform for fear of negative repercussions from co-workers your organization will suffer" (Bregman, 2015, par. 3).

Complying

So, how will you avoid conformity and become successful? Before I begin discussing how you stave off conformity, it's important to understand the differences between compliance, conformity, and obedience—and how these affect your business.

Constable, Schuler, Klaber, and Raskauskas (1999) defined compliance as a condition where "one must adapt his/her actions to another's wishes or roles" (par. 2). Feldman (2011) stated that compliance is "behavior that occurs in response to direct social pressure" (p. 591), be it from family members, bosses, or even children seeking to acquiesce to a specific request (Cialdini & Goldstein, 2004). That being said, the compliant person has a chance to follow through with the request (Breckler,

Olson, & Wiggins, 2006). But what makes compliance effective? Psychologist Robert B. Cialdini (2007) and Forest Time (n.d.) addressed six principles and techniques of influence that are commonly used to ensure compliance:

- **Reciprocity:** People feel obligated to repay something a favor completed by a person due to a sense of obligation.

- **Commitment and Consistency:** People will go to great lengths to ensure a decision aligns with their personal experiences and beliefs. The more committed a person is to a past decision, the greater chance the same person will repeat it.

- **Scarcity:** People look at opposites more favorably if these are only available for a limited time. This is commonly found with "Collector's Items," "Special Edition" items, and "For a limited time!" in consumer items.

- **Liking:** People are more likely to purchase a product from someone likable, more so from a trusted friend or family member. This is why word-of-mouth reviews are very effective for any business.

- **Authority (or detached deference):** People are more influenced when items or circumstances are referred or endorsed by people of authority in their field, such as doctors, athletes, or popular celebrities to a certain demographic.

- **Conformity (or social proof):** People perform a behavior when others around them do so and are applicable within the circumstances.

Buying "impulse" items, subscribing to a cute video related to cats, purchasing a candy you never wanted from a child, and going to the movies because everyone around you has seen the movie and you fear missing out from the discussion are examples of compliance techniques that influence your behavior. Look at the things you have bought within the past week. How much of that was completely necessary? How much of it was influenced by someone else—including friends, family, favorite celebrities, or doctors?

Successful People Don't...

Table 3: Summary of compliance techniques.

Technique	Characteristic	Example
Foot-in-the-door	Asking a person to agree to a small request, only to later ask to comply with a larger one.	Alice borrows $10 from Bob. Later, Alice asks Bob to borrow $100.
Door-in-the-face	Asking someone to agree with a large request with the expectation of being refused, following with a smaller one.	Alice wants Bob to give $100 to her, knowing he would reject. Later, she asks Bob to borrow her $10 dollars.
That's-not-all	Offering an item at an inflated price with additional incentives.	"You can buy this item at $100 or ten easy payments of $10 (plus shipping and handling)!"
Not-so-free	Offering free samples in order to ask customers to buy their product through reciprocity.	Alice gives Bob samples of a $10 product, hoping that Bob would purchase it.
Bait-and-switch	Committing someone to a course of action, later switching to another, oftentimes undesirable, alternative	Alice asks $10 to Bob for a $15 item of lower quality.

Note: Adapted from *Understanding psychology, tenth edition* by Feldman, S., 2011, McGraw Hill.

The Need for Acceptance

Conformity, just like the other habits that successful people *don't* do, has a purpose: the need to fit in and be accepted. We've all experienced that need at some point in our lives because it's a technique that helps us towards our survival. There was a time in our human history that it was critical to survival and that technique is still operating today. There is actually a purpose for groups exerting social pressures for people to conform and adapt. For instance, in order to keep law and order in our country, the government will insist on a degree of conformity. However, there are times when conformity isn't beneficial and, as a result, successful people understand that—but, at these very moments, they have the choice to stand up and be different.

As part of the process to update your mind and reach your peak performance, take some time and see if you can identify when and what happened in your life when these error messages could have taken root. Think for a moment: Was there an event or experience where conforming at the expense of your identity or beliefs happened? It may have been in school, or with friends in a social situation. Maybe you witnessed your parents conforming to work or political pressures, and this experience influenced your psychological development as it misinterpreted these experiences.

Successful People Don't…

For example, you see your father allowing his friends to influence his decisions and he seems to be happy on the outside, but inside he may be battling with his decisions. As a young child, it would not be easy to understand those nuances, and these beliefs can be set and operated early, below your conscious awareness.

No More FoMO

Thanks to the rise of social media and the integrated use of smartphones, there is a new dilemma to face: *fear of missing out* (FoMO). Przybylski, Murayama, DeHaan, & Gladwell (2013) defined FoMO as "a pervasive apprehension that others might be having rewarding experiences from which one is absent" (p. 1841). By staying connected to *every* available source you can find regarding what others are doing with their life, you can find a leg up and "compete" with nothing. Bloom and Bloom (2015) described how these people "either overcommit and fail to fulfill many of their commitments, or choose to avoid agreements and commitments as much as possible," creating their poor planning skills (par. 7). As a form of social anxiety, FoMO sufferers compulsively project their experiences through social media. As another modern aspect of conformity, a 2017 study by Eventbrite, Ipsos, and Crowd DNA, reported that 78% of Americans aged 18 or older attended at least one event in the past year, but half of

Millenial respondents "attend live events, so they have something to share online" (Seaton J., 2017, par. 2, 8). As a result, FoMO is also the result of a need for conformity when, in reality, the experiences shown by others are not rooted in reality. Lai, Altavilla, Ronconi, and Aceto (2016) related FoMO to the "fundamental need to belong, defined as a desire for interpersonal attachments as a fundamental human motivation" (p. 516). In any case, you must be careful and define your intentions when choosing to go through any event: do you want to take this action because of yourself, or is everybody around you talking about it and you only wish to belong?

Obeying

On the other hand, obedience is defined as "the act of following orders without question because they come from a legitimate authority" (Constable, Shuler, Klaber, & Raskauskas, 1999, par. 5). To a certain extent, some obedience to authority is necessary to live in a healthy and productive society. Citizens need to follow the laws and must respond to them when they are broken. Leaders must be both respected and held accountable for their positions. Stanley Milgram (1963), one of psychology's pioneers and creator of the now-infamous Milgram experiment on authority, agreed to the notion that authority is necessary: "Some system is not forced to respond, through defiance and submission, to the commands of others" (p. 371). Firefighters, police, parents, and teachers are considered as authority figures in any healthy society.

Dangerous Conformity and Business Culture

While obedience is often considered an important extension of a healthy society, *blind* obedience can bring dangerous consequences to any business. In 2015, Volkswagen was purported to have installed "defeat devices" in their vehicles to hide how their vehicles would produce up to 40 times the federal legal limit on emissions tests (Chaleff, 2015, par. 1). As a result, the company has faced up to $18 billion in fines for every car sold that breached federal emissions standards, recalled millions of cars at a potential cost of $7.95 billion (Hotten, 2015); and was barred from receiving a loan from the European Investment Bank after misleading authorities over a €400 million ($472 million) loan. The loan was supposed to develop more energy-efficient and environmentally-friendly engines (Ewing, 2017).

In the same year, Japanese technology conglomerate Toshiba was mired in an accounting scandal that involved "booking future profits early, pushing back losses, pushing back charges" and other inappropriate or fraudulent accounting practices (Carpenter, 2015, par. 5). Also, a "corporate culture of obedience" that stifled any dissent or ethical concerns, the pressure to "inflate profit numbers" and mask away any losses, and company factionalism fostered a toxic environment that ravaged Toshiba's financial standing amongst its peers (Shanmugam, 2015, par. 5). Complicating matters is the fact that Japanese business culture exhibits obedience and deference to superiors, where "the members of an organization are strictly demanded to obey superiors" (Chang, 2009, par. 3). But business scandals like these at Volkswagen or Toshiba happen within our business environments all the time. As stated by Chaleff (2015), "the short-term financial rewards of silencing dissent will become a corporate disaster" (par. 6). These events happen when we blindly follow authority without taking ethical concerns seriously (UT McCombs School of Business, 2013).

Hugos (2009) defined the root of many unethical business decisions as "malicious obedience," a negative aspect of the "traditional business model" where only those at the top give orders, and the rest follow without question (par. 2). In these organizations, the "cultural reinforcement of deference to authority adapted to a business setting can also force people to unwillingly accept and internalize these aspects of malicious obedience (Ashkenas, 2011, par. 2). Should this continue to spread out, innovation and creativity can grind down into factionalism, bureaucracy, and a group desensitized to various ethical concerns. Hess (2013) considered that rules and regulations "necessarily exist to establish a basic framework within which an organization operates," but they must allow the employee to adapt any response to "solid individual decision-making in a crisis" (par. 6, 8). If not, any "slavish obedience" to company policy will only hurt the people—and employees—intended to serve (par. 5).

Table 4: List of causes for problematic compliance.

Reason for Problematic Compliance	Cause
Ignorance	Originated from a failure in "culture and management"; training, suppression, or lack of encouragement
Fear of consequences	Originated from company expectations to strict conformity
Company protection	Originated from employee's irrational expectations to defend the company.

Note: Adapted from "Think for yourself: The danger of blind obedience," by M. Hess, 2013, CBS Interactive Inc., https://www.cbsnews.com/news/think-for-yourself-the-danger-of-blind-obedience/.

You see, we've explored the role of compliance and obedience and its ties to business success. But what about conformity? Look at this statement from Pech (2001):

> Everyone falls victim to the influence of conformity. We get to see the latest movie or wear the new fashion in footwear and clothes. We attend

a particular university because that is where our friends go. We agree to absurd extremes of behavior in the name of political correctness. Conformity declares agreement with the norm, recognition of the group and its membership, an unwillingness to be isolated (p. 568).

In reality, everybody has felt the pressure to conform in order to fit into a certain group. Constable, Shuler, Klaber, & Raskauskas defined conformity as "changing attitudes and beliefs to match those of others within the group" (par. 1). To successfully conform, the person must consider someone—arguably a leader——to maintain "legitimacy and credibility, if only to facilitate the group's change" (par. 1). Conformity differs from compliance over the aim and course of action intended to achieve; for compliance, it is a simple task, whereas for conformity it involves changing one's attitudes or beliefs, often slowly, with the help of a facilitator to engage (par. 2) slowly. Conformity also differs from obedience regarding the role of submission to authority: whereas conformity involves cognitively adjusting to a leader's or group's circumstances, obedience refers to following what an authority says without any cognitive discussion (Miller, 2014; Brody, 2013, par. 10). But, in reality, why do we conform?

Epley and Gilovich (1999) discussed in their research how conformity produces "internal conflict"—a person may believe that a course of action or specific behavior would be "immoral," yet not doing so forces the person to feel "ostracized" and ridiculed (p. 578). In business, conformity is much more complicated; from "modeling the behavior of others in similar [or desirable] roles, to agreeing to team decisions without any recourse of dispute, the person's "preferences and beliefs" are put into question (Gino, 2016, par. 7). Here are many reasons people choose to conform:

- **Social pressure:** Three types of social influence are identified: *informational* (or social proof); *normative*, where people are expected to conform to the positive-reinforcing expectations of a trip (Lord, Lee, & Choong, 2001; Deutsch & Gerard, 1955, p. 629); and *value-expressive*, where the person finds a psychological footing with the group and conforms through admiration (Lord, Lee, & Choong, 2001). Gino, Kouchaki, & Galinsky (2015) also stated that the more successful a person is at portraying authentic experiences, the more interpersonally connected he or she is judged to be (p. 983).

- **Status quo comfort:** People conform to the things they know. Gino (2016) regarded status quo practices are important to develop our performance, but can also de-crease and constrain any attempts to innovate and integrate into peak performance. Henderson (2016) defined this phenomenon as the *status quo bias*, where the "allure of inertia" hinders the ability to make better decisions in the long run over short-term comfort (par. 12). Fleming, Thomas, & Dolan (2010) referred to the status quo bias as the "suboptimal acceptance to a default choice option", and in their study discovered that "participants are more likely to accept the status quo when faced with different choices, leading to more errors" (p. 6605, 6607).

- **Interpreting information in a self-serving manner:** Described as "motivated skepticism" by Ditto and Lopez (1992), this means that the "information is consistent with a preferred conclusion and, consequently, less information is required" to reach a decision (p. 568). In other terms, we favor the information that best conforms to our beliefs because we consider them as assets worthy to be protected and, thusly, will make things hard to change and update (Taber & Lodge, 2006). By looking at information that merely reinforces our glitches, we "subtly stack the deck against good decisions" (Gino, 2016, par. 17).

Even though everyone has conformed to appease a rule or fit into a group or subculture, there are four categories of conformity as addressed by Kelman (1958) and McLeod (2016), and an additional one to consider:

- **Compliance:** As discussed, compliance within a group context involves acquiescing publicly to majority thinking even if one disagrees privately in order to "gain specific

rewards or approval and avoid specific punishments or disapproval" (McLeod, 2016; Kelman, 1958, p. 53). Should
there be no reasons to comply with the group, then
compliance ceases to function.

- **Identification:** Also known as *group membership*, the
  person conforms to the expectations of a social role; in
  Kelman's words, "the individual actually believes in the
  responses which he [or she] adapts through identification
  but their specific content is more or less irrelevant"
  (McLeod, 2016; Kelman, 1958, p. 53).

- **Internalization:** This occurs when there is both public and
  private agreement to public conformity. Also known as
  genuine acceptance, the person sincerely believes that the
  majority group has greater knowledge, to which the minor-
  ity cannot easily change (McLeod, 2016; Kelman, 1958, p.
  53).

- **Ingratiation:** Considered a much more opportunistic
  variant of compliance, ingratiation involves conforming
  "to appear more amiable to another person or group," become more attractive, or receive a favor from another person (Waude, 2017, par. 1; Pandey & Rastogi, 1979, p.
  221). Different ways to ingratiate with others include
  showing an interest to an admired person, flattery and
  compliments, and body language.

Figure 5: Types of conformity.

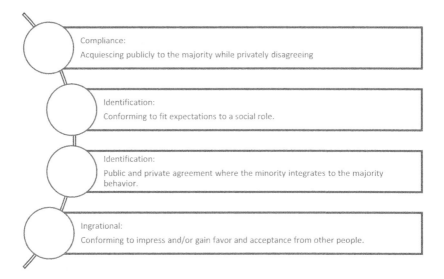

Note: Information adapted from "What is conformity?", by S. McLeod, 2016, *Simply Psychology*, https://www.simplypsychology.org/conformity.html.

The Value of Nonconformity

We humans are a *very* malleable bunch, and the way we conform to meet other's expectations is nothing short of interesting. And, as I said earlier, conforming is never inherently bad. That being said, excessive conformity to appease or look for a favor slowly whittles away at your identity. To be successful, you must creatively adapt to the business circumstances that challenge the value of your work. Managing others' expectations is fine, but placing your skills and abilities in a conformist box saps your chances to succeed in the future. Without looking ahead, there is never a chance to grow and develop your resilience and independence. Conformity is, in fact, the antithesis of success since, without it, you lack the authenticity to speak for yourself and communicate effectively with your clients. As described by Livni (2016),

> Remember, however; not even rebels can break all the rules or create chaos on the job. Be flexible and agile, and rebellion will speed up processes and be appreciated […] You'll stand out, feel better about your work, and be more successful in your career as your true self emerges and your value becomes apparent (par. 11).

Nonconformists are innovative. Pech (2001) referred to innovation as an important concept to develop the "role of organizational creativity" through transformation, revision, and "active learning" (p. 566). By looking beyond conventional ways to solve problems, nonconformists are committed to developing new ways of thinking, new values to structure a business, and new opportunities to grow (Oppong, 2016). Thinking differently enables others to look at the world through a different lens, and achieve greater opportunities to develop their skills. Even consumers embrace something Brooks (2014) titled *creative choice*, as a tendency exists to "seek differentness by selecting original, novel, or unique consumer goods" (par. 5)—in other words, even consumers seek something different to purchase *most* of the time!

To make a point, Henry Ford has said, "If I had asked people what they wanted, they would have said faster horses" (Vlaskovits, 2011), and there have been many famous experiments done to prove just how people will conform to fit into the group. People will change their "opinion" just to get along with the other people and not be marginalized. To remember, however, that conformity has a sensible purpose at certain times. But feeling the persistent need to conform may be coming from negative life experiences, including bullying or having an adult who was very influential in your life creating that need to conform.

There are many success stories of entrepreneurs who broke the mold and didn't conform. For example, Steve Jobs came out with the iPod at a time when MP3 players and Walkmans dominated the market. Think of how hard he had to sell his idea to his team of investors only to begin funneling money into research and development. Why not just make a *better* MP3 player? Because Steve Jobs was a trailblazer. Also, Larry Payne and Sergey Brin were repeatedly told they had a bad idea in their hands, that the marketplace was too full with search engines and dot-com skeletons. Yahoo and Alta Vista were giants, but Google saw each company's glaring flaws and pounced on the process to success!

Stories like these are the ones we, as entrepreneurs, love to remember and emulate in our own fields dreaming that, one day, we *become* the next giant-killer or industry disruptor. It takes guts to go against what people are telling you. You may question if they may be right. But what if they're actually *wrong*? You'll never know until you try. I created this book because I've done things differently all my life. I've always looked for new and better ways to do things. I've always desired to become a serial entrepreneur. Yes, there were times when I ignored some sound advice. But there were also times where, after taking a chance, I forged ahead and proved to *myself* that I was right. But always remember your goals, for success has many parents, but failure is an orphan.

A Little Creativity

British psychologist Dr. Jeremy Dean (2009) referred to creativity as "a much-coveted asset" because unorthodox thinking can offer us "wealth, fame, and status" (par. 1)—and if you choose to, a little of transparent, unpopular and rule-breaking creativity to develop your nonconformist side. Brooks (2014) considered this an "unpopular choice" of "products and brands" that are disrupting social norms and conduct (par. 5). In addition, Pech compared the difference in a conformity-based business model, which creates "more of the same," and an individualistic and nonconformist culture developed through employee productivity: "Creative thinking leads to change, and if that change provides social or economic benefits, the result becomes an innovation" (p. 559).

That said, it does not mean that any attempt at nonconformity needs be chaotic; instead, it is important to be both "flexible and agile" when developing any nonconformist plan, which will allow others to observe the value of nonconformity in the company (p. 566).

Avoiding similarity involves downgrading styles of consumption by losing interest in material impressions (Brooks, C., 2014, par. 5). Belleza, Gino, and Keinan (2014) noted how "nonconformity leads to positive interferences of status and competence" when nonconformist actions are *intentional* and *aware* of what is intended to be broken (par. 3). As an example, a person who wears a yellow tie instead of the normal drab colors issued by others can create a positive statement that calls attention to its dissimilarity.

Figure 6: Behavioral manifestations of nonconformity.

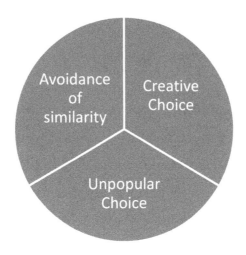

Note: Adapted from "Dressed for success? Harvard researcher says you may be doing it wrong" by C. Brooks, 2014, http://www.businessnewsdaily.com/5979-the-benefits-of-being-nonconforming.html.

Bad Ideas

According to American biochemist and author Linus Pauling, "The best way is to have a lot of ideas, and throw away the bad ones" (as cited in Thorne, 2015, par. 17). In fact, why are we afraid of bad ideas? What circumstances are we exposed to in bad ideas that are oftentimes impossible or undesirable to accomplish? Marketing strategist Jared Coker (2016) explained the circumstances and the many excuses that ultimately force them into the status quo: that they sounded "too aggressive, doesn't fit to the marketplace, [or there is] not sufficient talent" to develop (par. 2).

New ideas are the ultimate rejection of conformity, for they challenge the expectations of what can be done in order to improve a company by confronting long-established power structures and their actual perceived value or lack thereof (Coker, 2016, par. 5); rejuvenating company knowledge through new hires, teaching, or research (par. 6); force company authorities and the old guard to relinquish control (par. 7); and force us to engage with our fears (par. 8). Bad ideas should never be avoided—in fact, they should be fully embraced.

In a 2011 study about the duplicitous and contradictory value of creativity, researchers learned that people rejected novel ideas out of certainty even if they looked to creativity as a "desired goal" (Mueller, Melwani, & Goncalo, 2012). Likewise, the double-standard stigma against creative people is shown in the school system, where "creative kids are seen as more disruptive" and refuse to "follow the rules" as expected by authorities (Westby & Dawson, 1995). According to researchers, uncertainty leads more likely to unrecognize and disavow creative ideas, looking at the world with fear and apprehension (Dean, 2011). Regarding the conforming values of certainty against creativity, Konnikova (2012) acknowledges the differences:

> As a general rule, we dislike uncertainty. It makes us uneasy. A certain world is a much friendlier place. And so, we work hard to reduce whatever uncertainty we can, often by making habitual, practical choices, choices that protect the status quo (par. 3).

In essence, bad ideas are never inherently *bad*—they are only misguided attempts for success. Maybe your employees offer certain off-the-cuff suggestions that seem bizarre, senseless, or even downright incomprehensible. Some may radically change the course of the company in a direction you may never be comfortable with. Others are out of step with your company values and culture. But if you wish to be successful in the long run, you need to pay close attention to the creative folk, the dissenters, and the free thinkers in the business. Bad ideas are beneficial as the first step for "processing your thoughts for potential ideas," to which a change in both approach and environment are necessary for generating new, future ideas: "A bad idea today is worth remembering and even documenting because the timing may be off" (Wright, 2017, par. 12).

Successful people don't worry about what other people think of their ideas. That doesn't mean they don't listen to good advice. When a successful person has a great idea, something they wholeheartedly believe in, they will continue to pursue it in spite of people telling them that it will never work. Throughout history, there are many incredible examples of how this process has led to some of the greatest products ever invented. So, if you're an entre-preneur and find yourself worrying too much about what people think of you, or think of your idea, there is a good reason why. You see, it's in our nature to want to be liked, to fit in and this thought process goes back to a time when if you were not accepted and ultimately rejected, you could die. So, it makes sense why someone would be worried about not being liked because the primitive mind is trying to survive.

Dix et al. (2006) referred to a neat trick to *encourage* the creation of bad ideas because, "In practice, the majority of bad ideas are extreme variants of existing and potentially good ideas" (sec 1.1, par. 3). By exchanging the term "bad" with "silly," it allows people to gauge expectations and challenge contradictions. Moreover, engaging in critical thinking, problem-solving, and design explores the relationship between "dimensions, properties," and other criteria for bad ideas (p. 5).

Figure 7: Development process of Bad Ideas.

Note: Information adapted from *Why bad ideas are a good idea* by A. Dix, et al., 2006, *Proceedings of HCIEd.*

Successful People Don't...

Have you ever heard the story of how the infant incubator was created? Dr. Martin Couney was a pediatrician who was born in Germany in 1870 and is the inventor of the baby incubator. Premature birth was one of the highest causes of infant mortality during the early 20th century. In fact, 36% of all infant deaths in 1925 were due to premature birth. Dr. Couney's own daughter was born premature, and because of her father's care, she survived. The reason I'm telling you this story is to point out that Dr. Couney was not heralded as a champion, in fact, quite the contrary. He faced a lot of skepticism from the medical community who did not believe that his methods would work. He wasn't able to get any banks to finance the production of the incubators because they never believed that hospitals would put something like that into service. Dr. Couney had to do this all by himself.

It would've been easy for Dr. Couney at this point to give up. A lot of people would have given up. However, Dr. Couney knew that he had something different, something special, even though no one else could see it. What makes this story even more interesting is the method Dr. Couney needed to use to get his invention financed. Criticism from the medical community was already significant and now he would face even more criticism because of the way he chose to finance the development and production of this life-saving technology. You see, he decided to take these premature babies that he was trying to save and put them in an exhibit, in a sideshow, a carnival act so to speak. The advertisement invited people to come and see the tiny babies in these little glass enclosures. At the time these carnivals and sideshows featured many of these oddities, and Dr. Connie realized that this may be the only way he could finance his project. The first exhibit using these incubators was at the 1896 Berlin exposition. A local hospital gave him several premature babies simply because the hospital had determined that these babies were going to die. The incubator technology was a success and resulted in saving each of the infants' lives. The purpose and intention of Dr. Couney was to show this technology and how he could save the lives of these premature babies and finance the future use and development by charging admission fees to see the tiny babies. It worked. Visitors watched these little premature infants receive treatments, grow and survive.

As Dr. Couney continued to successfully save these children, hospitals in the USA began referring parents with premature babies to Dr. Couney in Germany. He accepted these children at no cost to the parents, and this was because he was still funding his operations from the expositions and fairs. It was estimated that this breakthrough technology saved about 90% of the premature babies placed in his care.

In today's society, Dr. Couney would have never been able to use the unique funding source he deployed in the early 20th century. Besides the expositions in Germany, Dr. Couney featured the babies at Coney Island as well as World's Fair expositions including New York City's World Fair. In Atlantic City, he placed a permanent infant incubator exhibit across from Million Dollar Pier. It began in Atlantic City in 1902 and patrons paid one dollar to view the babies and listen to lectures on how the program worked. At one point the admission was dropped, and donations were accepted instead. The exhibit was in place as early as 1902.

Eventually, the technology became accepted by hospitals, and by 1940 Dr. Couney closed almost all the exhibits. The one in Atlantic City closed its doors in 1943, and Dr. Couney passed away at his home in Coney Island in 1950. How close did he come to giving up, to accepting and conforming to what the medical community was telling him? How many children would have died without this pioneer who challenged the status quo and defied the critics? Dr. Couney didn't worry about what other people thought. Successful people don't worry about what other people think about them or their ideas. Do you? If you said yes, then there is a reason why you do. An error message has developed, and the Inspired Performance Program can help you correct that.

This is why the Inspired Performance Program encourages you to develop the skills inside you to encourage nonconformity in the business culture. There's no reason to stay in your business' comfort zone if only to assuage your fear of success or the future. It's a new time for innovation, and your nonconformity to break the rules can become the difference between an average, run-of-the-mill company, and a successful business with the power to change the world. By not conforming to others' expectations, you're free to develop your values and align your business success!

#4. Blame

Successful people take responsibility for their own situations.

The Dance of Blame

We all know someone who refuses to take responsibility for their actions. Someone that blames everybody in the world except themselves. Someone that appears to have a valid excuse every time he or she is asked to do something. Someone who cannot take any criticism in stride and chooses the safest way to protect themselves. Dealing with these types of people can be equally tense and frustrating because they become roadblocks to your business success. It can be uncomfortable or undesirable—and you may even walk on eggshells for it—in order to avoid delegating important tasks to them. You can fire them, but you know replacing them could take an inordinate amount of time and expense. In the end, you are forced to choose between staying in the status quo and making a radical change.

On the other hand, we all know someone who takes too much responsibility for their own good. Someone that everybody––and even you—dump the work on out of confidence that he or she can handle it. Someone who is an excellent and diligent worker, and also an overachiever. Someone who has a hard time collaborating with teams and despises any attempts to delegate their work, or say no and recognize their limits. These people are treated as star employees by everyone due to their diligence and the fact that they rarely cause any problems solely by their performance. However, working with them can also be frustrating because they cannot engage successfully with company culture. By taking too much responsibility on their shoulders, misbalance occur, even from well-meaning people.

Responsibility and blame are a two-way street, and everybody must learn how to recognize our share to be successful. Taking responsibility for your work is a hard proposition when things go horribly wrong, but this also enables you to become different, develop self-respect in your work, become respected by your peers, and grow your business to success. Audiences, investors, and consumers alike will develop a healthy sense of trust that will create a glitch-free relationship in the future. And, by creating a business culture that encourages people to take responsibility for themselves, everyone will grow into successes, too!

Why do We Blame Each Other?

That being said, why do we blame each other? What can we gain from blame? Is there a good explanation for why people blame other people whenever something goes wrong? Of course there is! Understanding why people do it is halfway to the solution.

You may find yourself deflecting responsibility. Or you may not even know that you're doing it at all. If you've been walking for twenty years with a sprained ankle and you limp, then someone asks, "Why are you limping?" You're surprised to hear them say that because you have been limping for so long, you can't see it anymore. It's important to note that it can be occurring in seemingly benign situations.

Look at this example:

> You're late for a doctor's appointment, and you blame your tardiness on the traffic when in reality you left 20 minutes later than accounted for. If that doesn't fly when you run it past the receptionist, you rationalize it to yourself by blaming your spouse for making you drop off a package in the FedEx drop box on your way. You justify the detour to the FedEx drop box put you right into traffic, and now the receptionist seemed skeptical. For crying out loud, why doesn't everyone just understand that it's not your fault for always being late or not getting things done on time? Is this something you recognize in your own life? If so, there may be a good reason for it. Now, I can already hear you say, "I knew it wasn't my fault."

There is a young lady that comes in on a regular basis because she has convinced herself that she suffers from anxiety and depression. In most cases, I don't see someone for an extended length of time. In her case, however, she has benefitted from the sessions by working on life skills. Her self-esteem was danger-ously low when we started working together, but I witnessed an incredible change in three months. She dresses with a more stylish and age-appropriate flair, clearly demonstrating she takes greater care of herself overall. At the same time, she mentions that she gets anxious and believes medication is the answer to eliminate these negative emotions.

To address her concerns, I ask her to describe a situation where she gets anxious, to which she mentioned certain details about something she's been afraid to tell her father about. I then asked her if there may be an alternative solution to medication, to which she replied, "I can't see one." She blamed others for her problems; a behavior formed early in life from emotional concus-sions, a coping mechanism to deflect her pain. Even if she was right in the fact that, as a child, she wasn't responsible for these actions, her avoidant behaviors surfaced in a feeble attempt to pro-tect her to the point of believing that medication would help her handle and even eliminate—albeit temporarily—the anxiety. Now this behavior was showing up in another form, avoiding the solu-tion to her current problem and expecting a medication would help her handle the anxiety. The solution she couldn't see was to tell her father about what she was avoiding, thinking it would be a problem, and it probably would. However, she could not avoid the issue forever. A deadline was fast approaching, and there was no way to avoid it. I was able to help her understand that by talking this situation head on, deal with it now; then the anxiety would stop. In my book, You Must Be Out of Your Mind, I discuss that any time you feel an emotion, then your mind is requesting an action. Fear is used to create an action and avoid or escape a threat. Anger is used to attack or extinguish a threat. She was anxious because she *predicted* how her father would respond to what she needed to tell him as many scenarios ran through her mind. Her subconscious mind was trying to protect her from the scenarios she was imagining even though they weren't happening right now. The imagined and predicted reactions she was anticipating from her father were seen as threats and her mind was responding to the perceived threat. Makes sense, right?

Understanding this concept is key to our program. When we fear something that happened twenty years ago, that is an error message: Your mind is calling for an action for you to do something about it, even if nothing can be done. What can you do NOW about that? NOTHING! However, your mind sees the disturbing high-resolution images stored in memory and thinks they are still happening right now. Error message. Anxiety is on the other side, the future. It is viewing the high-resolution images of something that you're imagining and reacting to it in real time. Once again, an error message. What can you do about something that is not happening? NOTHING! So, the solution for her was to deal right now with the situation, and there would be no more imagining what her father would say. Problem solved.

Is this happening to you? Dwelling on future events and predicting reactions. If you have been doing this for a long time, walking with a sprained ankle, then your mind will create a work around to these unsolved problems. If you have been predicting other people's reactions, and your predictions are not met with reality, then your mind will avoid responsibility and blame the other person for not reacting the way you had predicted. Can you see how easily this happens? If I predicted a reaction and it became my reality, then the person doesn't meet my reality. Whose fault is it? Not mine, it must be theirs. Then this behavior follows me throughout my life, and I don't recognize I do it anymore. I blame other people when my expectations are not met. That's why the key to fixing a problem is to recognize it exists; thus, if you're always blaming other people when things don't go your way, then it will create a problem in the way you run your business, or deal with your friends and family. You may reach a certain amount of success, but these behaviors will hold you back. Successful people understand that inherently or have learned it through experience and adapted. Are you able to accept that you have this problem, and are you ready to change it? If so, the Inspired Performance Institute's programs can help you reach peak performance and develop a greater sense of responsibility towards yourself.

The Blame Game

Research says there's no way of predicting what type of people play the blame game, to which I confidently reply: I can tell you *who* is prone to blame, I see it all the time. It arises for people who have suffered disturbing or traumatic events at some point in their lives. Blame is a way of dealing with a situation that doesn't turn out the way people predict, expect, or create, to which they don't want to take responsibility for it since their reality is affected. When you blame, your mind will use that lie to protect you and keep you safe from any perceived threats.

On the other hand, there are people who blame themselves for anything and everything that goes wrong. Once again, this is coming from experiences earlier in life: from receiving blame from parents or influential people to failed marriages and extreme financial hardships, young and inexperienced minds look for a multitude of reasons to analyze why the people around them failed, concluding that, if they had just been a *better* child, *none* of this would have happened. It's not true, but they don't have enough life experience to *know* that.

Here's an example: A 35-year-old woman told me she had an overwhelming feeling of being worthless. She was constantly afraid that she would be fired from her job as soon as they realized that she was worthless. Her husband knew that, so he took advantage by mistreating her. I informed her that she felt that way because certain life events produced it. She then remembered the first time: when she was a six-years-old, her abusive father beat her with his belt for dropping a glass of milk and put her in the hall closet for what she imagined was a full day. And such abuse left her with a sense of worthlessness that is still as prevalent today as when she was a child. Only this time, it created negative behaviors that affected her personal and professional relationships.

I asked her to imagine that if we went into the parking lot and saw a man beating his six-year-old child with his belt because she dropped a glass of milk, would we think that child is worthless? No! But can you imagine why the child would interpret this event differently? What could make this person who's in charge of my survival do this? The child will attach a meaning of worthlessness to the experience, especially when taking into account the *lack* of life experience. When you look at why someone would keep blaming themselves, you can hear negative expressions like, "Nothing ever works out for me," or "I have the worst luck!" People who blame themselves are doing so not necessarily for reassurance or modesty; they truly believe they're at fault for everything that goes wrong in their life. If you just tried to tell them it's not true, you'll be met with rejection. The solution is to update those disturbing or traumatic events from earlier in their life, so the mind will no longer use that information in the present. Of course, when there is no reasonable explanation for an outcome then the person may blame it on fate, karma or a higher power. Perhaps they're being punished for some reason.

In another chapter, we will also examine another behavior that has some ties to blame. I'm talking about someone who experiences success but feel like they just got lucky. Once again, successful people don't blame other people and also don't believe in luck. The solution is to address the underlying causes of why someone blames other people or why they assign blame to themselves. That's exactly what the Inspired Performance Program (TIPP) does.

Signs of a Toxic Culture

In many companies, open lines of accountability and communication foster an important sense of community. But in other toxic environments, where petty politics are rife, and competition is fierce and often unethical, a culture of blame saps any available energy into negativity. A blame culture is "A set of attitudes such as those within a particular business or organization, that is characterized by an unwillingness to take risks or accept responsibility for mistakes due to fear of criticism or prosecution" ("blame culture," n.d.). In this type of work environment, gossip, arguments, backstabbing, and ambiguity toward group responsibilities demoralize employees and damage any trust in the company (Karten, 2013) because "It is sludge in your [business] engine that slows down the gears and eventually corrodes them" (Ryan, 2016, par. 3). In many cases, circumstances in the blame culture go unquestioned and are unchallenged by employees and employers alike for fear of rocking the boat. As a result, avoiding responsibility compromises safety and forces people to "pass the buck" to other scapegoats (Bond, 2007, p. 1).

Ryan also described certain signs of a toxic culture:

- **Lack of communication:** If people smile, joke, or even have an honest conversation about group goals, that is a sign that communication has been frigid within the company. With this in mind, sometimes problems that can be misconstrued as "poor communication" can very well be a lack of group structure, which can muddle lines of communication (Markman, 2017).

- **Power plays and hierarchy:** Business can be as dirty as office politics and power plays. When people care more about titles and job descriptions than the company's overall health and well-being, there is a problem. According to an office politics survey from Robert Half International, three-fifths of 400 surveyed workers "believe that involvement in office politics is at least somewhat necessary to get ahead" (King, 2016, par. 2).

- **Bureaucracy:** When company rules and policies become much more important than customer service, safety, and even good judgment, that is a sign of a toxic blame culture in your company. A "rule and compliance-driven" company that "fertilizes a culture of back-covering, responsibility-shifting, and finger-pointing" (Ward, 2017, p. 3) demoralizes employees from engaging in creative problem-solving techniques and sap away at business innovation in the long run (Hamel, 2014).

- **Lack of mid- and upper-level interaction:** Research by Mastroianni and Storberg-Walker (2014) on employee perceptions of workplace interactions revealed that "feelings of well-being were enhanced by work interactions, which were trusting, collaborative, and positive, [making them feel] valued and respected" (p. 798). On the other hand, detracting interactions between coworkers and friends include distrust, disrespect, and lack of collaboration (p. 807), which can be amplified through uneven interactions within mid- and upper-level management involving a lack of collaboration within other groups.

- **Employee unhappiness:** Keeping employees happy and motivated "help organizations survive," are "more productive," and allow employees to become self-actualized (Lindner, 1998, par. 8). Conversely, if employees are unhappy and management and leadership do not take employee happiness (or unhappiness) into account, these can have disastrous effects on your business. Keep in mind that motivation has two aspects: as an "energizing force," and ability to accomplish goals (Meyer, J.P., Becker, T.E., and Vanderberghe, 2004, p. 992).

- **Punitive business culture and fear:** Kamenetz (2013) reported that "A culture of fear is toxic, whether it's the deliberate by-product of intimidating or an accidental chilling produced by a punitive management style" (par. 7). Threats, fear, and disagreements, most often as an attempt to give up control, only forces employees to look for other jobs where they feel they will not be haphazardly punished (Yon, 2014). Allowing employees to make mistakes within a controlled environment and encouraging their successes boosts employer empowerment and motivation.

- **Unreasonable requests:** Unreasonable requests that step over the line of job descriptions can be a setup for failure if not careful. Weak and inflexible boundaries break your sense of safety and compromise your ability to work successfully. The best way to place bosses in their place (no pun intended) without blame is to "confront, reform, undermine, expose and even unseat [toxic] leaders" and reminding yourself of a company's culture (Lauer, 2005, part. 1).

- **Grapevine communication (this means gossip!):** Formally speaking, gossip can be defined as "informal and evaluative talk in an organization, usually among no more than a few individuals, about another member of that organization who is not present" (Rooks, Tazelaar, & Snijders, 2001, p. 91). While efficient *if used properly*, this type of grapevine communication can be fast-spreading, uncontrollable, and damaging to both individuals and the company (Crampton, Hodge, and Mishra, 1998, p. 568), which can be exacerbated by the communication's importance; "ambiguity and lack of clarity"; an "insecure and threatening" environment; and a climate of distrust (p. 571).

- **Lack of employee latitude:** When leaders refuse to encourage employees to be creative and innovative—since managers "are the most knowledgeable about which employee work outcomes should be creative, and they have considerable influence over the context within which creativity can occur" (Zhang & Bartol, 2010, p. 707). If, on the other hand, employees are not empowered and motivated to make their own decisions (p. 108), this will eat away at employees' "job satisfaction, exhaustion, and depression" (Warr, 1990, p. 285) by undermining employees' "control over potential tasks" and job demands, or the "psychological stressors involved in accomplishing the workload"(Karasek, qtd. In Warr, 1990, p. 285).

- **Culture of fear:** While having reservations about job performance, a culture of fear is at the extreme of a grossly inefficient workplace, which is why "employees today often face intense pressure to meet ambitious targets with smaller teams and fewer resources—and expect repercussions if they don't" (Meinert, 2015, p. 1). In such a blame-based environment, it becomes hard to build trust and "Fear erodes joy in work, limits communication, and stifles innovation", and "Fear fosters short-term thinking as people search to avoid reprisal, perhaps at the expense of others in the system" (Suárez, 1993, p. 2).

Table 5: Signs of a Toxic Culture.

Signs of a Toxic Culture	
Lack of communication	Punitive business culture
Power plays and hierarchy	Unreasonable requests
Bureaucracy	Grapevine communication
Lack of mid- and upper-level interaction	Lack of employee latitude
Employee unhappiness	Culture of fear

Note: Adapted from "Ten unmistakable signs of a toxic culture," by Ryan, 2016, Forbes, https://www.forbes.com/sites/lizryan/2016/10/19/ten-unmistakable-signs-of-a-toxic-culture/#3f92541c115f.

Promoting a Just Culture

Instead of promoting a toxic culture, it is important to promote a "just culture," one that encourages employee accountability and safety without any office politics or recklessness. Eurocontrol (n.d.) defined a "just culture" as "a culture in which front-line operators are not punished for actions or decisions that are commensurate with their experience and training, but also a culture in which violations and willful destructive acts by frontline operators or others are not tolerated" (par. 1). In a just culture, there is no use to blame departments or the public for any avoidable mistakes; against the grain, "organizations with a just culture are as willing to expose areas of weakness as they are to display areas of excellence" (Frankel, Leonard, & Denham, 2006,

p. 1962). Through this model, there is an ability to distinguish between "human error, at-risk behavior, reckless behavior, malicious, willful violations and the corresponding levels of accountability" (Pepe & Cataldo, 2011, p. 51). This allows employers, managers, and employees to recognize the consequences of their actions within the company culture.

Why is addressing blame important for any successful business? Before addressing how to eradicate blame, it is important to define blame. According to philosophers Tongazzini and Coates (2016), "To blame someone is to respond in a particular way to something of negative normative significance about him [or her] or his [or her] behavior" (par. 1). Blame can happen every time a specific wrong has been committed, such as a disgruntled customer or an avoidable work accident. In this case, blame can be used as either a form of punishment or a way to keep track of one's failure to abide by certain standards of behavior (Pickard, 2013, p. 616, 617; Tognazzini & Coates, 2016). Blame is also irrational in the sense that, tied with resentment, it can spontaneously "erupt" and avoid responsibility or air out frustrations (Pickard, 2013, p. 615). This is why research has shown that "in organizations where blame is the norm, group members are likely to be less creative and perform poorly" (Bryner, 2010, par. 3).

Shifting the blame to someone else never works either, as this leads employees to suffer withdrawal, lack of engagement and motivation, justification, and defensiveness, only exacerbating tensions in the workplace ("Why," 2016, par. 2). Without this engagement, "the antidote of job burnout" (Bakker, Schaufeli, Leiter, & Taris, 2008, p. 187, 188), sufferers and all sense of creativity is destroyed—more so today, where "there is now a widespread belief that all mishaps and accidents are predictable and preventable; hence, if mishaps occur, someone must be blamed" (Lau, 2009, p. 1). With engagement, employees are energetic, enthusiastic, and immersed in their work to the point that self-determination is present, "being driven by the mere pleasure and satisfaction of taking part in an activity" (Bakker, Schaufeli, Leiter, & Taris, 2008, p. 187, 188; Martins, Rosado, Ferreira, & Biscaia, 2017, p. 40). In an engaged, blame-free environment, the "psychological presence" of engagement exhibits three important factors (Saks, 2006, p. 601; Mons, 2016): *alignment,* or experiencing a sense of meaning in their work; *psychological safety*; or dedication to the rule won't end in undesirable or negative consequences; or *psychological availability*, or accessing proper resources.

Figure 8: Values of Engagement.

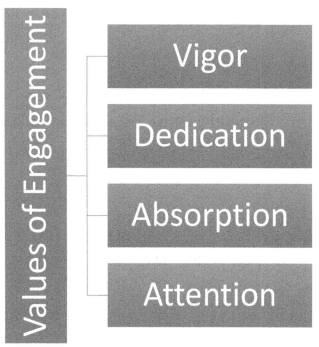

Note: Adapted from "Antecedents and consequences of employee engagement" by A.M. Saks, 2006, *Journal of Managerial Psychology*, 21(7), 600-619; "Enriching or depleting? The dynamics of engagement in work and family roles," by N.P. Rothbard, 2001, *Administrative Science Quarterly*, 46, 655-684; and "Work engagement: An emerging concept in occupational health psychology," by A.B. Bakker, W.B. Schaufeli, M.P. Leiter, & T.W. Taris, 2008, Work & Stress, 22(3),.

What's the Point of Making Excuses?

We've all made excuses at some point in our lives. Sometimes, we make excuses so we can deflect any criticism and project it on someone or something else. At other moments, we make excuses to escape from going to an undesirable event or taking an undesirable—but necessary—course of action. Our kids may have even learned to say to a teacher that "My dog ate my homework!" when, in most cases, they never even bothered to complete it in the first place! The fact of the matter is, excuses are another form of blame—and it can be disastrous for any successful business if they aren't kept in check.

Schlenker, Pantone, & Christopher (2001) defined excuses as "self-serving explanations, or accounts, that aim to reduce personal responsibility for questionable events, thereby disengaging core components of the self from the incident," and excuses on any case are contradictory since they are both "universally condemned while being universally used" (p. 15). At best, excuses are "a social lubricant vital to the smooth operation of daily life" (Goleman, 1984, p. 4)—meaning that these "white lies" allow us to compassionately deflect or make people feel better about themselves or their actions. At worse, excuses serve as "chronic evasions of responsibility borne of *irrational fear* [emphasis added]" (Goleman, 1984, par. 7), forcing excuses to distract them from reaching personal goals and insights. Excuses like this one are disempowering and divisive—and, as a consequence, more than one-fifth of Americans "overuse excuses to the point that may be detrimental to their emotional health" (par. 3).

Excuses are a form of self-handicapping and self-sabotage, in which people place obstacles before taking any action, under the subconscious expectation that failure would protect their fragile self-esteem (McCrea, 2001, p. 275). A 2008 study on the effects of self-sabotage on performance, McCrea (2008) concluded that excuses form a plateau or a sense of satisfaction with person, thus negating any motivation (or embarrassment) to succeed (p. 276; Carey, 2009). This form of self-handicapping lends itself to rigid, irrational beliefs that occur when their needs and contacts are placed in contact with humans' self-destructive nature through experiencing adversity (Kaya, Uğur, Şar, Ercengiz, 2017, p. 870). Additionally, three characteristics are important in any form of self-handicapping: the *handicap*, the *reason*, and the *precedence of the strategy before the performance* (p. 872). For instance, a person who did not prepare for a major presentation did not sleep properly, and after the presentation's (perceived) failure by the person serves to protect his or her self-esteem. The *handicap* is not sleeping properly; the *reason* is the use of sleeplessness as an excuse, and the *strategy* involves not sleeping in order to fail the presentation.

Because "[p]eople use excuses when their self-esteem is threatened by past or expanded poor performance" (Caron, Whitbourne, & Halgin, 1992, p. 90). The attribution bias "overempasize[s] to dispositional explanations for behavior at the

117

expense of situational explanations" (Grimshaw, Baron, Mike, & Edwards, 2006, p. 12). This is what occurs with victim-blaming, which occurs when people question what a victim of an adverse circumstance could or should have done differently, such as in the case of a crime (Roberts, 2016). Unlike other types of excuse-making and self-handicapping where the motivation is external as a measure to project the person's self-criticism or self-sabotage to others, victim-blaming occurs under the *just world hypothesis*, or the idea that people deserve to pay for the consequences of their actions, be it good or bad, even if—through objective terms—has no bearing on the victim's character (Grinnell, 2016). In other terms, if someone goes through something negative, then they must have done something wrong to deserve it (Single, 2017). This is also reflected in a 1989 study by Konovsky & Jaster (1989) on impression management, concluding "businessmen and women were more likely to defend their questionable behavior by using excuses and justifications than to openly concede errors of judgment and behavior" (p. 391).

Figure 9: Graphical description of self-handicapping.

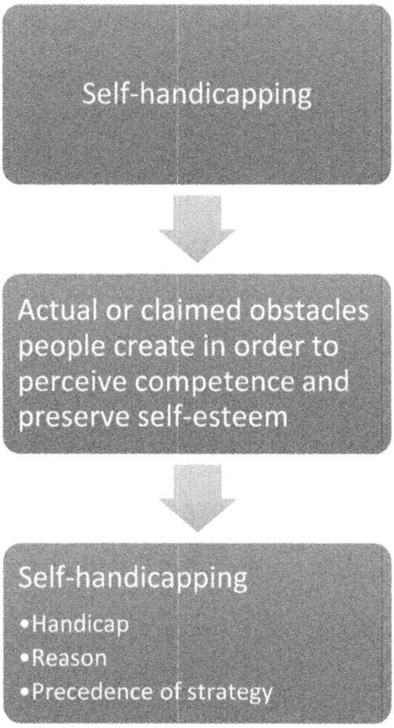

Note: Adapted from "Self-handicapping and irrational beliefs about approval in a sample of teacher candidates" by Kaya, Uğur, Sar, & Ercengiz (2017).

An important aspect of blame is *projection*, a defense mechanism that distorts people's reality by rendering themselves and others "unaware of their conscious and unconscious unwanted impulses" (Abeles, 2016, par. 1). But for every aspect of blame, including blame-shifting and victim-blaming, both the "just-world hypothesis" and rationalization involve a complex relationship between the external loci of control: whereas the external locus of control assumes "some outside force [...] is ruining your life", an internal locus of control makes "you believe that *you* are in the driver's seat" (Booth, 2016, par. 3). Blame is triggered by external laws of control, as you feel powerless over the circumstances, including fate, luck, or others. On the other hand, an internal locus of control is important for business as "[e]entrepreneurs are usually motivated by the sense that they can make things happen" (par. 16); with research findings placing an importance on increased academic performance, effective health-prevention behaviors, and greater social and political activism (Tracy, 2013, p. 6). They avoid the pain of *learned helplessness*, where people believe outcomes cannot be controlled by themselves (p. 7) against "the relationship between behavior and event" (Dweck, 1975, p. 675).

Learned Helplessness & Your Personal Power

A 1973 study on "reinforcement responsibility" by Dweck and Reppucci revealed that "children are more likely to give up in the face of failure [...] took less personal responsibility for the successes and failures they met with" and, should they take responsibility, attributed the outcomes of their behavior to ability rather than effort (Dweck, 1975, p. 674). This study reinforced the concept of learned helplessness, where repetitive and consecutive exposure to negative events will reduce their motivation, interfere with their performance, and trigger anxiety and depression as an "expectation of uncontrollability" (Pittman & Pittman, 1979, p. 39). Hiroto (1974) also defined learned helplessness "failure to escape" because, as per the original experiment, the "incentive for initiating responses had been lowered" and any expectation of independence is destroyed (p. 187). To better understand this concept, think of the locus of control as a continuum between internal and external factors; in a sense, learned helplessness represents the worst extremes of both factors—internally, they redirect the focus of their attribution to themselves; externally, they perceive any action they undertake will be tainted by circumstances out of their control. In essence, the blame in learned helplessness is twofold.

According to Wakeman (2010), learned helplessness is disastrous for any business, and workplace surveys proved that three out of ten workers believe finding any aspect of learned helplessness aids company success, yet four out of five leaders do not drive teams to accountability. If not, employees progressively begin to believe "that the odds are stacked against them, that they are the victims in most circumstances, and that they deserve special consideration of their 'circumstances' when they don't hit their goal" (par. 2). To Hough (2014), this exceedingly passive behavior will "flat-line productively, dent creativity, and see both physical and human resources paired into endorsing topic behavior" (par.

8). Even worse, the enforced negativity that learned helplessness provides is almost encouraged.

This is why establishing clear lines of communication and a clear procedure of accountability—both personal and team-related—creates opportunities to enjoy a sense of pride and ownership in their work, addresses what skills should be improved, and encourages trust and responsibility into the company brand. Bivins (2006) reported that a person must be held accountable if the person is functionally and/or morally responsible for an action; any harm occurred after taking the action; and no legitimate excuse for the action occurs (p. 25). For management professor Norman Bowie, "A responsible being is a being who can make decisions according to his or her insights. He or she is not under the control of others' (qtd. in Bivins, 2006, p. 23). Accountability is important because leaders "are answerable and willing to accept the outcomes or results of a project or activity," while responsibility encourages people to take the necessary steps to ensure accountability (Zenger, 2015, par. 6).

One thing is to take very little to no responsibility for one's actions. Another thing is to take too much responsibility to the point of overextending themselves. Karmin (2015) noted that, in some cases, people carry an excessive burden to "keep from feeling guilty and irresponsible for being blame[d] for others' failure," even though this thought is irrational (par. 4). In addition, research revealed that people with greater levels of self-control "may feel tired, annoyed, and perhaps even resentful" out of other's excessive (though not uncommon) reliance on their skills, even though they feel "respected and valued" by the challenge of other's expectations (Koval, vanDellen, Fitzsimmons, & Ranby, 2015, p. 763). Emotional, atmospheric conditions stemming from a need to control or have leadership force overachievers to "align their interpretations and perspectives or bring the misunderstandings to work a compromise" (Scott, 2017, p. 3); otherwise, rivalries and resentments can occur within the team.

This is what makes the Inspired Performance Program's stance on blame: nobody needs it! Neither business leaders, employees, human resources, collaborators, and consumers need not lock themselves in a tug-of-war of blame that leads to nowhere. When each piece of the business equation recognizes *their* share of the responsibility for any situation, there will be fewer misunderstandings and distrust between the parties. The same blame-free tactic applies to teams in every shape: by staving off every impulse of blame in every situation and encourage people to grow empowered by the opportunity to not only take responsibility, but also reap the benefits of success. In the end, what is the only thing that matters: failure through complaining, or success by honest efforts? This is what the Inspired Performance Program aims to do:

take away the blame in any situation by focusing on the actions that bring about change.

#5. Fail (to Appreciate Failure)

Successful people don't separate their successes from failures; rather, they see failure as part of the journey for success.

How Failure Breeds New Business

Have you ever failed at anything? If you say *no*, then you've probably never attempted anything. Successful people fail all the time. However, successful people see failures as a part of the process towards success. Even I know and recognize I've failed before. However, I don't see those failures as a failure; I see them as a formula for reaching a successful outcome. There have been many products throughout history that had seen many failures before they experienced success. In one of the earlier chapters, we discussed how the infant incubator came to light even though Dr. Cooney met with heavy criticism. His development could have been a failure in the wrong hands. His persistence to overcome the critics was the key to its success. For this reason, let me illustrate a few examples of products that could have been considered failures *if* the people gave up too early:

- Don't you love bubble wrap up? You love the sound of popping those little bubbles, hearing them crackle. But did you know that in 1960, it was originally designed to be *a new textured wallpaper*? Even though it was branded as an

125

initial failure, later it was marketed as housing insulation. And then IBM decided to use it for packaging for a computer in transit to keep it safe. It was an overnight success when, by all accounts, it started as a complete failure (Daily Mail Reporters, 2011).

- Apple founder, Steve Jobs had a lot of failures on his way to success; in fact, some of those failures cost him his job and the ability to control the company he founded in 1976. The steady string of failures forced the board of directors to oust him, but Steve Jobs never stopped believing in his ideas. He eventually returned to Apple in 1997 and turned the company around with the IMac and Ipod So, would Steve Jobs be the success he was without any of the failures? This is why I say that failure is just a part of the process of achieving success and the most successful people know this better than anyone.

- You may have used a lubricant called WD-40; but do you know where the name comes? The 40 represents the fact that it took 39 *failures* before they came up with the right formula! What would have happened if they would have given up after 39 attempts? Originally designed as a degreaser and rust protection solvent for the aerospace industry, it became a popular product amongst employees and engineers to the point that it eventually got packaged into aerosol cans and started to be sold in retail markets in 1958 (Madrigal, 2011).

Most people are afraid to fail. Makes sense, who wants to be seen as a failure? The fear of failure stops most people from attempting a new project or starting their own business. Here's the truth, everyone fails. Some failures are small, and some are epic. There is a tendency to see successful people as lucky, success just fell into their laps, or it was more about who they knew than what they knew. There is a definite connection to success and who you know, and yet that doesn't mean it's going to be an automatic success. Ever try to get money or support from a successful person, and they turn you down? When this happens, a person who doesn't understand success will see this as a sign of disrespect. They have so much. Why not help me out? That's why they have so much; they don't waste money on things they don't believe will work. So, you need to look at your idea, is there a fatal flaw that they see and you don't or don't want to. If you have a good idea, it's much easier to deal with successful people.

Because successful people have attempted endeavors and failed, they have more experience in overcoming adversity. They can see things more clearly. One of the most valuable things you can get from a successful person is their time. And their resilience is infinitely more valuable than their money or time spent on perfecting their company. Money and time come and go, but the marks of their resilience last forever. Time is precious. Money comes and goes, time just goes.

Failure and its Stigma

We see successful people in a different light, especially those with nice cars, big houses, and expensive vacations. You may not notice, however, but these people are human just like everyone else, worrying in secret about making the mortgage payment or paying the electric bill. When you look through that lens, you'll be amazed when you talk to these people that they had their phones turned off or electricity disconnected. When you listen to them speak, it's common for them to tell you the inspirations experienced during those trying times. This way, you'll learn that failure is part of the journey on your road to success. Does that mean you should embrace failure, and see the valuable lessons it brings? Of course! You see, without appreciating failure, it is difficult to appreciate success.

A Lesson in What *Not* To Do

On a regular map, it looks like Orlando and Los Angeles is about 12 inches apart, making it look shorter than it is. The same is true with success: It always seems like it shouldn't take so long to get there. Achieving success is never easy; in fact, it's hard work, and the failures along the way seem to make the trip longer. Keep in mind, however, that our minds are playing a trick on us when, in reality, the failures make it shorter. Isn't it better to find out sooner that something isn't working? Look at Thomas Edison: when asked about how many attempts he had taken at making the first electric light bulb he answered that he did find a lot of ways not to make a light bulb He never saw his attempts as failures; conversely, he recognized the value to learning what not to do. That's all failure is, a lesson in what *not* to do. The key to success is not giving up; instead, adapt your plan and make some tweaks based on the lessons of finding out what *doesn't* work.

Mark Twain, perhaps America's most beloved writer, and (nowadays controversial) humorist, is most recognized for creating *The Adventures of Huckleberry Finn*. For a guy with what could be considered a minimal formal education, his writing chops were pretty impressive! He worked as an apprentice in a printing company when he was 16 and loved spending his evenings reading books at the local library. Travelling across the country with the Confederate Army, Mark Twain began to write and to develop the dry wit we know and love.

When we think of a great leader, I think of someone like Winston Churchill. By all accounts, he was born into wealth, and the best of educational opportunities were at his fingertips. Although he had all this opportunity, he struggled in grade school. By the educational standards of the time, he would be seen as a failure; yet, he rose through the system to lead Great Britain to victory in World War II. During his school years, he was routinely punished for his poor academic performance. The same held true during his military service. He applied to the Royal Military College and was rejected for infantry service because of his poor grades, eventually being accepted in the cavalry where topics like algebra and British literature weren't as important. And do you believe that those early years of failures developed the great leader? Probably so.

Here are a few of his famous quotes on failure and perseverance.

"Success is not final; failure is not fatal: it is the courage to continue that counts."

"Success consists of going from failure to failure without loss of enthusiasm."

"Never, never, never give up."

On a personal note, something I discussed in my book "You Must Be Out of Your Mind.," I tell the story that has had a significant impact on my life. When I was a young teenager, enthusiastic about being the best tennis player I could be, the tennis pro at our local club gave me some amazing advice. His name was Vic, and I considered him a mentor. He would exchange tennis lessons with me in exchange for me helping practice with his students during lessons. After their lessons, he would hit with me and give me a tough workout, honing my skills. After one of the lessons, he sat down with me and said, "You want to be a great tennis player don't you?" I confirmed with an enthusiastic yes. He then gave me the secret, that's what he called it. He said, "lose a lot." I didn't understand right away. He explained that I would need to challenge myself by playing above my level, play better players. The early results would be a lot of losses. Those losses would teach me something every time if I just paid attention. What did they have that I could learn from, how did they hit this shot or that shot? In a short time, Vic said I would improve faster than playing the people at or below my level. His advice was simple, you learn from your losses. In fact, sometimes more lessons come from failure/loss than from success. It's just a loss, just a number. I still live by that advice today.

The Idea of Failure

In a hyper-competitive world such as this one, people find it hard to wrap their minds around the idea of failure leading to success. In one extreme, people are so afraid of feeling like a failure that every time any attempt to relate to clients or customers they can come across as desperation, if only to ward off the feeling of failure - but desperation, in and of itself, becomes a failure to relate: "Humans can work like a wolfpack when in groups and if they get a sniff of desperation they will either ostracize the perpetrator or target them unkindly" (Beaumont, 2015, par. 1). Trying too hard to become relevant or doing too much to please clients also invites a fair share of trouble, since this can show a lack of confidence in your brand and places doubt in your abilities as a marketer and a business leader. Baer (2015) reflected how failure at cleverness, bribery, and false marketing crosses the line from catchy and clever to desperate and just downright unethical, all of which are negative signs of a failure to relate.

Have you ever been fired from a job for some vague reason? Did your marriage fail to work out? Have you ever been passed over for a job promotion you thought you had in the bag? Have you ever been so close to following your dreams when, for some reason, the rug was pulled from under your feet? Everybody has faced failure at some point in their lives—we may not like it, but failure is as human as living, breathing, and dying. More so in business, a cut-throat arena where the chances to succeed are slim, but the chances to fail are overwhelmingly numerous—and not always in our conscious awareness, where our own unique set of atmospheric conditions can signal any danger. A failure like this can be overwhelming, disheartening, and traumatizing—but can be a necessary opportunity to grow into a mature business leader, athlete, and leader.

But before we describe how successful people don't fail (to appreciate failure), we must first address: why are we so obsessed with winning? Schwartz discussed an important limitation in the concept of winning: "The pursuit of any challenging goal is usually long and difficult, but the pleasure of victory tends to be fleeting. As any gambler knows, there is more pain in losing than there is pleasure in winning" (Williams, 2016, par. 2). To explain this, researchers (Medvec, Madey, & Gilovich, 1995) looked at athletes' emotional reactions through recorded NBC footage of the 1992 Summer Olympics, which revealed that "bronze medalists tend to be happier than silver medalists" due to their thinking— whereas silver medalists believe they could have won gold based on their effort, bronze medalists are happy that they could have placed at all (p. 603). Victory is addictive, and it can also be vicarious—you only need to look at a soccer field, a basketball court, or a golf course and see how coaches and parents disparage children for not fulfilling their unrealistic expectations. Yes, winning "generates intensity, determination, and effort, and often success can fill out life with meaning" (par. 30). But a competitive mindset is not without its problems.

An excessively competitive culture feeds off individualism, a value so ingrained in American culture that any attempt to introduce it in a business setting becomes "mindless, automatic, but powerful principles" for any organization (Son, 2013; Pfeffer, 1999, par. 1). It promotes self-fulfilling prophecies that offers severely unequal results, as "leaders will unwittingly act to fulfill" someone's poor expectations (par. 7). It fosters a simplistic differentiation between "winners" and "losers" (Williams, 2016, par. 29) and promotes a sort of self-righteousness for the winners and rumination by the losers; in fact, "the stronger the relationship between an organization and its members, the greater the willingness of individual members to engage in behaviors that support the group" (Fisher & Wakefield, 1998, p. 24). Most importantly, it forces us to seek validation through winning, and alienates others as enemies, mostly out of "insecurity and fear" (Griffiths, 2010, p. 228). This is not to say that competition is wrong; rather, "competition helps individuals to recognize their strengths and liabilities and improve their personal competence" (Tauer & Harackiewicz, 1999, p. 210). But winning should never be about proving, vanquishing, or eliminating; instead, winning is about using the best circumstances of peak performance and making them work to your advantage.

Is Failure Not an Option?

There is a famous quote from the NASA flight controller Jerry Bostick, when he stated during the return to Earth of the damaged Apollo 13 Mission, "Failure is not an option." So, why do we hold failures out to be a loss instead of a gain? Because of the way we reward success. For instance, school grades are used as a *tangible* way of measuring success, a sign of intellectual superiority. If success is a sign of intellectual superiority, then it must be that failure is a sign of intellectual *inferiority*. That must be true, and logic would tell you that. It's not. Our educational system is only one way for someone to be successful. There are many stories of people with little to no education who have been successful.

When people say, "Failure is not an option," it's uttered by everybody who believes they have nothing to lose—or cannot afford to lose. For many who face absurdly high stakes, or when any failure can put many lives and livelihoods in danger, thinking like this is a necessity. But when people "get so desperate that they are willing to resort to immoral reasons to win, then such thinking can be dangerous and problematic to the health of a business (Stallard, 2014, par. 13). In many companies adopting this mantra, employees feel fear at every turn, which forces people not to take risks or challenge themselves to the point that companies degenerate into "a stagnant non-competitive culture with low engagement" (Hassel, 2014, par. 5). Through personal experience and observations from students, Harke (2014) exposed how students feel when reacting to failure:

> They return to college feeling somewhat defeated, and many question their self-worth and their ability to succeed. Their self-efficacy has been diminished by the browbeating received from family members, or they have spent the holiday break beating themselves up over the idea of "not being good enough" (2014, par. 2).

In the author's case, failure should never be considered taboo—just that students should be exposed to failure and learn how to adopt a "lesson learned attitude" that brushes off any self-blame and take greater responsibility for themselves (par. 8). A "failure is not an option" attitude fosters irrational thinking by assuming they are doomed to failure—when, in reality, there was a lack of effort into succeeding (Allen, 2014, par. 1). Instead, you should cultivate a competition-free "heroic mindset" that courageously takes action to embrace new ideas—without the glitch of fear (Gots, 2011, par. 7).

Why Businesses Fail

According to the Bureau of Labor Statistics (BLS), 679,072 businesses were created in the United States in 2015, and over 78% of small businesses survive during their first year (Bureau of Labor Statistics, 2016). However, even if you may have read depressing statistics of small business failure rates when, in reality, business failure rates fell by 30% in the past 30 years due to changes in small business operations, less competition due to fewer companies being created; a more careful evaluation of business opportunities; improved talent; and technology (Shane, 2017). Consumer spending, about 70% of our economic output, has grown significantly due to improved debt and fiscal prudence. And Americans are feeling optimistic and are more willing to take greater risks in their business (Passione, 2014). Still, businesses fail, sometimes out of bad choices, sometimes out of fierce competition, other times from misguided efforts to succeed. So, why do businesses fail? Or better yet, why do businesses begin in the first place?

Shepherd (2003) recorded that people choose to manage their business not only due to "personal profit," but also out of a passion and drive to offer an innovative (or improved) product to the community, or as a form of realizing ethnic identities or family unity (p. 319). Carter, Gartner, Shaver, & Gatewood (2003) identified six reasons individuals start a business:

137

- Innovation, or the "individual's intention to accomplish something new" (p. 14);
- Independence, or "an individual's desire for freedom, control, and flexibility" (p. 14);
- Recognition, or the need to seek approval or status from others;
- Roles through identity or imitation;
- Financial success, or making more money;
- And self-realization, or "pursuing self-directed goals" (p. 14).

Figure 10: Reasons Individuals start a business.

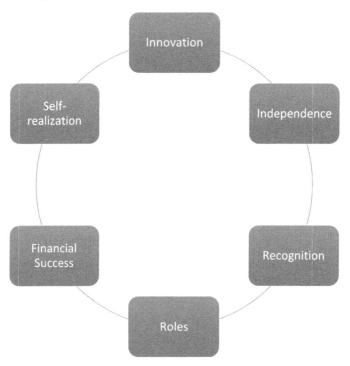

Note: Adapted from "The career reasons of nascent entrepreneurs," by N.M. Carter, W.R. Gartner, K.G. Shaver, & Gatewood, E.J., 2003, *Journal of Business Venturing,* 13-39.

In another survey, Mask (2014) reflected four different types of small business owners: *passionate creators*, those who feel passionate about their work and feel pride and accomplishment for the things they do; *freedom seekers*, those who choose to be in charge of their time and career; *legacy builders*, seeking stability for their families and retirement with practicality; and *struggling survivors*, who fear failure and consider closing their jobs and feel significantly overwhelmed. As you can see, a diverse list of reasons for people to build their own business. That being said, why do businesses *fail?*

Titus (n.d.) defined business failure as a "firm's inability to exist due to loss of capital or insufficient return on investments" (p. 2). Shepherd noted how "business failure involves an involuntary change in both the ownership and management of the business owing to poor performance," which is personally devastating for everybody involved in the business, especially for those who are self-employed (Nemaenzhe, 2011, p. 319). Creating a new business, let alone a startup, is already a precarious, uphill battle filled with uncertainty: The market can be hot at one moment, and unseasonably cool the next. A bad online review from a disgruntled customer can eat away any customer loyalty in the community.

Family infighting can spill over into further competition. Lack of capital or management incompetence can dilute any trust the employees have in the company. And, even if the business has done everything right, a sudden competitor can disrupt the business to the point of failure. To this, Goltz (2011) described that many business owners blame "the bank, the government, or the idiot partner" that brought them to ruin, when in reality the owners themselves may have contributed to the failure (p. 1). In any case, business failure is "the defining moment that unfolded over time, creating losses for investors and creditors alike" (Dias & Teixeira, 2014, p. 2).

There are many circumstances that explain business failure:

- **Lack of business experience:** Greenstreet (2016) noted how business owners are overburdened by the many roles they have to take on at once, "from marketing to selling or management and finance" (par. 11). As a result, Fotopulos (2010) noted that prospective business owners should engage in formal or informal apprenticeship positions in order to receive an inside look at the business. On the other hand, if prospective owners do not have enough experience, then the business will suffer from poor organization and resource allocation (Titus, 2016, p. 4).

- **Inadequate financing:** Many business owners have no cash cushion or, even worse, financial literacy. According to reports by market data aggregator CB Insights on startup post-mortems—or "an essay that tells the rest of the community what went wrong" (Griffith, 2014, par. 1)— 29% of companies "ran out of cash"; 18%, pricing and cost issues; and 13%, disharmony among the team or investors (par. 1). This common phenomenon is known as *undercapitalization*, or "a lack of sufficient capital to conduct normal business operations and service debts" (Premier Quantitative Consulting, Inc., 2015, p. 1), and this lack of planning is detrimental to any business. Moreover, bankruptcy is often the consequence of inadequate financing, when a company "ceases] to exist" through "voluntary [...] or involuntary means" (Walsh & Cunningham, 2016, p. 168).

- **Lack of adequate cash flow:** In 2010, a Discover Small Business Watch survey revealed half of small businesses in the United States had "cash flow problems" (Huebsch, n.d., par. 1), meaning that businesses spend more than what they earn. For business owners struggling with cash flow, they also struggle with projecting their revenue and their distribution (Titus, 201, p. 4). Even if a business receives more than enough revenue to maintain the business, you need to constantly keep track of anything that comes and goes in the business to ensure success.

- **Poor business planning:** For both long and short-term business planning, business leaders must endure "where the organization will be in two or five years, listing specific, measurable goals and results" (Silver, n.d, par. 1). On the other hand, lack of planning will create "shortages or delays of necessary materials" (par. 2). For any reason, business planners need to account for any circumstance, including cost structure, business strengths and weaknesses (Titus, 2016, p. 4). In addition, Fell (2016) determined that business planning will "develop deep, relevant insights about your customers, employ a bold, strategic focus on the priority markets and products/services and bring it to life with a strong execution plan" (p. 20).

- **Management incompetence:** using the example of the military, Furnham (2017) explained six circumstances to describe the consequences of incompetence: a waste of human resources and "economy of force" (par. 7); outdated traditions coupled with a "tendency to misuse available technology"; selective bias with items that conflict with perception; an excessive mixture of overestimation and underestimation; indecisiveness; and "an obstinate persistence in a given task" (par. 8). In this case, "incompetent" managers lack confidence and feel a need to soothe their egos through incompetence (Flaxington, 2013, par. 4). For this reason, leaders need to set goals, understand active listening and communication skills, and set goals to retain managerial competency.

- **Ignoring the competition:** As explored earlier, the creation of a business forces leaders to face many disadvantages, including very high barriers to entry and steep prices for failure, and very few businesses make the cut. While worrying about the competition will only fuel any business inadequacies, by all means, you shouldn't ignore the competition. However, "Certain competitors, or rivals, can instill a motivation to perform that goes above and beyond an ordinary competitive spirit or the objective stakes of the contest" (Kilduff, Elfenbein, & Staw, 2010, p. 932). Collaboration may be necessary in some cases, but entrepreneurs need to understand the rival company's circumstances (Saltzman, 2014).

- **Uncontrolled business growth:** Hamilton (2014) noted that business growth can be "a measure of validation for our ideas and all of the hard work" (par. 1). Even if this progress can be sustainable, excessive growth can be hazardous to the bottom line. Common growth problems include a significant decrease in morale and a decrease in productivity; a rapid increase in staff turnover; cash flow shortages; and losing touch with competitors (Business Queensland, 2013). In other cases, debt can quickly pile up and force employees to take on more work than usual.

While it is important to understand what factors contribute to business failure, there are other consequences of failure and the toll it takes on business leaders. Financially speaking, one of failure's consequences is a loss or reduction in personal income due to dwindling profits and falling revenue. Another consideration is any miscalculation to the *opportunity cost*, or "benefits foregone by a particular use of resources" (Palmer & Raftery, 1999, p. 1552), on explicit—which involves money— or implicit —which involves analyzing what could have been made with the already-owned resources (Kennon, 2016). Ucbasaran, Shepherd, Lockett, & Lyon (2013) noted how "entrepreneurs with high opportunity costs are more likely to be more impatient for success and invest more aggressively in their ventures, thereby increasing the chances of large financial gains [or] losses" (p. 175)—and the opportunities to succeed or fail are greater by the increasingly large amount of risk.

Socially speaking, any type of failure serves as stigma (a social devaluation of a person deviating from a social unit's norms), which precipitates the degradation of close relationships. In such cases, "a failed venture equals a failed entrepreneur, with many viewing failures as a reflection of one's own character or incompetence" (Junn, 2016, par. 2) because the failure is perceived by entrepreneurs as something avoidable and within their control. Lee, Lumpkin, & Bangar (2015) described how the stigma of failure differs between cultures:

> In Silicon Valley, business failure is often considered a stepping stone for future success; in Japan, entrepreneurial failure is a matter of shame to the extent that top managers of failed firms may commit suicide to avoid entailing stigma (p. 358-359).

As another consequence, entrepreneurs can suffer negative discrimination from future employment opportunities and social exclusion, because the entrepreneur's reputation depends on how the "fall" can be externally attributed—and how other businesses and startups react to these circumstances (Ucbasaran, Shepherd, Lockett, & Lyon, 2013, p. 177).

Psychologically speaking, "business failure has parallels with the loss of something (or someone) important" (Ucbasaran, Shepherd, Lockett, & Lynn, 2013, p. 178), meaning that business owners and leaders can suffer from the consequences of grief. Because business owners believe failure can be "personally relevant and motivationally incongruent" that damages the entrepreneur's identity (Jenkins, Brundin, Wiklund, 2010, p. 3), entrepreneurs face the uncertainty of grief. Two effects of psychological failure include a sense of hopelessness that undermines any future value in creating a new business and, infused well, failure serves as a motivation to develop new skills and create new ventures through the lessons learned from failure (p. 179; Shepherd, 2003, p. 320).

Stroebe and Schut (2010) proposed an interesting, dual approach to grief, where the sufferer has the flexibility to avoid and process the grief. In loss orientation, people learn to cope by "working through and processing some aspect of the loss experience" through memories of the deceased (business), including successes, failures, and enforces a re-evaluation of the person's identity (p. 277; Shepherd, 2003, p. 322; Nolen-Hoeksema & Larson, 2013, p. 65). On the other hand, a restoration orientation allows grievers to focus on "the concrete changes that have occurred as a result of the loss," like paying bills, declaring bankruptcy and setting aside what assets are to be liquidated (Nolen-Hoeksema & Larson, 2013, p. 65). This does not mean that they are actively avoiding the grief; rather, these represent proactive solutions toward "secondary sources" that are also important to take care of (Stroebe & Schut, 2010, p. 278). In any case, it is important to know that both types of grief oscillate depending on both the griever's wishes, circumstances, and explanations (p. 278)—every event is an opportunity to learn, grow, and develop character and resilience.

Berber (2013) noted a very important point about failure: "A society that worships winners tends to make horrible choices, whether considered from a moral, or a practical, perspective" (par. 2) because it oftentimes misconstrues past successes—and not a reaction to failure—as indicators of character. Successful people do not take risks; whereas those that experience failure must "adapt and change" (par. 11) to the surrounding circumstances, using past failure as a measure of what *not* to do. For British writer J.K. Rowling (2008), "failure meant a stripping away of the essential" (p. 3), of re-evaluating the circumstances or attitudes on failure. Without a healthy understanding of failure, success is liable to breed complacency, "a reinforcing signal that no corrective action is necessary," (Sitkin, 1992, p. 234); in turn, complacent individuals fail to innovate when most needed. Because of "low attention and low stimulation," they find no need to change routines, search for new information, or try something new (p. 235). As a result, homogeneity permeates throughout the system, making changes to the status quo inevitably harder (p. 236)—and a company that aggressively shies away from making mistakes or (safely) addressing any failure only breeds insecure employees (Serrat, p. 2).

American psychologist Henry Murray described a need: *infavoidance*, as the need "to avoid humiliation", "embarrassing situations or to avoid conditions that may lead to the scorn, derision, or indifference of others," and "to refrain from action because of the *fear of failure* [emphasis added]" (Schultz & Schultz, 2009, p. 188). In other terms, the fear of failure forces people to "experience apprehension and anxiety" since people learn that failure is negative and are apprehensive to experience it (Conroy & Elliot, 2004, par. 273). This occurs because failure-averse people feel that "the self is unworthy of love and is in danger of being abandoned" and actively try to not repeat the negative experience again (Elliot & Thrash, 2004, p. 958). In other risk-averse companies, whenever a failure is attended to negatively or unacceptably, this will only force it to recur (Serrat, 2010, p. 2)—in fact, it should be treated as "a deviation from expected and desired results" (p. 2).

It's Okay to Make Mistakes

If you remembered when I discussed the role of perfectionism and procrastination—and now, there are significant overlaps to experiencing failure, which can be experienced in five ways: shame and embarrassment; devalued self-esteem; uncertainty; losing interest; and upsetting others (Sagar & Stoeber, 2009). It can be *socially oriented*, where "individuals feeling pressured to be perfect because of beliefs that significant others have excessively high standards for them to meet" (Conroy, Kaye, & Fifer, 2007, p.

148

238). It can also be *other-oriented*, which involves "setting unrealistic standards for others by expecting that they will be perfect and stringently evaluating their performance" (p. 239). It can still be *self-oriented*, because people have the "tendency to set unrealistic standards for one's self" and forces the person to try to meet self-imposed expectations (p. 239). If these circumstances are not addressed properly, it may lead people to become "failure deprived"; that is, when high achievers suddenly face failure and end up distraught and "unable to cope with simple struggles" (Bennett, 2017, par. 17).

Mistakes, no matter how rational, irrational, or deliberate, happen—and as leaders, we must learn how to deal with them appropriately. Anderson (2013) noted how mistakes could be valuable tools for opportunity:

> Mistakes are the pathway to great ideas and innovation. Mistakes are the stepping stones to moving outside the comfort zone to the growing zone where new discoveries are made, and great lessons are learned. *Mistakes are not failures* [emphasis added], they are simply the process of eliminating ways that don't work to come closer to the ways that will (par. 5).

Making mistakes are important ways that force you to confront your glitches, and it is very important to learn, own, fix and place new safeguards to learn new ways about how the world works. And they do not deserve to be scorned; rather, *our* reactions to our mistakes and failures determine any future success. As an example, a study by Kapur noted how three types of learning experiences: *direct instruction* where teaching occurs, and then students are given opportunities or practice; *vicarious learning*, where students study and evaluate their peers' solutions before receiving proper instruction, and *productive failure*, where students are expected to learn by exploring procedures on their own—and even failing them—later, using that information for later recall (Kapur, 2014, p. 1008,1009; Paul, 2012). This type of learning encourages leaders to choose challenging problems, elaborate and explain how to work around the circumstances, and compare and contrast solutions to the problem (Paul, 2012). And, in the Inspired Performance Program, we aim to show you how failure is an important value towards future success!

#6. Luck out

Successful people refer to "luck" as what happens when preparation meets opportunity.

Imagine this peculiar scene: You stop by a gas station, and you suddenly look at a line that's been forming inside. You then notice that everybody queues up at the cash register because they are all buying tickets for tonight's big jackpot! After pumping some gas, you mull it over in your thoughts and then decide to go ahead—after all, why not give a little kiss to Lady Luck once in a while? What's there to lose? Surely, you've been lucky before, so it hurts no one to "invest" a dollar or two of your hard-earned money in a dream? After filling up your car with gas, you dart into the convenience store and make the line buy a ticket with the other folk. Once it's your turn,

Luck has nothing to do with it, because I have spent many, many hours, countless hours, on the court working for my one moment in time, not knowing when it would come. –Serena Williams

you're suddenly mulling over the many choices you can make: do you use birthdays or favorite numbers? Do you take a quick-pick, or are you fine with choosing well-played numbers? Whatever strategy you choose, that's the one you use to pick your numbers, pay the cashier, dump the ticket in your car, and go home.

The next day, everybody in your neighborhood woke up learning that a new millionaire was in their midst! You search frantically in the house for that ticket you're sure you've bought in that gas station until you realize that you left it in the car. As you dart to the car in your pajamas, you suddenly find it in the glove compartment, wrapped in candy wrappers and tissues. After picking it up and looking at how the numbers match up, you become jaw-dropped at becoming the lucky winner of an eight-figure jackpot! Oh, the dreams you've once wasted hours thinking up are now a reality within your fingertips! You now look at yourself as the luckiest person in the world!

Even though you may have wished for years to have even the tiniest bit of luck as those multi-million jackpot winners on television with grinning faces and the cardboard checks, did you ever stop to think that maybe they were in the right moment at the right time with the most favorable atmospheric conditions to them? Think about it: In our example, the person was at the right gas station, gauged the most appropriate course of action and planned accordingly, picked the right numbers based on past choices that failed or won him very little money, and hid the ticket in the right spot in order to retrieve it at the most appropriate moment. To you, that's luck. But to me, that's what happens when success meets opportunity—in this case, the success being that the person became a millionaire, and the opportunity is buying the ticket.

Successful people learn how to determine the best circumstances to take action while keeping in mind the atmospheric conditions that followed it, be it positively or negatively, our attitudes. It's best and more convenient not to judge ourselves for the past, anyway, because these have served us as ways to protect our bodies, minds, and egos from danger, regardless if it's warranted or not. No two people respond equally to the same event, nor do they develop the same set of atmospheric conditions that gear them towards self-protection and self-preservation. Through these, people learn how to adapt to the environment because their minds couldn't have produced any different thoughts based on their experiences. For our new millionaire, should he not win the lottery, it makes no sense not to judge himself nor his actions because of failing to achieve his goal once when he learned how *not* to achieve it plenty of times before. This is why, in Webber's (2017) words:

> People who spot and seize opportunity are different. They are more open to life's forking paths, so they see possibilities others miss. And if things don't work out the way they'd hoped, they brush off disappointment and launch themselves heading toward the next fortunate circumstance. As a result, they're happier and more likely to achieve their goals (par. 4).

How many lives have been transformed by luck? Moreover, how "life and death, reward and ruin, [and] happiness and despair" are much more enjoyable when they are coupled with greater amounts of effort and hard work (Wiseman, 2003, p. 1)?

Why Do People Feel "Lucky?"

So, why do some people call successful people lucky? For starters, it takes some pressure off of them. It gives them a reason why they haven't been successful. It's important for them to come up with an answer, to defend themselves from what they believe is how they are seen by their friends or family. In most cases, the person looking at other "successful people" has felt that they are not lucky, bad things happen to them all the time. What other reason could it be? This thought process has developed over time and is the result of some unfortunate events and experiences that were unexplainable. Add into the equation little to no experience with success, and it's the only explanation they can rationalize. It's exasperating for these people when they're doing things right, and the successful person might be a jerk. How can he or she be rewarded when they are not nice people? Bad things can happen to good people, and good things can happen to bad people.

Can success just fall into your lap? Not really. Money can fall into your lap without you doing anything. Take for example an inheritance from a relative. However, that may not have anything to do with success. To be truly successful, you must develop a positive attitude *towards* success. When you talk with "success-ful" people, the one common theme is they don't feel lucky. Success is hard work. The great Arnold Palmer once said, "the harder I work, the luckier I get" Golf is not a game of luck even though, at times, you get some breaks like a favorable bounce, and those breaks can work both ways. Just ask anyone who plays a lot of golf. A bad bounce is no more bad luck than a good bounce is good luck. It's what happens, and everyone is subject to it.

A Game of Chance

So how does someone become successful without luck? They put themselves in more positions to benefit from the good breaks. When we see someone who is successful, we only see or hear about the good breaks they received. For this reason, success-ful people don't focus on the bad breaks. All types of chances be-ing equal, these types of people take "greater advantage of" chances than the average person who doesn't take them. Our brains are programmed to focus on the negative; it's a survival in-stinct. Our brains are designed to look for trouble, scanning the horizon for danger. Have you ever wondered why the news is so negative? It's because "If it bleeds, it leads," since people watch and, when people watch, they can sell more advertising. Unfortunately, it's true: The news will always focus on the tragedy because they know that's what people want to see even if they say they don't. It's subconscious. You can see this by watching people drive by a car crash, straining and searching to see the carnage. Do they want to see people hurt or killed? No, but our minds see this stroke of luck by trying to learn and observe as a key to self-preservation.

What is Luck?

Adler & Guelen (2001) define luck as "a mysterious power that affects outcomes favorably or unfavorably, above and beyond the influence of ability, motivation, and chance"(p. 197). Luck is a way to attribute an external locus of control to positive and negative events that seem "inexplicable" and are often unpredictable to determine absent of any reasonable explanation. It serves as an *attribution*, or a way to explain or attach meaning to other events, where people often see causalities and coincidences when there aren't any (McLeod, 2012). In addition, "lucky" actions mean that the event matters to them because taking advantage of their atmospheric conditions, these circumstances can't be easily replayed—conversely, "the more often something happens to someone, the less luck is involved" (Levy, 2012, par. 11).

Another relationship to luck, chance involves events genuinely out of our control: "They may be formative events which are usually not considered as irrational by a member of a given society" (Delacroix & Guillard, 2008, p.1). Whereas luck is an *attitude* surrounding an event, chance involves the actions or circumstance itself, including mathematics, probabilities, and opportunities. Say that you have a one-in-ten chance of randomly choosing an apple from a bowl with an assorted amount of fruit. You don't know if there are two, three, or four apples—but your circumstances ask you to pick just one apple. If you succeed, then you may be considered lucky; if not, then you may be considered unlucky by other people. For this reason, Ossola (2015) noted that, even if chance events cannot be predicted or fully avoided, "people can do a lot to put themselves in a particular place and time and hope that it's the right one" (par. 9; Pink, 2003, par. 9).

On the other hand, if you've heard from people that "Everything happens for a reason," even though many Americans believe they are the masters of their own fate, a "belief that important outcomes are predestined and beyond our control" (Jacobs, 2014, par. 2). A study by Tang, Shepherd, & Kay (2014) noted that believing in fate eases the value of difficult decisions, more so if their consequences are ambiguous or difficult to determine (p. 1046). Drawing conclusions from this study, Jacobs (2014) described, "we all have many difficult decisions to make in our lives, and finding excuses to avoid them hinders us from developing the emotional maturity necessary to comfortably deal with ambiguity" (par. 13) because understanding the concept of fate "helps us make sense of events that have already occurred" (Routledge, 2014, par. 7). On the other hand, excessive fatalism "can undermine personal responsibility" because people believe they are no longer in control of their actions and their consequences (Herbert, 2013, par. 3).

This fatalism extends to American culture: According to a 2011 Pew Research Center report, 3% of Americans "believe that success in life was determined by forces outside our control" (Rampell, 2011, par. 2), and 22% of college graduates "believe they have little control over their fate" (par. 4), even if a separate report on economic mobility revealed that "Americans actually appear to have *less* control over their success in life than their [Western European] counterparts do" (par. 6). Even different cultures handle business through a strong sense of fatalism; for instance, whereas American culture "is marked by a strong sense of belief in the power of an individual to control his [or] her destiny," Latin American cultures look at "the human condition as a product of destiny," which marks many delays in production as something that can't be avoided (McKinniss & Natella, 1994, p. 61-62).

You see, luck, chance, and fate are words that are interchangeably used by many, when in reality they have different meanings and expectations of success. All of these involve aspects of life that are out of our control and are probable or common enough actually to happen. For philosophers, three theories explain how we react to luck: the *probability theory*, where an event is considered lucky or unlucky due to its sudden and improbable occurrence (Hales, 2012, p. 491; Hales & Johnson, 2014, p. 510); the *modal theory*, where a lucky or unlucky event happens because of its fragility—meaning, "that would have been very different if it would not have occurred" (Hales, 2012, p. 491; Hales & Johnson, 2014, p. 510; Carter & Peterson, 2017, p. 2176): and the *control view*, where "if a fact was lucky or unlucky for a person, then that person had no control over whether it was a [valid] fact [or not]" (Hales & Johnson, 2014, p. 510)—"fact" denoting that the person knew no outcome of its course of action.

Let's return to the lottery ticket example from the beginning and how each of these circumstances play out on our own understanding of luck:

- If you'd explain luck using the probability theory, winning a jackpot is lucky because the event was sudden, improbable, and the person faced impossible odds.
- If you'd explain the event using the modal theory, winning a jackpot is lucky because the atmospheric conditions, fragile enough, collided to have you win the ticket.

- If you'd explain the event using the control view, winning a jackpot is lucky because the person had a measure of control through buying the ticket, stopping at the convenience store and eyeballing the line, and so forth.

Figure 11: Theories of luck.

Probability Theory of Luck	Modal Theory of Luck	Control View
An event is considered "lucky" or "unlucky" due to its sudden and improbable occurrence	A "lucky" or "unlucky" event happens because its occurrence was fragile enough to	The person has some control over the "lucky" or "unlucky" event.

Note: Adapted from "The modal account of luck revisited," by J.A. Carter & M. Peterson, 2014, *Synthese,* 194, 2175-2184; "Why every theory of luck is wrong," by S.D. Hales, 2016, *NOÛS*, 490-508; and "Luck attributions and cognitive bias," by S.D. Hales & J.A. Johnson, 2014, *Metaphilosophy,* 45(4-5), 509–528.

Heuristics & Algorithms

If you've noticed all around you, people are trying to predict what will happen next. Meteorologists attempt to predict how the weather will look like in the next hour—whether it rains or snows, whether it's hot or unseasonably cold. Psychics and mind readers take cues from their client's body languages to predict the actions their clients want to hear. Even your parents have warned you once or twice about a potentially negative course of action, only to scold you with "I told you so!" when it happens and an odd sense of bewilderment when it doesn't. And once again, back to the lottery analogy, you pick six numbers that you *predict* will make you successful—if those are the winners, great! If not, then no harm was done, except by spending two dollars from out of your pocket. Because you predicted or expected these events in the same way they happened, does that make you lucky? Still, if the knowledge gave you a sense of control over your future, are you also lucky?

As Ropeik (2011) discussed regarding the appeal of futurism, any type of knowledge, even incomplete, gives you a sense of power that feels reassuring (par. 5). In the end, predicting can make you feel good for a moment, but it's as flawed as any expectation—and any unfulfilled expectation can be costly to react and fix (Poon, Koehler, & Buehler, 2014, p. 208). In addition, three circumstances allow people to make inaccurate predictions: first, focusing on current interventions to address future expectations (p. 208); second, "barriers [obstacles or demands] may be discounted in the self-prediction process" (p. 207, 2012); finally, people do not place equal weight on the options available to predict the behavior (p. 207). So, these circumstances apply to gut feelings and intuition, oftentimes used as indicators of luck.

An algorithm is a specific process used to make a solution much more clear and focused (Myers, 2010, p. 371). Think of mathematical equations like the Pythagorean Theorem and the Quadratic Formula, where you only need to plug in some numbers and use some arithmetic to reach an *exact* solution. Think of a recipe that you have to follow to the letter if you wish to have an edible meal! Or how about computer programs or any type of equipment? For instance, Francesco Marconi, strategy manager for the Associated Press, used algorithms after moving from Italy to the United States to understand how to "achieve sustainable success" (par. 3). However, the jury's still out to determine if following an algorithm is a measure or a factor for luck.

A heuristic, however, is "a simple thinking strategy that often allows us to make judgments and solve problems" (Myers, 2010, p. 371) because they are quick solutions that help us to survive and react fast. But, while heuristics aren't as methodical as is the case with algorithms, they are fast, quick, and efficient—while being error-prone, inconsistent, and "can lead to completely incorrect solutions (Indiana University, 2010, par. 3). In essence, heuristics are quick, but they don't have to be accurate. Gigerenzer and Gaissmaier (2011) described how heuristics are useful for two reasons: the *accuracy-effort trade-off*, where "heuristics trade-off some loss in accuracy for faster results pg. 457), and *ecological rationality*, where "it is adapted to the structure of the environment"—in other terms, the atmospheric conditions surrounding your thinking determine what heuristics are appropriate and (mostly) adaptive (p. 457).

One type of heuristic is the *hindsight bias*, which is the "tendency to think, after the fact, that an event was predictable, even when it wasn't" (Frank, 2017, par. 11). Even if an event is unpredictable or uncertain and would have happened anyway, people tend to believe the past is "solid, knowable, and more pre-dictable" than expected (Roese & Vohns, 2012, par. 4). This hap-pens because of the way memory works through making connec-tions with related or unrelated circumstances that make a thread into something jumbled or new (par. 5).

Hindsight bias is very problematic in a business setting be-cause it perpetuates overconfidence since it uses selective in-stances to confirm something that happened before (Dame & Ged-min, 2013, par. 9), impairing our ability to make informed decisions with flawed information (par. 10). It precludes us from learning from our mistakes (Dean, 2012), more so when studies have shown that people claimed they could predict an event be-cause they were told to do so (Arkes, Faust, Guilmette & Hart, 1998, p. 368).

Another type, the *availability heuristic*, enables that "we tend to estimate the likelihood of an event or outcome based on how readily we can recall similar instances" (Frank, 2016, p. 17; Pachur, Hertwig & Steinmann, 2012, p. 315) through "memory and metamemory" or, in the case of the latter, the processes where people can refer to memory (Carlston, 2010, p. 85, 86); Metcalfe & Dunlosky, 2008, p. 351). This flaw is commonly found in businesses such as investments, where many decisions are made without looking at the whole picture—especially if we're actually swayed by anything "relevant, recent, or dramatic" (Franklin Templeton Investments, 2012, par. 8). For instance, a business owner that succeeded in securing one contract would immediately believe that there are many other accessible opportunities when there may not actually be one at reach; as a result, those perceptions "can easily slip out of line with reality" (par. 8).

There are many more heuristics, but these all serve as glitches and error messages that are perpetuated through past experiences. These rules of thumb are quick, helpful, and plentiful, and help free the mind for processing other things. But they can also be dangerous traps that "potentially trip us up in our ordinary judgments and choices, in everything from health to finance to romance" (Herbert, 2010, par. 12). Because heuristics serve as measures to ward off uncertainty—a term used in a managerial context to denote how a decision maker does not know all the possible options with their consequences and probabilities" (Artinger, Petersen, Gigerenzer & Weibler, 2014). On the outset, heuristics are treated as rational choices; however, these come from the most irrational circumstances, such as trauma, embarrassment, and fear. Some occur because of "habit and experiences" (Herbert, 2010, par. 16), ease of memory and comfort. Thus, luck can be considered a heuristic—a tool that can be used to find control by "reduc[ing] to manageable proportions the number of possible solutions through which the decision maker must sift" (McKenna, 2000, p. 223). Psychologically, the illusion of control is the belief that people overestimate and expect circumstances where they believe they have control (Ejova, Navarro & Delfabbros, 2013, p. 498; Langer, 1975, p. 311). You can only have so much control of circumstances, but you can't control *everything* around you. That being said, what you *can* do is harness the necessary skills to succeed. Conversely, luck is "a fortuitous happiness," to which any success appears to be "uncontrollable" (Langer, 1975, p. 311).

Luck also serves as a *self-fulfilling prophecy*, or "a false belief that leads to its own fulfillment" (Madon, Willard, Guyll, & Scherr, 2011, p. 578). Think of a time you thought of something that brought you success and fulfillment—if you tell yourself, "I am smart," then you will do things "smart people do—even if you normally don't think of yourself as smart. Watzlawick (1984) reported that self-fulfilling prophecies create conditions because "the action that is at first neither true or false produces a fact, and with its own 'truth'" (p. 393). Positive perceptions of luck lead to feelings of confidence, control, and optimism" (Maltby, Day, Gill, Colley & Wood, 2008, p. 656). And a prophecy that we know to be a prophecy can no longer fulfill itself because it needs a human agent—that's you—to take the prophecy to completion (Watzlawick, 1984, p. 401).

Know When to Fold 'Em

Let's use poker as another example. Think of this question: Is poker a game of chance, or skill? Some would look at poker as a game for a lucky break, while other, much more successful people would describe it as a process of good and bad breaks, with formulas or algorithms. Famous poker player Annie Duke defined it this way: Whenever she played poker, she used what she described as learning to be *outcome blind*—whenever she played a hand, Annie knew the cards she had in her hand and what had been played, but she didn't know what the other players had in *their* hands and what cards remained in the deck. Based on her atmospheric conditions, she'd choose to make a calculated guess--either move forward or fold. If she folded, then the cards played after were not as good as hers, she accepted the outcome with the understanding that she had made the best decision based on her information. No regrets, and no second-guessing. She never chalked it up to bad luck if she lost a hand, and it wasn't good luck when she won; Annie was making educated decisions based on wisdom according to her skill and experience. By accepting the fate, being outcome blind, allowed her to stay present and focus on the current game. In addition, staying present and focusing on the right now is also an important key for you. By focusing on what's in front, you can make the best moves based on what you know and never second guess, just learn from the experience. Whenever Annie lost a hand, she saw that as another experience to draw upon in a future game (Meyer S., 2014).

There is a formula or algorithm that allow people to achieve sustainable success. It can be replicated or modified as necessary. You can make it your own. You have unique skills and potential. There's more than one way to achieve success. Your personality may be soft-spoken; therefore, you need to surround yourself with people that admire or respect that style. When you hire people that support your vision and style, it allows you to spend more time on the things that matter. That way, you'll maximize your potential in your life. When you understand your strengths and weaknesses, you can achieve greater levels of success because luck can run out, there's no skill involved, and it's difficult to repeat. Once you acquire a skill and make it your own, success will follow. Keep in mind: there will be a series of events that will ensue and some will benefit you and some won't. This isn't luck; this is life. If you view it as either good or bad luck, then you miss the opportunity to develop your unique skills and experiences. Use outcome-blind thinking to make the best decisions based on what you know at one moment at this time. With more experience under your belt, your algorithm or process begins to adapt.

When you have set goals, it's much easier to calculate when to hold 'em or fold 'em. Without goals and plans, you once again are subject to random percentages in your favor. When there isn't a clear plan, it's more difficult to say no, and you end up spending too much time on something that has no value. Instead of working *harder*, it's time to work *smarter*.

With your plan of clearly defined goals in hand, it's time to execute the plan. However, to be successful, you must anticipate there will be roadblocks and obstacles that stand in your way. That isn't bad luck; it's what happens when you start to take action. Look at football: the quarterback sets a play for his team, and other teammates execute it. At the same time, they study the other team's defensive strategies and have to prepare that their plan may be countered by the other team's defense. Likewise, you need to be flexible and adaptable as you go on without becoming victims out of lament or bad luck. If so, it isn't all your fault, and you can correct that way of thinking by rebooting and updating your mind.

Superstitions, Revisited

Luck is also what makes superstitions common, popular, and enduring in every culture around the world, since these affect human behavior and, to an extent, business performance. Rituals and superstitions occur as people attempt to exert some power over others in order to "ward off bad luck" (Everett, 2010, par. 8). Positive superstitions, like good-luck charms, wearing lucky underwear, and telling someone to "break a leg" before a play reinforce positive values and actions toward self-improvement and personal growth; conversely, avoiding stepping on cracks on the floor, black cats, and opening an umbrella inside a house are "directed toward the avoidance of the bad luck and harmful consequences for the individual" (Sagone & De Caroli, 2014, p. 319). This is why the fact that luck is unpredictable in business: while a moment of bad luck can destroy entire careers and reputations, a stroke of good "luck" can improve one's chances of success (Wiseman, 2003, p. 2).

If you remember the book's discussion on worry from previous chapters, you may have learned that worry involves a superstitious avoidance mechanism because, not only do worriers believe that their worry subconsciously wards off catastrophe, but it also helps them maintain a certain sense of community. In a sense, worry is a form of superstition: When you worry, you fill your mind with irrational predictions—glitches—about the future. What ifs and negative thoughts cloud our judgment rationalized as self-discipline or anticipation. And worry, like any other superstitious behavior, can develop into obsessive-compulsive disorder (OCD), where rituals become compulsions that interfere with a person's functioning (Albert, 2004, par. 5). Controversial English writer Caleb Williams Salesby (1908) relayed the consequences of worry:

> Ignorance is not bliss, for ignorance leads to superstition, and superstition breeds more worry and misery and fear, that were even produced merely by man's knowledge of death or his intercourse with nature (p. 273).

For many, rabbits' feet and four-leaf clovers serve as tools to bring about good luck, fame, and fortune. But there is also a product of magical thinking, a belief that "certain actions can influence objects or events when there is no causal connection between them" (Risen, 2016, p. 183). If we perform rituals because they give us some illusory control over our actions, then it also helps by placing a "sense of meaning" in our actions, and "improve[s] our performance and thus *indirectly* affect our fate" (Hutson, 2012, par. 3). In addition, magical thinking happens because of *teleological reasoning*, or the belief that "everything happens for a reason." Some people assume everything has "intentions or goals," even if these circumstances are "evidently purposeless"

(Hutson, 2012, par. 5). Both magical thinking and teleological reasoning are related to fatalism because a "[b]elief in destiny helps render your life a coherent narrative, which infuses your goals with a greater sense of purpose" (par. 6)—and this type of thinking works even if the circumstances are negative.

To a certain point, every belief is some desire for control, more so if understanding our circumstances includes looking at patterns around us, making connections and drawing conclusions that fuels our disbelief coupled with a disincentive to question and discriminate our judgment (Diaconis, 1983, p. 1; Szalavitz, 2012, p. 5). In business settings, superstitions can be problematic because of the waste of "pursuing unrealistic expectations" from managers, leaders, and employees who feel pressured to perform and improve (Orr & Orr, 2014). However, expectation is important in luck because "lucky people are more willing to embrace the circumstances that are deemed through the challenges they embrace" (Oksman, 2016, par. 10). Instead, business leaders can use magical thinking to their advantage. At the same time it's important for improving motivation, confidence, and remembering life successes (Szalavitz, 2012, p. 10; Narvacan, Atienza-Bulaqueña & Evangelista, 2013, p. 156). Superstitions also serve as tools to activate the value of self-efficiency in business, the belief that people have the power to succeed while performing a particular task (Damisch, Stoberock & Mussweiler, 2010, p. 1015;

171

Lunenburg, 2011, p. 1). Through *magnitude*, or the belief someone can complete the task; *strength* measures how confident at completing tasks with differing levels of difficulty; and *generality*, or understanding how self-efficacy spreads to other areas and/or abilities (deNoyelles, Hornik, & Johnson, 2014, p. 257). Regarding the relationship between self-efficacy and luck, "The more people believe in *good luck* [emphasis added], the more optimistic, hopeful, and confident they tend to be" (Damisch, Stoeberlock, & Mussweiler, 2010, p. 1015). For instance, a 2013 study on Sicilian teenagers evaluating superstitious beliefs revealed that students with external loci in belief based their self-efficacy on luck and superstitions, while those with an internal locus of control did not while relating to luck in a negative fashion (Sagone & De Caroli, 2014, p. 323). This is why Lunenburg encouraged workplaces to choose individuals with high self-efficacy for promotions, training and development programs, and engage in greater challenges without frustrating or burdening their expectations (pg. 4). Conversely, people with personal lucky charms also enjoy a greater degree of self-efficacy, though not because of it—it only serves as a form of psychological insurance that makes people "set higher personal goals and expectations and to persist longer at the task" (Schuster, 2010, par. 8).

In the end, *you* make your own luck, and you are responsible for maintaining it. Use every resource at your disposal, including the tools you are provided through the Inspired Performance Program—in order to reach the unprecedented levels of success for your career and your personal life. You can use all the lucky colors and stars and underwear you love, but do keep in mind these are all glitches and error messages lodged in your past. By making your own luck through effort and taking hold of every available opportunity—while seizing "intuition, positive self-fulfilling prophecies," (Wiseman, 2003, p. 3), you learn how to grow the ability to develop strong connections with other "lucky" people. As noted by Jenkins (2014), "Every bump in the road, every spell of bad luck, should be seen as an opportunity to learn and progress. How you rise to that challenge will determine your chances of success" (par. 16). This is why optimism is important and the one that takes advantage of the opportunities of "luck." Even if luck is a good coping mechanism for success, you don't need it to succeed––that's what hard work is for!

#7. Stray from Their Lane

"Hire people who are better than you are, then leave them to get on with it…Look for people that will aim for the remarkable, who will not settle for the routine." David Ogilvy – Advertising executive considered the Father of advertising.

Why it's Important to Stay in Your Lane

Successful people don't attempt to do things that someone else is better equipped to handle. You've heard once or twice about the need to "stay in your lane" when it comes to people's private affairs. It usually translates to: "Mind your own business!" "Don't meddle in our personal affairs!" "Don't barge right into someone else's things!" In many cases, staying in your lane means respecting other people's boundaries—unless these broach into yours—or reminding others that no one knows how to do the job better than you do. Focus on your own responsibilities, and don't worry about others unless they ask you, so you don't risk neglecting your own responsibilities by helping others. Through this saying, you're supposed to think over what are the areas you need to go through to follow your hopes and dreams, without stepping on others', respecting people's choices, and asserting your leadership. Even more, you must stay in your lane, even if other people believe your choices are pointless or easily misunderstood. Geiger (2016) echoed this sentiment on leadership: "You must own your area, your realm of responsibility. If you are a leader, you have been given responsibility for a group of people, and no one should outpace you in passion or concern for the area you steward" (par. 5).

I Struggled with Staying in My Own (Entrepreneurial) Lane

Most successful people understand the importance of "Staying in Their Lane." What does that mean? It means they know what they know and know that they don't know. Early in my entrepreneurial development, I struggled with this area. I believed that, if I couldn't do anything by myself, it couldn't be done fast enough. When I would follow up with someone on a project I assigned them with, I would be impatient with any unforeseen delays. As a result, I stopped delegating because it wouldn't fulfill my unrealistic standards of how good or fast it should be. Not only would I struggle with the delegation, but also it would affect my hiring practices. It's human nature to want to surround yourself with people that you can relate with. Because of this, I needed to learn that it was essential to find people with strategic technical skills that they can contribute to the company. That way, the company would grow beyond the comfort zone in ways I couldn't take it alone. Employees would develop the skills to manage projects and manage opportunities on their own. A common mistake for someone developing their skills is to understand that they don't have to be the smartest person in the room. Handing off a project can be scary, especially when you did everything by yourself for so long. When you start building a business, you wear many hats. The key is to figure out which hat fits you the best. In the early stages of a company, you have had to handle the accounting, paying the bills. When you are making enough money, you need to hire a bookkeeper or accountant to take that off your plate. That's a tough one if you're paranoid about being ripped off. The best way to handle this is to maintain oversight, insist on receiving and then reviewing reports. When you can afford it, hire an independent auditor as a safeguard.

For a time, I considered myself a marketing person until I found people that were much better at it than me. Managing sales people is not my strength. Why? The reason is I don't need supervision and salespeople do. They need to be managed, preferably by someone who knows how to motivate. I motivated through action, and that's not enough. This doesn't mean I wasn't good at it, I was. But I wasn't the best, there are people who specialize in this area, and you need to find them and hire them quickly. When I ran one company, I hired a VP of sales to manage the team. She was a workhorse. There were no days off for her, seven days a week. Morning, afternoon, and evening she was available for her team. Sales and profits jumped. But one day, my assistant sits down in my office to inquire about something she noticed about the payroll. The VP was making more money than me, the boss. Why was I OK with that? Because she earned it: Her work ethic allowed me to work on the areas I was the best at. It was money well spent.

When you hire a super-star, you need to check your ego and pride at the door. It didn't diminish me; it made me stronger because I offered her what she needed, security. The skills she possessed were different than mine. I'm the risk taker, the one who will see the big vision and gamble my own money on it. The issue she had, as with most successful sales people, is the money came in fast and went out faster. Every week she would be requesting an advance to cover her Platinum American Express bill, or her x, y and z payments. One of my strengths was managing money, keeping the boat on top of the water. That is what separates the successful entrepreneur from the failing one. That doesn't mean I wasn't broke at times, wondering how to make payroll. In the end, I figured out a way to make it happen. When you understand the importance of hiring right and delegating, success is coming. In the end, I delegated responsibilities to people that were more than ready to handle the challenge, which gave me the freedom to pursue other projects.

Now, you get the value in hiring the right people, people not like you, and then delegating responsibilities to them. Is that it? No! Here's what's next. Six principles to develop and implement.

Number One: Keep an open mind and embrace open and honest dialogue. When your staff isn't afraid of losing their job because they disagree with you, that's priceless.

Number Two: Encourage risk-taking, within set parameters. Allow your staff to think outside the box and, within reason, implement their strategies. Now, remember, if something goes wrong, you share in the responsibility. Ultimately, you're the boss and all decisions, even the ones you delegated, land on your desk. Successful people don't blame other people. That's why it's important to set boundaries when you delegate, to mitigate damage from a bad or poorly executed idea.

Number Three: Keep on top of reporting. Tasks that have been delegated need to be monitored. This isn't micromanaging; it's prudent business practices. That way, if something is off course it can be corrected timely. Be fair to the person and give them some latitude and at the same time be diligent about what they are expected to deliver.

Number Four: Understand that the approach another executive is taking may not have been your approach. If it isn't broke, then don't be tempted to fix it. Remember, the whole point of delegating is to give you time to work on areas of the company that your skills are better utilized.

Number Five: Give credit where credit is due. This was an area I needed to work on. I just assumed people knew when I was happy with their performance. That is not how great leaders operate. If you don't feel comfortable recognizing achievements make sure you put someone in charge of that or a process that recognizes it. People want to be seen and recognized when they are succeeding. The mistake is only to notice the errors.

Number Six: When you delegate, make sure the person has the resources to carry out the project. If you're going to do something, do it right. Most great ideas fail because of a lack of resources. Not just money, whatever resource is required.

Jessica Jackley is an American businesswoman and co-founder of Kiva and later ProFounder, both organizations that assist individuals in receiving micro-loans—to entrepreneurs around the world. Her philosophy can be summed up in the following quote, "Deciding what not to do is as important as deciding what to do."

But today's leaders can't simply stay put in one lane, becoming an expert in their favorite topic; rather, they're forced to take multiple roles to address the fast-growing competition around them. Business leaders are not only bosses and managers in one setting; they can also be marketers and social media managers; investors and venture capitalists; handling vendors and consumers; entrepreneurs and ingénues; sales representatives and receptionists. Even athletes, at times, are forced to become entrepreneurs and sponsors to catch a trainer's eye. And students work as both interns and "employees" or mediators and communicators at the same time, though not to get a wage, definitely to enhance their learning experience. Instead of running an endurance lap around a circular track, today's business leader is forced to jump through many hurdles, each bigger and more complex than the last. As a result, "the entrepreneurial tendency to fly solo often becomes a habit, resulting in many entrepreneurs struggling to cope with business demands due to time constraints," sometimes of their own undoing (Niemand, 2013, p. 53).

What Staying in Your Lane Means

Herbert (2015) said to use the term "staying in your own lane" as a tip to help people understand how miscommunication and misunderstandings complicate the process of managing a business (par. 2). While the author didn't coin the saying, there is an important grain of truth to this saying: you must focus on the task ahead. But it's hard, you may say when so many things demand your urgent attention at once! Think about this for a brief moment: "[H]ow many years have been subtracted from your life and nights of good sleep lost to stressing about what others think, why someone does what they do, and so on?" (Divorced Moms, 2017, par. 1) You may believe it's tempting to multitask and fill many different roles when you (recognize) can only do one thing at a time. In this case, you need to understand your priorities and discriminate between what is urgent and needs your attention *now*, what can wait, and what you can toss off for a lazy day—and trust me, there's always *something* to do that you can give away!

By doing so much in so little time, their shoulders are burdened with so many tasks at once where they will eventually fail at all—and you may have heard this quote, "A jack of all trades is a master of none." No matter how big, medium or small a business is, taking on so many roles at the same time is a challenge that slowly fills the business leaders with stress and resentment and, if not taken care of appropriately, can lead them to burnout and lose all the hope they had in their business. And, as a result, that's a dangerous proposition where business leaders can't bear the consequences.

Instead, there is one important thing successful people know how to do to maximize their potential and achieve peak performance: *delegating tasks*. By delegating, you create the tools to train and develop your subordinates into receiving greater autonomy and authority in their job. You also free your time and money to man the sails of the project into new frontiers and face your growth with zeal. Everybody feels empowered through delegation if done so properly and efficiently. You can learn a lot from your employees' strengths and weaknesses by assigning failsafe tasks that progressively empowers people with healthy amounts of self-esteem in their abilities without looking at the work they're doing with dread. In addition, delegation helps you engage with your team's services so you can develop even greater ways to engage with your audience. Because of this, Sackett (2015) determined the perfect tool for leadership: "Part of it is patience. Part of it is loyalty. Part of it is a belief in your abilities and the environment" (par. 10). If you can successfully combine these three attributes—and many more—, you're on your way to creating an environment that heads straight to success!

What is Delegation?

Before we continue, let's define delegation as "a process whereby the manager transfers decision-making authority to a subordinate" (Leana, qtd. in Haselhuhn, Wong, & Ormiston, 2017, p. 1). Instead of simply handing out the direction to a subordinate with the expectation that the latter will satisfactorily finish those directions, delegation involves granting limited authority and complete control of any decisions to the subordinate so he or she can fulfill a predetermined task (Sagie & Koslowski, 2000, p. 81-82). Delegation doesn't mean that the person who delegates is completely removed from power; rather, the act of delegation is elastic and subject to many factors, including subordinate performance and any changes in job requirements. Delegation is also referred to as *decentralization* by scholars like Iqbal almost interchangeably, only differentiating when "organization structures and procedures which essentially call for the formulation of policies and decisions at the lowest possible levels" (p. 2). This is why delegation, unlike direct instruction, involves high amounts of job capability (or the ability for the person to do his or her assigned job), trustworthiness, and job experience are high (p. 83)—in other words, not everybody has the resources or proof to demonstrate he or she is qualified to do the job. If done right, delegating is important because it affords you an opportunity to tackle the important aspects of your project; it increases the morale, confidence, and productivity of your subordinates; and saves you precious amounts of time (McKay & McKay, 2010).

Table 6: Advantages and disadvantages of delegation.

Advantages	Disadvantages
• Eases leadership burden. • Engenders leadership confidence in employee job capability • Encourages risk-taking • Trains subordinates for future tasks • Increases motivation and employee participation • Human resources becomes much more efficient • Trains managers to "get it done through others" • Promotes mentoring and information-sharing from managers and leaders • Contributes to a more equitable power distribution • Promotes company democratization	• Leaders are unaware about delegation • Unwillingness to take risks • Inability to accept subordinate inadequacies • Fear of disclosing sensitive information • Aversion to organizational environment • Fear of exposure and misuse of authority • Losing competent subordinates, control, and confidence in detailed work • Exposes employee prejudices • Desire to set a right example

Note: Adapted from "Why managers don't delegate and how to get them to do so?', by J. Iqbal (2017), *Journal of Managerial Sciences*, Vol. 1(2), p. 59-65.

Here's an example: Imagine you were a kid and your mom suddenly told you to take out the trash. You groan, but you can't argue with her; she's your mom, and she's *directing* you to do a chore. For those brief moments, taking out the trash is (and should be) your main job. You're free to do anything else after you fin- ished what your mom told you to do with her satisfaction, after she checks that you placed the trash bag in the bin and nowhere else, like the garage or the shed. But if your mom suddenly shifted her approach to chores and gave you three days a week to pick when to take out everybody's trash—and one of those has to be on the weekends—, then she's *delegating* a task to you. She'll still be there, offering you guidance and helpful suggestions should you need any. But to fulfill her requests, you're on your own: you get the prerogative of picking three days where all you have to do is take out the trash.

Of course, this example is not without its limitations: first your mom gave you the ability to choose because you were already *capable* to do your job and within the allotted timeframe. Then, your mom placed her trust in you—not that you wouldn't fail on your first two or three times setting an appropriate trash-collecting schedule on your own without a few hiccups, but she also trusted you wouldn't *bail* on her delegation. Finally, your mom knew you had the appropriate amount of experience to take out the trash with minimal supervision and maximum accuracy. It might be tricky at first on either side, the mom never nagging the kid to take out the trash for the umpteenth time and the kid being told what to do for the umpteenth time. For both sides delegation can be rewarding; for instance, mom can spend those extra minutes she used to check the kid actually took out the trash in doing something fulfilling, and the kid can appreciate having more grown-up responsibilities (the act of choice is grown up by itself!)...for the first few days, at least.

By delegating authority to others, you "foster a more efficient use of resources and facilitate the emergence of more agile and responsive organizations, thus enhancing overall performance" (Fontaine Ortiz, Gorita, & Vislykh, 2004, p. 2). In organizations with a centralized hierarchy, a core group of leaders often makes the decisions for the rest of the company. In other, oftentimes, smaller organizations, one person's in charge and must pick up one, two, or even several missing roles in the case he or she needs to cover for a missing or dismissed employee (E-Myth, 2009). For every business, leaders *know* what work needs to be completed, but often don't know how to articulate or get people to work on it (Borzykowski, 2015, p. 9). And for many who are so passionate and involved in their ventures, any threat of negative action forces people to spring into action whenever trouble arrives. This is why staying in your lane through delegation is important, because you will learn how to reinforce your strengths and work on your weaknesses as you help others navigate their own limits: "Keeping an eye on the big picture is important, but you need to take a step back and let your associates do what they do best. Then you can do the same" (Roach, 2017, par. 6).

In extreme circumstances, managers and leaders are very reluctant to give up even a modicum of control to his or her subordinates. This could be damaging for both the hierarchy and the company because leaders feel massive amounts of strain that barrel through the company—for leaders, they keep carrying too much weight out of pride, reluctance, or both; for subordinates, they can't learn more of the company's inner workings because they're left out of making any worthwhile decisions or contributions to the company. This reluctance falls under the self-enhancement bias, where there are "some perfectionists who feel it's easier to do everything themselves, or that their work is better than others"—in other words, "Everything you can do, I can do better!" Bragging rights, entitlement, and fear all interact into what can be a pernicious display of glitches and negative self-reinforcement of people's negative attitudes, which only contributes to the self-enhancement.

Kruger (2016) determined three circumstances where people are prone to self-enhance their skills: to feel good about themselves (par. 6); because people don't have the ability to process any information or insight about their performance or lack of skill (par. 8); or the events are skewed towards the *atmospheric conditions* outside of his or her control (par. 10). Like any other subconscious error message, self-enhancement helps us protect our egos and our fragile self-esteem; however, when the ego takes

187

over, self-enhancement can cut off empathy to others and their work. At the same time, self-enhancement isn't bad, since it shows that, as I discussed earlier on "luck" and its needlessness, it helps us look at ourselves as boot-strappers of our own destiny (McLeod, 2011). Returning to delegation, self-enhancing managers feel they are the only ones capable of doing their work or, at the very least, believe their share of the work is better than others, regardless of any factual or concrete evidence. So, it's not all about pride or fear of loss; it can also be a tool that both leaders and employees can take advantage of successfully:

- For employees: Can you think of a time you held up your share of the work?
- For leaders, managers, and supervisors: Can you think of a time you've delegated your work successfully?

By determining how delegation can be productive to people's prospects, both will gain free time and "valuable knowledge and experience" that is commensurate with their experience (Wakeman, 2015, par. 5).

But what is the best structure to enforce delegation? One part of delegation involves power, and granting it to a subordinate is a serious responsibility. You can take the *structural approach*, where the "power in organizations stems from sources such as hierarchical authority, control of resources and network centrality" (Menon, 2001, p. 155), meaning that any delegation comes from the top. You can also use the *motivational approach*, where you can offer people to feel energized through intrinsic motivation that involves meaning, competence, self-determination, and impact (p. 156). Or you can use the *leadership approach*, where you can empower your subordinates by "providing an exciting vision for the future" and encouraging them to take on an increasing amount of important challenges (p. 156). You can use one approach, or combine all three—most leaders do that. Keep in mind how your delegation style, including your temperament; the team you're working with; communication skills; the schedule; priorities; and you and your team's place within the organization. This way, any delegated interaction will be important for your team's future!

The Role of Empowering Your Employees

But how to begin taking important steps towards delegating your tasks to employees? Remember that, when you delegate, you don't simply assign tasks to others and expect them to perform at your intended level of expectations; instead, it's best to look at the strengths and weaknesses of others and give them tasks of increasing complexity depending on their skill set, their levels of responsibility, and their value to team contributions (Landry, 2012, p. 56). After all, you wouldn't tell your three-year-old to finish an eight-year old's homework, right? So not everybody is expected to excel in addressing complex customer service requests––but that doesn't mean that they won't have a chance to work at customer service. But someone with certified accounting skills shouldn't limit his or her skills to accounting; rather, it's better to incorporate a progressively complex set of tasks through delegation. Feel free to strike a balance between what people know and what they're expected to reach, and you'll see the results of their empowerment in no time (Rue, 1987, p. 175).

People need to feel empowered to make their own choices. They like to choose between a *reasonable* set of options where they can weigh their expectations and enjoy quality at the same time—it's better to choose one set of pants from eight choices rather than one out of eighty. They also like to feel free to apply the skills they learned through life to the task at hand, given enough time and latitude to solve the challenges. This is the reason why, in order for delegation to work and for delegated employees to function at their peak performance, they need to see the value of *empowerment* in you: "No matter how an employee is performing on his or her current task, your appreciationfor the employee as a human being should never falter and always be visible" (Heathfield, 2017, par. 7).

By empowering your employees, they now have the "blessing" to do their job on their own. As they grow in your development, they'll naturally feel like big fishes in a small pond, achieving mastery of their abilities yet dangerously treading towards the comfort zone. As a result, it's important to use every tool at your disposal to delegate through empowerment, through simple things like sharing information, allowing employees to sit in on meetings and conferences and share their views freely and without prejudice. Empowered people are motivated to succeed, and you want to use that healthy dose of success to enhance their job involvement and magnify the need for greater organizational commitment and decision-making (Ongari, 2009). When was the last time you carefully listened to employee's suggestions about the way things are run in your business? You may dismiss their concerns as petty complaints, but no: they carefully interact with a complex set of atmospheric conditions that are not like yours, and their perspectives on the job can be the tool needed to bank on their (and your) success. When you do, they value their place in your business as they continually strive to improve their performance as they keep a healthy perspective on their place within the company. Don't neglect empowerment, and success won't neglect you.

Ongari (2009) discussed five aspects of employee empowerment that make it a successful endeavor:

- **Job control:** If you remembered from previous chapters on control, control could be defined as "a psychological construct reflecting on an individual's belief in his [or] her ability to affect a change in the desired direction, in the environment" (Carayon & Zjilstra, 1994, p. 33). And how much control they get is important; a study by industrial psychologists on employee latitude revealed that the extent of their freedom to make choices on their work "affects their health, their morale, and their ability to handle their workload" (American Psychological Association, 2013, par. 2). On the other hand, people in "high-stress jobs with little control over their workflow" can lose years of life, die younger, and become less healthy under the stress of helplessness (Raedeke, n.d., par. 1). This is why control and latitude shouldn't be neglected in employee engagement.

- **Awareness of work context:** In high-security or public safety jobs, awareness of people's surroundings is not only important—it's the distinction between life or death, a safe outing or an avoidable disaster. In other cases, the automaticity and repetition of the job drag on for many employees, making them work on autopilot because they feel like they're not challenged enough. To avoid this, empowered employees know that awareness makes them "better able to see the impact of their behaviors" (Ellard, 2017, par. 2) which, in turn, leads to experience mindfulness that allows them to enjoy their job performance (Reb, Narayanan, & Ho, 2015; p. 180). Beyond simply "getting the job done" and calling it a night, awareness of things like deadlines, reviews, and customer interactions are necessary considerations for them to experience the value of their work.

- **Job accountability:** Accountability is a scary word because it conjures up negative glitches and error messages of pink slips and waiting in unemployment lines—or even worse, jail—if some element of the work is wrong. But if you wish to be successfully engaged, then you must be accountable for your portion of the job: "Accountability is about delivering on command. It's taking responsibility for an outcome, not just a set of tasks. It's taking the initiative with thoughtful, strategic follow-through" (Thoms, Dose, & Scott, 2002, p. 307). Nobody likes an employee who can't hold his or her end of the bargain, which is why values like "integrity, honesty, and courage" are valuable to both empowered managers and subordinates, leading to greater amounts of trust in the employee (Forbis, 2014, p. 2)

- **Sharing responsibility for the unit and organizational performance:** Responsibility is another word that seems to be taken out of context. Everybody has different respon-sibilities within an organization; for instance, in a family unit, adults are responsible for working while children tend to be responsible for studying and respecting their parent's wishes. It's the same in business, and responsibility is tan-tamount to unlocking your maximum performance. Because leadership is "multi-faceted," sharing responsibility is a way to increase your input while spreading out the risk to other, able-bodied leaders that can also handle a portion of your work; in this regard, a study on management concluded that "the implementation of shared leadership has led to high-performance teamwork" because everybody is responsible to pull his or her weight and show how valuable they are to the team (Hoberecht, 2011, p. 2).

- **Reward equity:** Not every person is necessarily motivated by money, healthcare, stocks, or a pension—though these are very important financial tools to have. Some choose to be rewarded for their time through a better work-life bal-ance. Others want to be challenged with more complex gigs and side projects. Still, others would like a gym mem-bership or free meals. In the end, letting employees see the results of their work allows them to increasingly contribute their skills to the company, because "if they don't feel as if they're adding value and are indispensable within the team—then your business is at a huge disadvantage" (Caan, 2015, par. 1). By allowing employees to experience equity with their choices, you create "loyalty, motivation, and drive" that significantly decreases turnovers and allows, even more, people to participate in many new teams (par. 15).

It looks like delegation is a pretty sweet deal to have in your company. But don't think of executive trips to your vacation home just yet! There's still a long way to go before you sow the seeds of proper employee delegation within your project. Keep in mind that not everything can be delegated (if you do, what work can you make for yourself?). Delegate tasks that are fun, reward-ing, and routine for your company. However, it wouldn't be wise to delegate confidential or personal (as in non-work-related) mat-ters to employees when they should be handled by you. It also isn't wise to tell a subordinate to praise, reprimand, or even change hir-ing and firing policies, as this can be a very conflicting source of grapevine communication between the team. Also, do consider twice delegating when an actual crisis happens, like the aftermath of a natural disaster, a data breach, or a sudden leadership vacuum since, no matter how many dry runs happen you will still be re-quired to use your authority and act with a swift response. Thus, it's important to create healthy boundaries of delegation between your subordinates and yourself. After all, you do need *something* to do!

Figure 12: Aspects of Empowerment.

Note: Adapted from "Managing behind the scenes: A view-point on employee empowerment," by H. Ongari, 2012, *African Journal of Business Management*, 009-015

The Micromanagement Disease

We already know why people don't delegate: there's fear, pride, and trepidation involved. But did you ever stop and think about people who seem to obsessively check others' work without even finishing their own work? One thing is checking for thoroughness and completeness. Another thing is thriving on the minutiae of splitting hairs unnecessarily, if only to show who has power or authority. Instead of transparency, leadership becomes an invasion of employee autonomy—and everybody ends up losing time, money, and opportunities to improve their delegation skills. This leadership style is called *micromanagement*, and you may have experienced this in the past with a critical or demanding boss. Or you may have been one before.

Many people micromanage when the leader "dictates the tasks to be done or directs how to do the work," even if the subordinate has been given enough latitude to work on the project considering the initial and subsequent constraints of performing the task at hand (Canner & Bernstein, 2016, par. 4). Or they micromanage because they want to ensure that employees are doing their share of the work due to past mistakes. In other cases, people micromanage as a way to overcompensate for their personal insecurities when there's no need to dwell on them. Micromanagers, like many addicts and alcoholics, are the last people to recognize that they are hooked on controlling others. Extreme micromanagers behave pathologically, refusing to accept personal responsibility or accountability and create scapegoats to blame for their own mistakes (White, 2010, p. 71-72).

Or they can be ambitious and power-driven—which is not a bad goal in itself, I might add, but it invites many circumstances that "force" leaders out of relevance (Murphy, 2017). Needless to say, micromanagement is dangerous and unproductive: according to Collins (2002), "low employee morale, high staff turnover, reduction of productivity and patient dissatisfaction" are consequences of micromanagement, leading to "decreased growth potential in the department" (p. 32). Even worse, there are those who believe that they're constantly hovered on while performing at lower levels than others due to performance anxiety (Lucas, 2011; DeCaro, Thomas, Albert, & Beilock, 2011). Which is why power is, according to Baer (2016), an oxymoron: "If you're secure in [your power], you don't feel compelled to control everybody around you" (par. 4).

Burnout!

To the other extreme, any lack of delegation and excess of overburdening yourself with work can lead you to suffer *burnout*, or "the mental and physical exhaustion you experience when the demands of your work consistently exceed the amount of energy you have available" (Knight, 2015, par. 2). When you're burned out, you feel lethargic from carrying so much dead weight on your shoulders. You may feel stressed, depressed, anxious and frustrated at the same time. And the worst part of burnout is its lingering grasp: one moment, you're working to your peak performance and the next you feel like crashing down in a lounge and sitting at home all day is better than working 40 hours for a job you lost all of your love for. When you burn out, you experience "a prolonged exposure to chronic [long-lasting] emotional and interpersonal situations on the job (Maslach, 2003, p. 189). As a result, you're emotionally exhausted because you lack any more emotional energy dried up by work (Cordes & Dougherty, 1999, p. 623); you feel depersonalized because you can't connect to others, so you begin to treat them as objects to achieve a goal instead of people (p. 623); and you diminish any personal achievement or, at the very least, spin it self-deprecatingly (p. 623).

The stress of a burnout strains business resources, making any type of recovery distressing and often traumatic. If you're burned out, you can easily quit your career and neglect all your work within company leadership. You become resigned to a "loss of motivation, [a] growing sense of emotional depletion, and cynicism" that suddenly engulfs your life, which is made even worse by entertaining the error messages created through the improper functioning of your skills (Carter, 2013, par. 2, 3; Dizik, 2016, p. 7; Michel, 2016, p. 7). Because you have too much to do, you begin to neglect your time, your boundaries, and your health as you treat everything that surrounds you with contempt. In the brain, burnout "can alter neural circuits, ultimately causing a vicious cycle of neurological dysfunction" that only encourages an even more "burnt-out" feeling among others (Michel, 2016, p. 13). For this reason, delegate carefully, with intentions and goals in mind. You'll learn how to empower others dangerously teetering toward burnout, and you can learn from yourself!

Delegating is hard at first—nobody wants to give up something special to them—but it's worth it in the end. It's an art that needs to be balanced among other projects as you discover new opportunities to organize your delegation resources to other people. No, you don't have to give up your own space to develop your delegation skills, however rusty they may be. That's why the Inspired Performance Program exists to give you an opportunity to gather how the subconscious mind works, how to transform their attitudes on delegation and create clear and sweeping exercises to anchor your past successes in your mind. Take this opportunity to take a stand against burnout and micromanagement, and take back your time so you can track new opportunities that will help you become even more successful!

#8. Refuse Help

"When you're drowning, you don't say 'I would be incredibly pleased if someone would have the foresight to notice me drowning and come and help me' — you just scream." – John Lennon

Why It's Hard to Ask for Help

Successful people work hard and are smart to let go of their pride and ask for help when necessary. This area ties in directly to Number Seven about straying from your lane. It is difficult at times to ask for help. I know I've struggled with this many times. Not always because of pride. There are times when you want to just figure it out on your own. This leads us to the classic stereotype of the man who refuses to ask for directions. Why do we do that? Must be rooted in our biology. Well, it's not important to understand why we do it, it's more important to address and correct it. There have been times when I just don't want to bother people and just do it. These are not examples of what I mean by refusing to ask for help. It goes much deeper.

The major reason people do this is because asking for help at times is perceived as a weakness. The fact is, the opposite is true. Asking for help, or accepting help when it is offered, is a sign of strength. So why do people refuse to ask or accept help? Most likely it is coming from experiences earlier in life. Perhaps a parent who with all the best intentions delivered the message to be independent and strong. A child may interpret this later in life to mean that you don't need anybody. This belief, if set early in life, will be having an effect still today. Successful people are not afraid to ask for or accept help. Is this something you find yourself doing? If so, our TIPP process can help.

When we accept help from other people, does this mean we are the only benefactor from the transaction? Not at all. People like to help; it brings them a sense of accomplishment. When your spouse or child helps you, they feel wanted and needed. Accepting help benefits more than you. Think about times when you have helped someone. How about a time when you helped them when they never asked for help? How did that make you feel? If you are the type of person who always refuses help from other people, then you establish a pattern of behavior. So, don't be surprised or disappointed when no one ever offers when you really need it. Your consistent refusal will keep people away for fear of offending you. Everyone needs help at times. Develop an attitude of appreciation when you are offered assistance. Even when you might not need it, it pays to keep that door open.

The issue of meaning can also be in the way for someone who doesn't accept help. What does it mean about you when help is offered? Do you look offended? Or, do you create an atmosphere of being offended? This will create a problem for your ulti-mate success. If you're the boss at work and someone offers to help, give them a chance, make their day. What a thrill for them to know they helped someone they admire and value.

Now, there is an opposite side to this coin. Are you some-one who takes advantage of people that help you? This is not right as well. This is also an impediment to success. True success comes from a spirit of give and take. Selfish people who are successful will at some point have it come back on them. Accepting help is a balance between how much to receive and how much to give. You could also be someone who helps everyone and feel taken ad-vantage of. This can also create an issue with your success. Don't give away the farm and leave nothing for yourself or your family. I've known people that help everyone and in essence, have aban-doned their family. Everyone loves them, except the people at home. Once again, balance.

In the last two weeks, how many times did you ask for help in order to finish a request that was unreachable or unreasonable. Or maybe you want to donate and volunteer your time and money to a noble cause, such as helping those with children with cancer or making your city much more transit-accessible for people with transportation challenges or special needs. Or perhaps you can ask others to sign a petition aiming to stop the plans to demolish an important, historical building, because they want to build a boring strip mall and a parking lot. Today, there are many ways to interact with others—through the internet, through television, through simple picket signs and calling people by name. But it's important to fight for something, for that's our right in this country, and it's a freedom each and every one of us needs to take advantage of to be successful.

Here's the problem with the circumstances of help: "A person dealing whether to ask for help is almost always in conflict" (DePaulo & Fisher, 1980, p. 23). Even if helping others is rewarding and makes people feel good, it also has a cost of time, money, and emotions for people, too. Those who give abundantly must also be ready to accept rejection from people who don't want to *directly* ask for any help, yet you are very sure that he or she only refuse out of pride or convenience. In their minds, past atmospheric conditions have determined that asking for help is (irrationally) risky and unnecessary, that they can pull themselves up by their bootstraps and do it alone, once again. Or help makes people feel vulnerable, and they associate vulnerability with weakness. Either way, refusing help seems unproductive at first glance—especially in times of crisis—, but it's important to look at the essence of what made people and their idea successful to determine the best course of action.

It's difficult at times to ask for help. I know; I've struggled with this issue many times, and it's not always because of pride. Most people refuse to ask for help at times because it can be perceived as a weakness when, in fact, the opposite is true: asking or accepting help when offered is a sign of strength. But people refuse to ask or accept any help due to past life experiences. Perhaps a parent, with all the best intentions, delivered messages of individualism and independence. A child may interpret this later in life to mean that you don't need anybody. If this mindset is developed early in life, it will affect a growing child's perceptions in the future. Think about your reaction when being offered help. Do you look offended? Or, do you create an atmosphere of being offended? If so, this will be problematic to your ultimate success.

People like to help because it brings them a sense of accomplishment and bonding. When your spouse or child helps you, they feel wanted and needed. In addition, accepting help benefits more than you. Think about times when you have helped someone. How about a time when you helped them when they never asked for help? How did that make you feel? If you are the type of person who always refuses help from other people, then you establish a pattern of behavior. So don't be surprised or disappointed when no one offers when you really need it, or other people continue to offer their services even though you don't really need it. Your consistent refusal will keep people away for fear of offending you, but

205

your consistent approval will keep people ready and willing to help. When you develop an attitude of appreciation, it pays to keep that door open.

That being said, are you someone who takes advantage of people that help you? Or are you someone who helps everyone and feel taken advantage of? While mistrust shouldn't be a precursor to helping, you must know that true success comes from a spirit of give and take. Selfish successful people will eventually have their negative actions come back on them. Likewise, kind and helpful people will have better days where they can enjoy receiving help from healthy relationships. This can also create an issue with your success. Don't give away the farm and leave nothing for yourself or your family; as another point, don't help everybody to the point that you abandon your family.

Successful people know that some help is necessary to succeed and reach a goal. But it's also important to distinguish *when* to stop receiving help and the message it brings to those around you. As a leader, your goal isn't to promote dependence on others; instead, you want to assert your leadership while slowly building up a loyal employee base willing to help you and collaborate with the necessary resources you need. You don't need to be an altruist to figure out what happens when you develop an altruistic company mission to give—and receive—help from everybody who wants to see your brand succeed. After you take the important steps to address these new concepts, you can create opportunities where you and your company can reach your peak performance!

Profit-Making Help: Corporate Social Responsibility

Whether you give out help to a single person, to a group, or to a community, you are engaging in a form of altruism—a "behavior that benefits others at the cost to an individual" (Kerr, Godfrey-Smith, & Feldman, 2004, p. 135). But cost need not always be money or resources; it can be time, fame, and an opportunity to enjoy a healthy tax break on many occasions. For instance, if you own a catering company and you choose to donate your services to provide lunch to a homeless shelter, you are engaging in altruistic behavior, since it costs you both time and money to prepare for a meal out of concern for other people's welfare—namely, the homeless residing in the local shelter. Of course, there are other ulterior benefits, too, since your company is also gaining exposure from your act of altruistic kindness. But doing that service matters for the community; as such, people are more than willing to support those that act unselfishly and whose values align with theirs. In addition, two types of altruism exist: *psychological altruism*, where people "act out of concern for the well-being of others, without regard to your own self-interest"; and *biological altruism*, where it helps the species' survival without benefiting something in particular (Taylor, 2011, par. 1).

In business, corporate social responsibility (CSR) refers to "transparent business practices that are based on ethical values, compliance with legal requirements, and respect for people, communities, and the environment" (Ronda, Baird, Kramer, & Woodford, 2002, p. 2). Companies engage in these practices because it pays to show respect and responsibility for the business' local community. You see this in action every time there's a major oil spill, and companies volunteer to clean up beaches, animals, houses, and supplies—and often provide cash—as a way to address their commitment to the local community's environment. Instead of looking at the business world as an entity full of competitors and clients that need to constantly take a swing at each other (Gratton, 2014), corporate social responsibility is no longer treated as a peripheral concern over profits, but as a way to develop resilient communities in which they can draw new opportunities––and profit—for the future.

Why do people install corporate social responsibility programs? Four theories are proposed: *slack resources*, where companies will invest money on corporate or social programs through profit remnants; *management practice*, where companies will use corporate social responsibility practices as a way to develop new profits and resources in order to ensure a better reputation; *penance theory*, where companies try to make amends for any damage they intentionally caused, like offering free food supplies after a hurricane; and *insurance theory*, where companies attempt to mitigate any potential damage from their course of action; as a result, companies invest in CSR practices because "they think it's the right thing to do ,or a good move for the business that pays off by improving the overall financial performance of the company" (White, 2016, par. 6). Not only does helping others feel good, but it also becomes a ticket to success when you develop the opportunity to help others.

Managers are more than willing to help employees succeed. Employees want to use their resources to help others. And prospective job applicants don't necessarily look at salary or benefits as a way to determine if that job is the right one for them; rather, they're currently choosing opportunities where they can give back and help others, as Millennials do—for instance. A study in 2009 reported 88% of females and 82% of males believe "it's important to be able to give back to the community through work" (Hewlett, 2009, par. 5; Stahl, 2016); 95% of females and 92% of males desire recognition from their superiors as a non-monetary benefit (Hewlett, 2009); 84% of Millennials have made a charitable donation in 2014 (Feldman, Hosea, Ponce, Wall, M, & Banker, 2014, p. 19); and their use of social media and technology has skyrocketed to the point that "[t]echnology has armed [Millennials] with knowledge and understanding of how other people live in societies and socioeconomic classes and countries around the world"—and has influenced the value of serving others (Stahl, 2016, par. 45). If you want to be successful at helping others be successful, arm yourself with the value of helping others as an important part of your brand!

Why People Refuse to Help

Now that I've discussed at length the value of helping others and how it impacts your business, let's delve deep into the heart of the matter: If people have more resources than ever to find the help they need, then *why do people steadfastly refuse to take it?* On many occasions, people refuse help because they never asked, they never wanted nor chose to be helped for reasons of their own. From the outside, the leader's actions look stormy and scary enough that you wish to spring into action and help them; but for the person on the inside, their actions make a lot of sense. Yes, they may carefully weigh your advice or any suggestions, but it doesn't mean they're actively seeking your help. In that regard, they never asked you to help.

For Flynn & Lake (2008), "In the context of helping behavior, help-seekers may routinely fail to appreciate the person's concern with rejecting a request for help, despite finding themselves in a similar position on a frequent basis" (p. 129). This means that help-seekers aren't aware of your intentions to help because they don't know how to ask for it. Or, they don't know that you want to help them because you don't make your intentions loud and clear. Perhaps they truly need help, yet they can't clearly explain their circumstances and how you or another person can contribute to the solution. Asking for help can be "uncomfortable, if not embarrassing," recoiling out of fear of exposing their personal, self-imposed inadequacies or attempting to stave off rejection (p. 140-191). Newark (2013) described this as a "missed opportunity" since "they may feel so bad about rejecting us that they become more willing to ask for help should the chance arise again" (par. 4).

Some people perceive themselves as a burden. The term *self-perceived burden* is used in palliative care to describe an "empathetic concern engendered from the impact of one's illness and care needs, resulting in guilt, distress, feelings of responsibility and a diminished sense of self" (McPherson, Wilson, Tubchuck, & Brajtman, 2007, p. 425; Gorvin & Brown, 2012). Applying this concept to other, non-terminal circumstances, people fear they're helping others by not asking for help because they feel they weigh down on others who have better things to do and, thusly, don't want to become an inconvenience. It becomes a rationalization because they attempt to justify their feeling of being stuck, even if it personally harms them in the long run. It doesn't help (no pun intended) that the helper isn't cognizant of the person's need, and believes he or she "has a greater chance to be refused" (DePaulo & Fisher, 1980, p. 24). In the end, they make mountains out of molehills since the problems they face are much more manageable than they first believed.

Other people are afraid of admitting they're out of control. This is true when more serious offenses happen, such as addictions or bad investments. In this case, fear rears its ugly head because it reveals people's weaknesses and only motivates rejection (Dean, 2008, par. 3). They fear being exposed for their personal failures, and they wish to keep a front of stability, even if their self-destructive behavior slowly chips it away.

Still others are afraid of asking for help because they fear they'll be owe favor—and they'll have to pay it back somehow. This reveals the concept of *reciprocity*, a compliance technique I already covered in our chapter on conformity—but if you need a refresher, "if someone does something for you, then you feel *delighted* [emphasis added] to return the favor" (Cherry, 2017, par. 1). It doesn't mean that you necessarily *like* the person who did you the favor; it means that you appreciate his or her actions in your favor and, in most cases, you are expected to comply to his or her requests should the need arise. This works so well as a tool of persuasion because it allows for cohesiveness in our society, including a fair and equitable "division of labor", trade and the exchange of goods and services, and other "interdependencies" to foster cohesion (Cialdini, 2007, p. 14). Reciprocity can be *instrumental*, where the person can obtain some value for the item, be it "good, service, or social outcome;" or it can be *symbolic* or *communicative*, where the "value is conveyed by the act of reciprocity"—in other words, you're doing a favor for doing a favor (Molm, Schaefer, & Collett, 2007, p. 200).

Think of a time a friend of yours gave you an item you've always wanted but never expressed it loudly (or implied): tickets to a concert or a basketball game, an expensive item, or a surprise weekend trip. As you're shocked at this act of friendship, you respond with thankfulness and the tacit expectation that you'll find a way to repay the gift. Breaking this down, those tickets and trips are a form of instrumental reciprocity, while your gratitude *and* the expectation to return the favor is symbolic reciprocity. To note, this reflects that reciprocity is "a multi-faceted concept of belief and behaviour, evident in various forms of interaction and leading to varied outcomes for individuals and society" (Lewis, Horton & Coddington, 2017, p. 165) regardless if the gift—and the subsequent favor—is good, bad, or simply weird.

Appearing weak is another reason people loathe seeking help. People hide emotions because they need to "stay in control,

213

look strong, and keep things at arms' length," which is especially true for men in business who are attached to the strings of societal expectations (Sundheim, 2013, par. 2). However, refusing to show weakness or any emotion at all, only deepens the emotional concussion and cuts through the person's apparent resilience. In fact, showing some vulnerability can help leaders become trustworthy in the eyes of teammates because "a team can't function without trust, and vulnerability is required to foster trust in others" (Berg, 2017, par. 5). By showing a personal, visceral awareness of your emotions to others, you can develop strength within your team, and encourage others to develop themselves and contribute to your business with honesty. After all, "someone can't get their work done on their own," anyway (Baker, 2014, par. 2).

Even worse for others, people refuse to seek help because they're afraid of—you guessed it—rejection. Langens & Schüler (2005) reflected in a study that "Individuals with a strong (relative to weak) fear of rejection feel more insecure in social situations and typically transmit feelings of insecurity to people around them [and] tend to doubt that they are liked and valued" (p. 819). And, in many cases, that includes asking for help. Because they're so afraid of being told "no," they refuse to ask anybody about their plight, which in and of itself becomes self-reinforcing, self-limiting and isolating. They need not suffer from social anxiety to realize how breaking off decisions based on fear of rejection can be detrimental to the health of a business venture since they, as Altman suggested, are putting themselves "into a position of being judged or evaluated" based on irrational thinking (2017, par. 2).

Also known as *rejection sensitivity*, people who fear rejection "may originally develop a self-protective reaction to parental rejection" (Downey & Feldman, 1996, p. 1328). In many cases, people are first exposed to rejection from parents or guardians during childhood by saying "No" to a child's deepest desires; the emotional concussion from childhood rejection at school, with friends and family, and society in general, compounds to make the individual relive the emotional concussion of rejection and brings that glitch to any modern-day interaction. In other circumstances, people who suffer rejection believe that they will be "unlovable," lonely, or worthless because nobody else looks at them the way they desire (Amodeo, 2014, par. 3); this is compounded in a study of rejection in relationship displaying that "participants who scored higher in rejection sensitivity were more likely to interpret their partner's hypothetical behavior as hurtful intent as *hurtful intent* [emphasis added], overlooking other potential explanations" (par. 6). Even if the study is focused on *romantic* relationships, it's not hard to extrapolate this to other non-romantic relationships with two or more people—*any* negative reaction from a person can be seen as a reflection of mistrust or negativity against the other one. Thus, if a leader cannot shake off rejection, then he or she will be at risk to suffer from unnecessary victim-hood.

Figure 13: Graphical description of the benefits of asking for help.

Note: Adapted from "Become a better leader by asking for help" by L. Corcuera 2014, Inc, Mansueto Ventures, https://www.inc.com/lorie-corcuera/become-a-better-leader-by-asking-for-help.html.

The Trouble with Self-Reliance

And what about self-reliance, that classic American trait? Nobody said that business leaders shouldn't be resourceful or self-reliant; in fact, that should be one of the first things they should have in their mental constitution! I don't argue that a solo entrepreneur has fewer chances to succeed than a start-up or a fully-fledged company developing a new project or idea because they have very little help, since any help is better than no help at all. What I do argue is that excessive self-reliance in business is "self-limiting" because, "In today's organizations, you can't be successful if you don't ask for what you wanted" (Baker, 2014, par. 3).

This is what Gaspard (2014) considered problematic about self-reliance: "This is the tragedy of the double-edged sword of reliance. On the surface, it's wonderful to be independent, self-sufficient, and resilient. But when you believe you must do everything for yourself, you create your own demise" (Gaspard, 2014, par. 6). No business should be an army of one, taking on too many hats that don't correspond to his or her talents; instead, there should be someone to take care of marketing; another person for coding and preparing the website; another person for publishing social media; and so on. By staying in your lane and delegating the appropriate tasks to the appropriate people, you receive more "insight and information" to the overall problems in your business (Meninger, 2016, par. 2).

In extreme cases, self-reliance can be distorted into arrogance. It's not a bad thing to feel proud in your successes, especially when they are hard-earned and warranted; but if this healthy, humble pride turns into an off-putting display of "aggression and hostility," then it can lead to problems in both professional and personal relationships (Tracy & Robbins, 2007, p. 506, 507). In essence, arrogance is a heuristic, an error message known as the *egotistical* or *egocentric bias*, where people have "the tendency to present oneself as responsible for success *whether you are or not*, and the tendency to believe these positive presentations" (Bordens & Horowitz, 2008, p. 54). And everybody suffers from it to an extent: according to a 1984 Journal of Personality study on this bias, it was determined that "in an informal group, each person present may be seeing himself as at its center" because participants see themselves as being more attractive, attentive, and much more impactful than what society suggests (Goleman, 1984, p. 6). In contrast, it's better to develop a humble—but confident and assertive—business environment as it is "collaborative" and "promotes a positive buzz, creativity, and effective teamwork" (Federer, 2013, par. 3), where you allow employees to make (calculated) mistakes and learn from them, who in turn develop confidence for the company's resources and each other.

Mentoring is Valuable

It feels good to help. As I've discussed throughout this chapter, people love to help and want to help others, so it's important to take out those glitches and error messages where you steadfastly believe that people won't help you because it happened in the past. Take a moment to look at the past few years of your life, and think of all the people you've helped and all the people that helped you. Doesn't it feel good to know that people are more than willing to lend you a hand—if you ask them, right? Most people don't want to lose sight of helping someone in need, more so if it will improve their lives in the making. If someone's new to a place, a company, or neighborhood, people (for the most part) receive them with housewarming food, gifts, and a pat on the back and the suggestion to call in case of any need. It helps to guide them towards how things work in that new environment and integrate them without much trouble. Think of Patel's (2014) positive consequences for help: "[...] asking for help can make it a lot easier to boost brand awareness and build up your reputation among other entrepreneurs [...] grow your network [and] can lead to business growth" (par. 4-6).

This is how mentoring also works: you've been helped by someone in business before, and you decide to help new employees to seamlessly integrate themselves into the company. *Mentoring* can be defined as "an indefinite, relationship-based activity with several specific but wide-ranging goals," where "the mentor is a facilitator who works with either an individual or a group of people over an extended period" in order to help them process new skills, abilities, and experiences that will improve their professional careers (Michael, 2008, p. 4). Closely related, but completely different, is *coaching*, where the training is "concerned with performance and the development of certain skills" (p. 4), which is mostly self-directed and limited to a certain amount of skills. Stewart & Harrison (2016) notes that this activity improves the mentor's personal development and communication skills, and contributes to "the success of an organization as it promotes a culture of belonging, support, and trust" (p. 14).

Krishnen (2006) described why mentoring is important for *protégés*, or "someone who is sponsored by someone who is more experienced and influential" (Brenner, 2014, par. 6):

> A mentor is a business investment. When business owners are mentored, 70% of their businesses live past five years—double the survival rate of non-mentored small businesses. 88% of those in this same survey called the mentoring experience "invaluable" to their business success (par. 2).

Additionally, mentorship can be used informally which, "coupled with a formal training program, increases the amount of knowledge absorbed by employees" (Stewart & Harrison, 2016, p.

14). This maximizes company resources by offering both "on-the-book" training and practical applications of the things protégés learned in the process. They learn how to integrate flexibility, develop resilience to unavoidable failure situations, and interact with other fellow protégéss within the job. (Those are the same things that make internships, recent graduate and young associate programs so competitive and desirable—if you're a business leader, you should *definitely* plan to install one—within your budget and limits, of course!)

When you enable a mentorship program, you begin to feel internal satisfaction for showing the ropes to new employees, who will benefit from your many years of wisdom and experience. You will feel a sense of self-rejuvenation from their energy, as your protégés will propose novel ideas that may further your company and give you a head start on the competition. Your job performance and leadership skills will improve due to the protégé's growing sense of loyalty to you and your company—but be careful *who* you are choosing to become your protégé, since any negative performance from the latter can easily damage your leadership and reputation. But most importantly, you'll develop a sense of *generativity*, or a growing contribution and an "immortal" legacy of your work for others to follow (Ragins & Scandura, 1999, p. 494). With generavity it doesn't mean that you'll live forever or vicariously through your protégé's accomplishments; rather, it becomes a tool so that others can understand the value of your success and your many contributions to the company. You'll also become a sounding board, a "sensor" of any workplace issues or dynamics that can become troublesome before these escalate—this can happen when you match "mentors and mentees who are two or three levels apart in the organizational hierarchy and who are not in the same immediate chain of command" (Wilson & Elman, 1990, p. 89).

But if you choose to undertake the path of mentorship, you must be ready to face disagreements and disappointments. Different work styles, career paths, and atmospheric conditions will be in conflict with one another, but take this time to understand how both mentor and protégé can learn from each other. In addition, any poor performance from a protégé will reflect badly on your leadership skills, since others may question your ability to choose people that will contribute respect and value to your business. This relationship is also rife for exploitation since there's risk of exploitation and preferential treatment on behalf of the mentor, and dependence on the mentor on behalf of the protégé, who may excessively rely on the mentor instead of developing new, enriching experiences. Or administratively, other departments don't feel as convinced or intrigued into bringing mentor relationships on board because it can be hard to convince them to implement a mentoring program when there's a lack of reliable, conclusive data (Erlich & Hansford, 1999, p. 100).

And most importantly, it takes time and effort from both parties to develop a successful mentor-protégé relationship. It takes many phone calls and face-to-face meetings, many e-mail tags and opinions, and many successes and failures, to create a successful mentoring relationship. Don't feel frustrated if you and your protégé aren't a perfect match at first; like any relationship, it should take more than a few tries to create a working relationship, one that satisfies both parties and reflects mutual respect. As time progresses, your relationship should markedly improve to the point where both parties benefit from the other's abilities while relating to one another. Remember that a mentoring relationship is not only career-focused, where you help broaden the protégé's career path while forging expertise; it's also psychosocial, where you are also responsible to become a confident role model of what the protégé should expect in his or her future career (Allen, Eby, Poteet, Lentz, & Lima, 2004, p. 128). As you invest in your protégé, and your protégé invests in you, a beautiful, professional relationship is in full swing.

Table 7: Benefits and Costs of Mentoring.

Benefits	Costs
• Generativity: "the contribution to future generations that gives a sense of immortality" • Internal satisfaction from making a productive use of these accumulated skills and wisdom • Self-rejuvenation from protégé(s)' energy • Internal satisfaction from making a productive use of protégé(s)' accumulated skills and wisdom • Mentor (s) improved performance by protégé(s) job support • Recognition from peers and superiors for developing talent	• May devolve into mutual exploitation • Risk of protégé displacement or backstabbing • "Nepotism" by giving protégé(s) an unfair advantage • Poorly performing protégés may reflect negatively on the mentor's judgment and competency • Difficulty to convince management or implement a mentoring program with a relative lack of data

Note: Adapted from "Burden or blessing? Expected costs and benefits of being a mentor," by B.R. Ragins & T.A. Scandura, 1999, Journal of Organizational Behavior, 20, p. 493-509; and "Mentoring: Pros and cons for HRM," by L.C. Erlich & B. Hansford, Asia-Pacific Journal of Human Resources, 1999, 37(3), p. 92-107.

In conclusion, successful people let go of their pride and any other error messages to ask for help. It can be "awkward and uncomfortable" to ask for help because anything can happen—begrudging support, rejection, doubts, or even outright denial, but having other successful people join your business during times of need will allow you to grow in the future. When you take a risk and ask for help, you're exposing yourself to people's true intentions, and you have the responsibility to choose those that will lead you towards success. In the Inspired Performance Institute's Executive Business Program, we feature short, time-tested methods that allow you to experience relief from past glitches, sweep distressing events from your mind, remember past successes and become the leader and mentor you wish to be!

#9. Fear Change

Successful people never avoid change—they embrace it!
I can't change the direction of the wind, but I can adjust my sails
to always reach my destination. Jimmy Dean

Everything Changes

In life, everything changes. People change, attitudes change, circumstances change. Change happens, and we can't avoid it as much as you want or desire to. Change is disruptive. Change is innovative. Change shakes up your business, your perceptions, and your life. It may be disorienting at first, but if you're willing to embrace change, you'll enjoy how you can use change to your advantage and succeed in the future, even if you won't see any evidence of change until months or years away. Today is the perfect moment where you can put in all of your hard work and experience the freedom to enjoy the value of your success. As a result, Brenner (2011) reported how changes determine the value of choice:

> While change may interrupt the usual flow of our
> daily lives and disrupt our normal functioning, it
> also affords us the opportunity, and the challenge,
> to examine our lives and to alter its course, if we so
> choose. Or to stay the course, making better

choices and decisions in the life we're already living (par. 7).

Don't be afraid to change or to embrace change. Instead, it's best if you become the person that *makes* change happen even though you're dealing with adverse circumstances and negative atmospheric conditions. Those that are truly successful know how to stop staying stuck in the "passive state of just watching how things unfold" to taking responsibility for their actions and establishing their choices today (Brenner, 2011, par. 3). Change appeals to movers and shakers, to those who want to make their own waves and disrupt the market with their new inventions. Change also appeals to those who want to break out from their comfort zone and think outside the box in order to become leaders in their respective fields. But there's always a catch: how should you, as a business leader, address people who fear change—and those who want to, but don't know how to start?

Change is Not Easy

So, why do people refuse to make changes even when the changes would be beneficial? There may be many reasons, but without a doubt, it's because our brains are hardwired for survival. People become so intimidated about making a change they'll end up doing nothing at all or accepting less than their abilities could deliver for them. The fear of change can be powerful. In order to be successful, you need to embrace change. I've met a lot of people that appear to be paralyzed, doing anything but what would be in their best interest. So, let's examine why.

Let's start with the easiest reason first. Change is not easy. Making changes involve taking risks and the fear of failure can be overwhelming. Fear has a purpose. Your mind produces this emotion to protect you from danger. So, why would it protect me from something that could be beneficial? Because of your "atmospheric conditions." The events and experiences throughout your life have taught your mind what to avoid. Perhaps you had taken some risks, and they ended up in a big loss. This loss is now still active in the thought process. Can you see why your mind would want to avoid another big loss?

Or, it could be fear of the unknown, not from an experienced event. The fear is produced from the standpoint of safety and comfort. Your subconscious mind is focused on survival. If there is no experience in taking chances, why start now? You're OK; you're alive. What's wrong with that picture? Successful people understand that overcoming these fears is the key to moving forward. Even the most successful people still experience some trepidation before making a big investment. The mind is making sure that you're looking at every angle, mitigating risk. Some of that fear is beneficial. The fear that is not beneficial is when the fear comes from old events and when you think about them you still experience the emotion. That's the glitch, the error message. What can you do about something that happened twenty years ago? Nothing. Fear is an emotion for action, escape a threat. It's impossible to escape a threat from ten or twenty years ago. That is exactly what the Inspired Performance Program (TIPP) fixes. The glitches or error messages that keep your mind in fear. Paralyzed or stuck as most people describe it.

Our imaginations can come up with fears that have never happened or, highly unlikely to happen. The problem with this brilliant feature we call imagination is it's operating within a brain that operates in real time. When our subconscious mind, our survival mind, sees images from previous experiences or imagined ones, it sees them as real and happening NOW. If we are imagining losing everything if this investment goes bad, isn't it obvious why your mind is using the emotion of fear to protect you? The way your mind operates is unique to you, based on your life events. If your experiences have been negative, then your mind will create thoughts and use emotions to avoid the danger. That can keep you stuck in a routine; something also called a habit or behavior. Overcoming this way of thinking is exactly what we do at the Inspired Performance Institute. We teach you how to stay present, in the moment and using your success and highlights throughout your life to your benefit. That's why people who start succeeding keep succeeding. They build on one success and use it to get to the next success.

Now, you can read all the self-help books or attend all the motivational seminars available, however, until you fix the glitches or error messages that have been built up over your life-time, success will be even more elusive. Our program is designed to fix the glitches, and then the other self-help books will make an impact. When you read those books, or attend those seminars and hear all you need to do is this or that, why can't you do it? The reason is a blocking belief, and that belief will not change until your mind is updated, rebooted, and adjusted.

Do you find yourself playing the what if game? What if the bank turns me down? What if people don't want my new product or service? What will people think about me if I fail? The problem with this way of thinking is, your subconscious mind sees these scenarios as real, operating in the present, when in fact they are not happening at all. The subconscious mind measures these pos-sible scenarios against any stored memories of similar experiences and will attempt to avoid hurt and pain at all costs, even potential success.

It would be great if we had a crystal ball and could see the future. That would make everything easier. Well, here is the next best thing. We can use our previous success and make sure our mind focuses on those events. However, it won't do that if the traumatic or disturbing events are still active. Those high-resolution images of painful times in our lives are interfering with moving forward. Now, once we clear those events, update your mind's experiences, your imagination can become a beneficial tool for success. Imagining your success, creating scenarios in which you succeed. That is the next step. Focused on goals and targets and your mind will see that as real as those imagined tragic scenarios.

The Inspired Performance Program works on two things, First, eliminate the way your mind filters through traumatic events and experiences by updating the memory and the high-res images stored. Second, creating a new way of thinking by using repetition as the tool. You see, when you repeat a new behavior, your mind builds a new neural pathway that eventually becomes the default pattern and overcomes the old code. However, if you don't ingrain the new pattern, then under stressful situations your mind will default to the old pattern or code. The TIPP process takes you through this and gives you the tools to change your life forever.

If you realize that you're resistant to change, then you are halfway there. Making changes is more than necessary, it's imperative. Why? Because the world is changing even if you're not. Older people who haven't embraced technology are at a huge disadvantage. We all know someone older who doesn't use a computer or email. So, what's wrong with that? They're missing the

231

major benefits to the advancements our society is receiving. Grandparents can Facetime with their grandchildren. If they can't travel due to health issues, they can be a part of their children's and grandchildren's lives. The memories created by these experiences are priceless. Change is constant. You're either keeping up or falling behind. Our world is changing so fast that keeping up is getting harder and harder.

I remember hearing from a friend that worked at a successful burger restaurant chain in the 1970's, and she told me how their management scoffed at the success of McDonald's. They said there was no way people would accept the McDonald's approach. The result, they are out of business. If you don't constantly make changes and adapt to the new business environment, you will soon be out of business. That's a fact. Now we have to understand the trends within age groups, the baby boomers, the millennials, Generation X's. Marketing to these groups is getting more and more specific. The younger the generation, the faster the changes in preferences. How you served the younger age group a year ago may be totally different next year. Here's a great piece of advice. If you don't like making changes to your business model, you believe in staying the course, then don't open a business. Work for someone else. Change is everywhere and happening at incredible speeds.

Here's the good news. If you fear to make changes, then take baby steps. Start showing your mind that change is not dangerous. We instruct people in the Inspired Performance Program to do several different things when they are building new codes and patterns. For example, brush their teeth with the opposite hand. Change the way they drive to the office once in a while. Drink their coffee with the opposite hand. It will feel uncomfortable at first. You're building new neural pathways. Eventually, the new code will be built, and it will not feel different or new. I sometimes say to someone going through our program that if you walked for twenty years with a sprained ankle and it heals over the next month, pretty soon walking without the pain will feel normal. Walking with the pain at one point felt normal.

Here's the best part. A code doesn't take that long to change. Your mind is designed to adapt. The TIPP process has you walk out behaviors over a twenty-eight-day period. Twenty years of a behavior can be adapted that quickly. Your mind is brilliant and focused on what's beneficial, appealing and possible. What needs updating for you? Let's do it!

There are many benefits to embracing change in your life. For starters, you grow as a person; you become more flexible. When you start embracing change, it becomes easier. Your mind will adapt faster; improvements will be beneficial. Your values may change for your benefit. Progress in your personal and professional life will create new opportunities. Then there's the snowball effect; one change turns into two changes, and two changes become four changes. The changes become faster and bigger. Plus, isn't it boring to always stay the same. Safe, but boring.

How I Changed My Golf Swing

Let me tell you a story of how I changed my golf swing to illustrate this point: I had just purchased a new set of golf clubs fitted to my personal swing. The professional golfer suggested a small swing change after viewing me on video replay I agreed and could see the benefit of making the change, so I set off to practice the swing change. On the weekend, as I golfed with a friend, I told him about my new swing. It made sense to him; in fact, he thought he could benefit from it as well. I informed him during that round that I wouldn't record my score, but I'd focus on the swing change. Even if he asked me what my score was during every hole, I constantly reminded him about not wanting to keep track of it. On the tenth hole, I told him that if I focus too much on my score, then my mind will want to go back to the old swing because it knows how to score better that way. If the score becomes a threat, then my mind will fix the threat and unconsciously repeat the old swing. You see, I needed to make the new swing safe and the only way to do that is to consciously repeat it until my subconscious mind programmed it. I needed to build the new code, and that would only come from repetition.

Why People Fear Change

For many, neuroticism is a constant character trait that precludes them from experiencing long-lasting personal and professional change. Neuroticism is described as a disposition to suffer from traits like anxiety, irritability, impulsivity, and rumination, which oftentimes happens as a result of *negative emotionality*, or "being disposed to more negative emotions than other people" (Baer, 2014, par. 1, 3). Even if everybody has suffered negative emotionality at one point or another in their lives, neurotics internalize their distress through rumination, while vocally and physically externalize their distress through anger and impulsivity (par. 4), to which their condition worsens by suppressing and "disowning" their feelings (p. 6). In addition, Furnham described neurotics as people who "see threat and danger everywhere [and] they are hypervigilant for possible threats" (Furnham, 2016, p. 10). However, don't discount neurotics as hopeless, for they do offer important contributions to a business; for instance, neurotic personalities "are motivated to work on behalf of their teams, who wind up appreciating their effort, in part because they exceed everyone's expectations" (Adams, 2013, par. 2). They can channel their hypervigilance and point out any holes or danger spots affecting the business. They can sweep the rumination of negative actions away and determine how to properly analyze the status of the business with new, creative ideas. There's always a way to change negative beliefs into good ones—and neuroticism should not be the exception.

In other cases, people with high self-efficacy can clash with others who are mandated to direct change. Self-efficacy refers to "beliefs about one's ability to complete a specific task" (Lunenburg, 2011, p.1). Like self-reliance, people with high levels of self-efficacy have an internal locus of control, believing that they are "masters of their own fate" (Furnham, 2016, par. 10). This can be troublesome for other workers who are used to a more regimented and structured approach, especially if that guarantees them a psychological sense of control. But individuals with high levels of self-efficacy are more willing to contribute to the company by their effort, performance, and persistence (Griffiths, 2015, par. 11). Also, they have a greater determination to "sustain their efforts in the face of failure" out of a self-perceived lack of effort, which gives them the opportunity to quickly recover (Bandura, 1994 (Bandura, 1994)). On the other hand, those with poor or very little self-efficacy will struggle to persevere in the face of change, and may quickly drop out of any challenge that doesn't fit within their comfort zone (par. 10, 11).

Or, it could be fear of the unknown, not from an experienced event since the fear is produced from the standpoint of safety and comfort. Because your subconscious mind is focused on survival, successful people understand that overcoming these fears is the key to moving forward. Even the most successful people experience some trepidation before making a big investment, as the mind is making sure that you're looking at every angle, mitigating risk. Some of that fear is beneficial. It's problematic when the fear comes from old events, and you can still experience the emotion even when thinking from it—that's the error message. What can you do about something that happened twenty years ago? Nothing. Fear is an emotion for action, escape a threat. It's impossible to escape a threat from ten or twenty years ago.

People observe different reactions to ambiguity. Some thrive on the uncertainty that ambiguity provides and they learn how to wade through it. Others with more structured work perceptions can't stand any ambiguity or unclear direction. In any measure, how we react to ambiguity will mostly determine our reactions to change, be it good or bad—from our perceptions, of course. Ambiguity tolerance is important because it determines the "willingness to accept a state of affairs capable of alternate interpretations, or of alternate outcomes" (English and English, qtd. in MacDonald, 1970, p. 791); or it can also be considered the way people react to ambiguity through "greater or lesser intensity" (McLain, Kefallonitis, & Armani, 2015, p. 2). Of course, it's unrealistic to expect that everybody in your company would have the same ambiguity tolerance as you—but it's not unrealistic to understand how resilient each of your workers are in light of the changing circumstances. Employees should expect *some* ambiguity and vagueness in the details of change, but not in the *intention* and *direction* that change can take; by navigating these conflicting aspects of change, they will be prepared to succeed in solving "monumental tasks" with expediency and minimal interference (Schulman, 2016, par. 12), even if it involves making many failures that aim to develop resiliency (Sandfeler, 2012, par. 12).

It's never wise to force change in your company if there aren't any reasons to warrant it or the change would be so overwhelming that you would lose the project's core identity. Some small-time changes may be welcomed by employees if these speed up bureaucratic and administrative processes. Other long-lasting changes may be viewed with suspicion by those both inside and outside, more so when it changes the core values your project represents. Thus, it's not easy to determine *when*, *what,* and *how* to foster change if your leaders and employees aren't on board with it. Keep that in mind as you consider the benefits and disadvantages of change at a certain point in time since the fear of the unknown is one of the main triggers of resistance to change. Baker (1989) described that employees "feel anxiety about how the change will affect them, their job performance, their relationship with other employees, and other job-related factors" (p. 53), and such emotions should be welcomed as an integral part of the change process. It's important to allow for resistance to change because it also serves to slow down the rate of change to a more manageable pace and that allows employees to comfortably adjust (p. 54).

Fear of the unknown is not diagnosable; rather, it can be described as a "mental obstacle" because it "curbs an individual's ability to perform to the fullest in various walks of life," including professionally (Perry, n.d., par. 1). Like any fear, facing the uncertainty of the unknown is uncomfortable at best, and terrifying at worst; as such, for those people who cannot tolerate ambiguity, they choose to run away from the fear to withdraw in their comfort at the cost of their personal development (par. 1). As a leader, your job is to guide your employees towards the future, but it's important to address to more fearful or apprehensive members the value of this change and how can they contribute their skills to the new project. Don't dismiss the fear of the unknown—address it promptly, so you can develop a proper understanding of the resources each team member contributes to the company.

Successful People Don't...

In other cases, people fear change because it conflicts with their self-interests: "Some want to maintain the status quo to better advance their own personal agendas; others have different motivations" (Brookings, 2017, par. 3). Each and every one of us is motivated by his or her self-interest—and there's nothing wrong with that. However, any attempt to change must be guided towards a healthy understanding of each person's roles and responsibilities, and how these will impact the development of a change. This is important because you must align your goals with people's self-interest (Rappaport, 2017). Unlike other factors of resistance to change, "self-interest exerts a much more automatic influence than influences concerning professional responsibilities, which are more likely to be invoked through controlled processing" (Moore & Loewenstein, 2004, p. 190). In addition, self-interest can be *parochial* because "[people] think that they will lose something of value"—which relates to any vested interests people have in the status quo. Instead, self-interest should be *enlightened*, where companies can still make a profit, but they also fulfill social, environmental, or managerial duties to their workers; this value is perfect because you are willing to commit your responsibilities as you guide them towards a season of change.

In 2014, 37% of CEOs and business leaders "were concerned about lack of trust in the business," less than half of "lower-level" employees "trust the companies they work for"

(Bingham, 2017, par. 1), and 64% "feel their organization treats them unfairly (American Psychological Association, 2014, par. 2). Lack of trust is pervasive in American workplaces, and this can derail any opportunities for change because employees can't trust their leaders because the former feel the latter aren't being honest about their intentions. In obvious cases, employees blame leaders for discrediting the formers if only to benefit the latter, "withhold full disclosure" in meetings from any important changes to employees (Llopis, 2011, par. 4), and take credit for skills and abilities they haven't harvested to the company. Because of this mistrust, people lose their motivation for fear of losing any control over the circumstances that may arise from change.

Use Social Proof to Motivate Your Employees to Change

And as a leader, your job is to encourage employees to develop enough motivation for the process of embracing business change. You can also verify your employee choices *before* having them on board by checking past references and ensuring that they have a history of working through change and adversity; treat them fairly in every step of the employment process; and, once on board, do not tolerate any deceitfulness or shady business coming from employees—instead, it's better to promote honesty and truthfulness in your business, as your problems are out in the open and everybody has the chance to deal with them. If not, you risk degenerating workers into cynical, indifferent employees without a motivation to change. This is why Bardwick (2011) encourages parties to become *actively engaged* in their work so that change can be productive, a combination of trust, commitment, and a sense of mission instilled by leadership (par. 7). If not, positive expectations can be distorted into cynicism, and any active engagement will be diminished because employees find no reasons to be on board with the value of change (par. 10).

In past chapters regarding conformity, I discussed a concept of compliance called *social validation*, where people perform a behavior when others around them do so. This is also known as *social proof*, Jost (2015) assured leaders to take advantage of this technique in order to embrace change: "If you want to 'unfreeze' prior opinions, it may be better to work with members of such groups *collectively* [emphasis added] rather than *individually* [emphasis added]" (p. 611). It's important to have most of your employees on board any change process because the more people join, the more others—inside or outside the business—are willing to join. Social proof can also be defined by Rao, Greve, and Davis (2003) as "using the actions of others to infer the value of a course of action" (p. 502); as a result, social proof can be used to your advantage because, as "people have grown to distrust brands," they have grown to use "peer reviews and peer actions" like social media commentaries, to make their own decisions "DeMers, 2015, par. 5). Be careful, however, for social proof is also dependent on context and culture: for instance, a compliance study undertaken in both United States and Poland in 1999 concluded that Americans are mostly led by the commitment and consistency principles, while the Poles are mostly led by social proof (Cialdini, Wosinska, Barrett, Butner, & Gornik-Durose, 1999, p. 1242). This doesn't mean that social proof is not important in an American environment, but in an increasingly multicultural environment, there are many more aspects to consider that enhance the value of social proof.

Types of Change

Change can be episodic, where it is "infrequent, discontinuous, and intentional" (Weick & Quinn, 1999, p. 365); or continuous, where there are changes that are "ongoing, evolving, and cumulative" (p. 365). In other words, change is neither black nor white, but is instead placed in a continuum where episodic change is mostly a one-time event, and continuous change happens constantly and with many moments of anticipation. For example, if your company changes its database collections systems from a manual system to an electronic, cloud-based system, this change is *episodic* because the change in the company only occurs once every couple of years, rendering it infrequent. On the other hand, if a company frequently offers professional development courses throughout the year, this type of change is *continuous* because it happens constantly. Keep in mind, though, that any long-term change follows a chicken-or-egg type of situation: for instance, are you instituting change because you want to introduce new products to the customers, or are your customers demanding new products because they expect you to change? This is why Norbutus (2007) noted, "Change is seen as part of the ongoing process of organizing, and equilibrium is not assumed" (par. 5); thus, it's important to balance any episodic and continuous changes so employees and teammates can get used to any values of change.

Remember: the goal of change is to provide positive outcomes for your company. Leybourn (2016) described outcomes as being "planned, slowly changing, and define the common direction for the organization" (par. 5), the result of your hard work and direction. One of the main outcomes is relevance by making your products and services attractive *without* compromising your company values (Joseph, n.d., par. 2). In addition, you'll begin to appreciate new developments and opportunities that each business member—including your clients—will enjoy. Of course, let's not forget the increased efficiency and productivity, the breaks in monotony and the ability to manage growth in a controlled fashion, among other perspectives (Joseph, n.d.; Moody, n.d.). But there is one major challenge that any change, planned or unplanned, needs to overcome to make it long-lasting for your project—your mind-set: "If you do not believe that you can change successfully, then you will continue to hurt yourself throughout this process. For change to work, you must believe in yourself and in the process of change you have selected" (Sicinski, 2013, p. 38).

Make Change a Consistent habit

If you wish the changes to stick, make the changes a habit. This is called *automaticity*, where "automatic thoughts and behaviors are ones that occur efficiently, without the need for con-scious guidance or mentoring" (Wheatley & Wagner, p. 991). Au-tomaticity may be unconscious, where certain events and pro-cesses occur without any conscious control due to *priming*, or a stimulus that influences unconscious behavior; or conscious, where certain behaviors reflect constant awareness, especially if these acquired skills become automatic through conscious pro-cessing (p. 991). Automaticity is important because, when you learn new habits and ingrain them, there's a greater chance for these to be automatically ingrained (Rykr, 2009, par. 12). With automaticity, any new change needs to be maintained through practice. For instance, if you install new software that employees need to learn as expediently as possible, it wouldn't make sense if they only trained and practiced once. To change this, you need to encourage employees to practice, practice, practice constantly, so that training becomes second nature—but be careful, since any other habit can turn into complacency if any respect to the job isn't developed!

In addition, the psychological principle of consistency also applies to any values that determine change, for "managers must convey a consistent, clear and straightforward message about the culture change and then be led by example" (Bello, 2014, par. 3). Don't force a change if *you* can't commit to it; otherwise, you may lose credibility as a leader because you couldn't follow through. Returning to the new software example, if you need to install new software which you're not comfortable using, your employees won't feel any encouragement to even try out the system. In this case, you must be prudent enough to give the change a try and be comfortable with it to encourage others to succeed.

The Comfort Zone

I've previously established that change is a natural process that shouldn't be avoided if you wish to become successful in your business. Change at any moment is thrilling, exciting, and invigorating, to the point where a successful company loves to find ways to encourage new ideas and developments so that everybody can benefit from them. However, there are many that are deathly afraid of *any* change—positive or negative—, more so if they can't avoid or swerve by it. Like any type of fear, it leaves them feeling stuck inside a box, where they enjoy their trepidation and make no effort to improve themselves or their surroundings. Everybody has a point where they become *too* comfortable with their environment, and we call this the *comfort zone*, "the psychological state of low stress and low anxiety that people feel when occupying familiar environments, performing familiar activities," but keeping themselves willfully stuck out of fear (Read, 2016, par. 6).

The comfort zone can be considered the ultimate error message one can have. Without it, we may face great danger. With it, we can't succeed as expected or promised. In this "anxiety-neutral" environment, there exists a "steady level of performance" that has little to no risk involved. You can't grow in the comfort zone. You can't develop your best skills if you're not exposed to a healthy level of risk because "growing, whether in the form of learning a new skill or taking your business to the next level, is not as straightforward as just going outside your comfort zone" (Iny, 2016, par. 3). Because life is a process of adaptation and growth where both "skill and courage" are important values to develop

(Molinsky, 2016, par. 2), the comfort zone is a place where experiences are at a plateau, where people avoid any unpleasantness.

Iny (2016) defined the comfort zone in a set of three concentric boundaries, where one builds upon the other: the *slow growth zone,* where growth happens by learning things for yourself, like watching YouTube videos and Googling throughout the Internet, finding a recipe for cinnamon scones; the *zone of destructive anxiety*, where growth is so anxiety-inducing that learning becomes cumbersome; and the *zone of proximal development*, where you can challenge yourself to grow at a steady, yet challenging pace. In this zone, you challenge your glitches and erroneous beliefs, develop a healthy sense of resilience and trust in your own abilities, and you become committed to develop your resolve over uncertainty by making peace with it—it doesn't mean that you *love* any random occurrence in your career, but you know how to handle yourself successfully with the help of others and the personal experiences you can apply to solve problems. When you push through the comfort zone, you will be ready to tackle any type of change in your life!

Figure 14: Graphical dimensions of the "comfort zone".

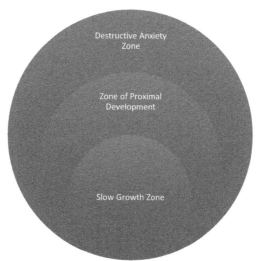

Note: Adapted from "What science says about going outside your comfort zone," by D. Iny, 2016, *Inc.,* https://www.inc.com/danny-iny/what-science-says-about-going-outside-your-comfort-zone.html.

You can't deny that wholeheartedly embracing change is an important value to look for in a successful business or employee. With the help of the Inspired Performance Institute, you'll be prepared to handle the circumstances and opportunities that bring about change. Some people may not like it, and that's okay––but don't neglect their objections, for they may have some salient points you may not have considered yet. Do recognize, however, that your business needs to evolve at some point, for it may stagnate if you let it. That's why our program allows you to sweep away any failed attempts or failure lodged in your subconscious mind as you anchor your successes with change. In the end, Ivtzan,

Successful People Don't…

Lomas, Hefferon, and Worth (2015) defined why change is valuable to anybody because, when change happens, our weaknesses are exposed, "some aspect of our world may have been changed, lost, decayed or wounded, and this, in turn, may press or force us to respond or move into a journey of change" (p. 179, 180). For this reason, change is invaluable: it exposes us to our personal weaknesses, but it dares us to think—and succeed—in creative ways.

#10. Feel complacent

Successful people never reach their ultimate goal. Why? Because they are always setting newer and bigger goals.

Complacency is a continuous struggle that we all have to fight. - Jack Nicklaus

Success is a Journey

Throughout this book, you've learned many tips and tricks regarding the top ten things successful people *won't* do. You learned that to beat procrastination, you need to tackle the fear you've entertained. You learned that worry leaves nothing to be desired because it saps away any opportunity to successfully develop your business while your mind is consumed with negative perceptions of the future. You learned that, while complying with certain requests should be expected by the different parties that make up your business, there's no reason to be afraid of finding new ways to stand out and avoid conformity with the rest of the bunch. You also learned that blame won't get you anywhere and taking responsibility for your actions will foster long-term success; that you shouldn't be afraid of failure—instead, welcome the opportunity of learning from your mistakes; that you don't need luck in order to succeed, but hard work and effort, both of which are entirely within your control; that you need to shake off your pride and reluctance if you wish to gain help from others; and that change is something that is worthy to be embraced. If you take these tips and tricks to heart, then you're on your way to success!

Success is not a destination; it's a journey. I've heard it said that you would never reach your ultimate success as long as you keep setting new goals. Successful people keep reaching for more. This doesn't mean they're greedy; they just understand that to maintain success you need to keep moving forward. Have a new goal to reach. The new goal could be to be a better philanthropist. See what I mean?

Are you complacent? Do you recognize the signs? Let's examine the signs and then take a hard look at your situation.

First, are you taking success for granted, believing that you're on a roll that will just keep going.

Next, are you staying focused on your personal and business life? You can become complacent in one and not the other. Focused so hard on your business and forget that your family needs you too. Keep checking out your competition, are they changing? As for your family, when was the last time you asked them if they're happy? The hardest line to walk is the line between success at home and success at work.

Next, are you looking for ways to improve your products or services? When is the last time you surveyed your customers or staff? Are you listening to them?

Next, are you reading and learning, taking courses and attending seminars. Not just seminars in your line of business, but personal growth seminars and workshops. Look for retreats or groups to join. I was involved in a CEO group called TEC, the Executive Committee. We had a Chairman and ten to fifteen CEO's that would meet once a month and share ideas and help each other with problems. It was a great tool. What are you doing to learn and grow?

Another thing to watch for when success comes your way is the trap of surrounding yourself with a staff that always tells you what you want to hear. They don't want to lose this job and may not tell you the truth, or you stopped listening. Either way, look for this trap.

Success doesn't mean entitlement. Success is earned, and no one owes you anything. You can expect loyalty. However, it is getting harder and harder to find it. The younger generation doesn't like being in one place too long. They are not necessarily disloyal; this is their world. If you don't understand it, then you will get surprised and possibly hurt. Keep your head up and be careful you're not letting your guard down.

Successful People Don't...

Keep innovating and setting new goals and targets. Keep listening to new ideas and encourage your staff to stay sharp and on top of new trends. Look for routines and challenge them, is it still the best way. Trust your instincts; you're successful for a reason. The lessons that got you to where you are were hard earned.

Minister Benjamin E. Mays said, "The tragedy of life is often not in our failure, but rather in our complacency; not in our doing too much, but rather in our doing too little; not in our living above our ability, but rather in our living below our capacities."

A Short Questionnaire

Take Blockbuster as an example. Their customer service was abysmal. A steady stream of late fees or charges for damaged or lost DVDs. I last visited a Blockbuster when they charged me for a DVD that they said was not in the case. I distinctly remember putting it in there and dropping it off. "Too bad," they said. "You owe us $40.00." That, right there, quickly ended my relationship with Blockbuster. Instead, I went to the theaters instead. Then Netflix came. Blockbuster stopped innovating and taking care of their customers. I wasn't sad to see them go. That doesn't make me a bad person, just a demanding customer. That's business. Either you grow or you die.

Let's examine the signs that could define complacency in your life or company:

- Are you taking success for granted, believing that you're on a roll that will just keep going?

- Are you staying focused on your personal and business life?

- Are you extremely focused on your business that you forget your family needs?

- Is your competition constantly reinventing themselves?

- As for your family, when was the last time you asked them if they're happy? The hardest line to walk is the line between success at home and success at work.

- Are you looking for ways to improve your products or services?

- When is the last time you surveyed your customers or staff? Are you listening to their worthwhile feedback?

- Are you reading and learning, taking courses and attending seminars? In other words, are you willing to continue learning?

- Are you surrounded with complacent yes-men who only say what *you* want to hear?

So, what should you do if you wish to *maintain* a successful business?

When People Are Complacent...

Not all businesses are created equal. Some struggle for many years with many items like cash flow and leadership, only to receive their lucky break and stratospherically rise to the top—only to fizzle out as quickly as they started. Others develop their brands through hard work and public awareness, slowly grinding their way to success to the point that they're at the top of their league—only to slowly hit the ground without noticing, leaving themselves in an even worse position than they started. The former case shows how fads are created, flourish, and die: A fad is a "short-lived phenomenon" that "generally surges into a peak of popularity, and then drops abruptly out of favor" (Munyikwa, 2013, par. 2), oftentimes maintained by social proof and group conformity and maintained by demand. It's not hard to think of fads that have invaded popular culture recently: memes, GIFs, emojis, fidget spinners, and popular video game apps, to which even businesses have jumped on that bandwagon. They can also be institutional, which directly affects business structures because they can transform the development of company process to the point of unrecognition. This is dangerous since businesses that suffer from "finite variability," to which companies "must constantly churn out new content and experiences to cater to their consumers' insatiable desire for novelty" (Eyal, 2014, par. 7). Trends, on the other hand, "take longer to build," wax and wane throughout the years, and have a harder time crossing borders (Staff Report, 1999, par. 2, 3).

The second case, however, is much more reflective of complacency. How does that make it dangerous to the health of a business? Let's take a look at a simple definition: Complacency is "a feeling of smugness or uncritical satisfaction with oneself or one's achievements" (Hurd, 2017, par. 3). Unlike pride and arrogance, the complacent person is not concerned with boasting of their actions to others as an attempt to prove something. Rather, someone who is complacent is someone so inured to his or her personal reality that there is no chance to improve or maintain their stature by force of will. Any change to the status quo of a complacent person will be met with "hostility or apathy," especially if these block any attempts for "soul-searching" and self-reflection in the process (Hurd, 2017, par. 3); as a result, such a person cannot bounce back from any setbacks, self-imposed or not, and cannot appreciate any constructive criticism towards his or her behavior.

When people are complacent, they are "easily frustrated," disappointed and angry because growth isn't as smooth as they expected to the point of submitting to depression (Hurd, 2017, par. 7). This is why a lack of growth exists related to this type of behavior since any growth is uncomfortable and plateaus any advancement of growth because of his or her lack of abilities (Schreiner, 2015, par. 4). Rick (2015) determined how the values of complacency are distorted:

> Complacency ignores opportunities, big and small. It turns a blind eye to serious and dangerous threats. It hushes innovative ideas. It stomps on energy, enthusiasm and anything new. It hangs on to the old ways of doing things with white, altruistic knuckles. It doesn't want to hear or see what is happening in the world. Learning new things is not up for discussion (par. 5).

Complacent people never learn from their mistakes because, deep down, they secretly believe that they never did anything wrong. Even if evidence exists of the detailed choices that need to be done if they wish to change their management and/or leadership processes, complacency keeps their feet grounded and without being moved. They are too comfortable to recognize their flaws and actively work towards correcting them, so any potential change will be lost as quickly as it was learned in the first place.

Think of a time you had an employee that could perform the work succinctly and at its pace. You know that employee has a proven track record of potential, but the employee can't reach it for some reason. Maybe the work you assigned to that employee is too complicated for them to do alone. Maybe the person lives in fear of being fired or suffers from the "impostor syndrome," which greatly paralyzes the employee's performance. Or is the employee not feeling challenged enough by the tasks you've given him or her, and wants to polish any skills or hidden talents? After careful deliberation of the employee's skills, you conclude that they are complacent in his or her skills. There are many reasons why complacency can happen: It can be a lack of innovation and creativity because of the drudgery felt by the employee—as a result, "bureaucratic cultures almost unanimously devote little thought to raising the bar and even less about why they toil at the low end of a sizable performance gap" (Ruark, 2017, p. 20). Maybe the employee believes the "old ways" of doing stuff is much better (Rick, 2015, p. 5); that being said, don't discount the employee's objections because they may have a point after all— remember, not every change is beneficial to the company in the long term. Once you address *what* drives people to become complacent within their circumstances, you can direct the employee to correct his or her mistakes successfully.

In organizations, complacency occurs due to a "mental shift" between "health-growth practices" and misplaced expectations, especially those that are self-imposed (Hitt, 2016, par. 9). As a result, they often resign to experience low expectations in their career values, especially if he or she struggles to find a "true purpose" in the work they enjoy (Llopis, 2013, par. 7). Employees have left their first love, their engagement towards their work and the values they longed to portray in their actions in favor of the business. As employees entrench their expectations into complacency, leaders need to take great care to "remain relevant" and direct them—not scold, punish, or dismiss employees—and encourage them to take back their sense of pride and ownership for their job because, "Being an effective leader is hard work— harder than ever before, because it requires continuous renewal and reinvention' from every source that impacts your actions (Llopis, 2016, par. 2).

Mediocrity, Complacency's Cousin

Alongside complacency is mediocrity, a condition where groups build a glass ceiling for themselves as a measure of inferiority and poor quality (Hermanowicz, 2013, p. 364). Their work isn't good nor bad; it's *average* enough that it looks good and sells well, but it doesn't become either a game-changer or a trailblazer at the onset of the project or business. That's why mediocrity is a frustrating result since the end result could have been better. However, do keep in mind what Grenny (2017) referred to concerning mediocrity: "Chronic mediocrity is a symptom of ineffective leadership, not anemic personnel" (par. 3). So, if you wish to address mediocrity and banish it from taking root into an already complacent staff, you need to address *how* have you been lax in your own perceptions of leadership. Before confronting others' attempts at mediocrity, you need to evaluate the mediocrity you've exhibited towards yourself. Challenge the comfort zone you've stayed in as a leader and show the attitude you want to showcase to your employees as you expose your company to new opportunities (Tartakovsky, 2015, par. 4).

Signs of Complacency

Here are ten signs of complacency in your employees, and how to stop them in their tracks (Llopis, 2013):

- **Disengagement:** In previous chapters, I discussed the role of active engagement in creating a blame-free culture—and you could argue that engagement works to ward off complacency, as well. In the Western world, however, employee engagement is suffering from critically low levels of workplace productivity. For instance, only 10% of European employees are engaged against 31% of North American employees (Eltringham, 2017, par. 1), and Australian and New Zealand employees, despite enjoying a high quality of life, only 14% are engaged (par. 2). To ward off complacency, learn how to become a leader, "inspire and listen to your teams, urge them to raise their expectations and achieve more, that will engage them" (Loveless, 2015, par. 25).

- **Lack of critical thinking:** Allen (2017) noted that critical thinking is important for employees because "Critical thinkers are willing to challenge assumptions, stay open to new possibilities and approaches, and be aware of the limitations and scope of analysis while remaining reflective and transparent" (par. 6). However, only 49% of employers believe their employees' critical skills are "average or below average" (Harris, 2015, par. 4), and 28% of employers rate college graduates as having "Excellent" critical thinking skills (par. 6). But finding "critical thinking" skills in employees is as vague as defining it; because of this, they look for people that can show an ability to think through their actions with logic and reasoning, and without a need for others' approval based on their decision-making (Fallon, 2014). If employees don't learn to develop important critical thinking skills, they will be swayed to complacency and make erroneous choices that will affect your company's direction, and its future because "[critical thinking] is a mental muscle; only repeated use makes it strong. And when we spend a long time in places that deliberately discourage critical thinking, we lose the opportunity to keep building that skill" (Selinger & Frischmann, 2016, par. 12).

- **Lack of employee initiative:** Sometimes employees struggle with being overburdened, under-qualified, or too in tune with the comfort zone regarding their job responsibilities (Hogan, 2016). Because they have no initiative or drive to succeed, they "will pass up valuable opportunities, reducing the productivity and effectiveness of your team" (Mack, 2017, par. 1). This is where creating a culture that focuses on rewarding (calculated and sensible) risk-taking behavior and addressing any imbalances within your group is essential. Get someone else on board that will lighten your team's load. Or give employees the opportunity to choose which tools are good for learning, such as respected online programs. In addition, a survey revealed 92% of employees "want their managers to ask for their opinions and ideas at work," and 89% "want their managers to involve them in decisions that are made at work" (Nelson, n.d.)—in other terms, employees want their opinions to be considered. Use these to your advantage, and you can improve their initiative.

- **Lack of personal investment:** Complacent people have no care to professionally invest in themselves. Maybe they stop at a comfortable degree, a position, and stop there.

Maybe their work is too comfortable for them not to feel the need to achieve further goals. To remedy this, not only is it important to encourage them with professional development courses tailored to their job responsibilities; it's also a good idea to engage employees' work according to their likes and dislikes. What if all of you dressed up for Halloween—just for fun? What if you spent one day after work playing board games and having a good time? Or why not set up a mentorship program? As employees learn how to invest in themselves, they also learn how to invest in each other and their business by giving them a sense of belonging. Personal development is important because it "is a continual learning process that helps in personal life, professional career development and also inter (sic) personal relationship development" (Konatham, 2017, par. 1).

- **No personal brand:** Everybody has a "personal brand", an image that identifies them and creates a "market" for their skills and abilities. *Everything* about you can be turned into a brand: your voice, your dress code, and your work attitudes are important to determine how much your "brand" is valuable to an employer. If you make no steps to encourage them and put yourself in the spotlight, it's easy to allow indifference and complacency to take root especially when, in many companies, success is not determined by the individual's internal sets of skills, motivations, and interests but, rather, by how effectively they are arranged, crystallized, and *labeled*. Lair, Sullivan, & Cheney, 2005, p. 306). In complacent people, they require constant reassurance and exhibit a lack of self-awareness to others' needs over their own. Since reputation is also part of a personal brand (Dabbah, 2017)—there is something as trying *too* hard. On the other hand, *not* trying at all gives complacent people a personal blank slate to work with, *if* they're willing to shake off the shackles of their complacency

- **Shortcuts:** It's important for employees to continue developing detail-oriented tasks even if they already know what to do. If employees lose any sense of competition and start taking shortcuts, which can be considered a form of "soft complacency," since "Resting too long on one's laurels prevents focusing on moving to the next step" (Pater, 2013, par. 4). Simple shortcuts are taken for simple tasks, and other processes get cut in order to accommodate employee laziness, and shortcuts breed complacency (Reyes, 2017). Beyond heuristics, taking shortcuts reflect poor leadership habits on one part, and employee laziness on the other— however, even the mere act of taking shortcuts reflects a misplaced creativity that could be better harnessed in other pursuits. Regarding athletes, "Situational complacency and too much confidence result in failure to recruit and use needed resources (insufficient mobilization), and an athlete is not ready for the game...an athlete tends to underestimate task demands and overestimate his or her own resources (Hanin, 2007, p. 51). Replace "athlete" with "employee," and you know the trick.

- **Fear of risk-taking:** As I previously discussed, complacency diminishes any type of risk-taking, even if it's important and valuable. Risks are important measures that improve the value of your business as long as they're calculated and within legal means. You can discover new avenues to which you can manage your product's growth (even by accident) and access an even greater number of customers willing to enjoy the product. If your company becomes complacent about these risks, you'll stay stuck with no means to grow in any other direction. For Jackson & Csikszentmihalyi (1999), complacency in risk-taking can be a symptom of the fear of failure, even though "[comfort and ease] do not make a good mindset for athletes [and employees] trying to achieve new skill levels or improve" (p. 44).

- **Loss of passion:** Passionate people love what they do and are involved in every step of the way. Vallerand and

Verver-Filion (2013) defined *passion* as "a strong inclination toward an activity that people like, find important, and in which they invest time and energy" (p. 36), in one sense it can be *harmonious*, where people are integrated with the object of their passion; or *obsessive*, where they have an "uncontrollable urge" to develop their passion despite the obstacles. If people lose the passion they previously felt for their work, they will lose the value of their grit, which "entails working strenuously toward challenges, maintaining effort and interest over the years, despite failure, adversity, and plateaus in progress" (Duckworth, Peterson, Matthews & Kelly, 2007, 1087-1088). When you learn how to find passion in everything you do––from learning transferable skills to saving for the future––, you begin to shake off complacency and set yourself free to maximize your growth (Williams, 2016). But, in order to let your passion flourish, you need to be proactive in searching something to be passionate about.

- **Disgruntled with career destination:** In many cases, people feel complacent because they don't know where they are headed regarding their careers or where they want to showcase their skills in the future. As a leader, it's important to address these valuable skills and encourage people to look into the future for what to expect when their careers take off in a certain time period. Learn how they can take responsibility for their career circumstances and do not allow them to wallow in pity, with blame or misplaced judgments. It's okay to learn that one choice they took previously was "wrong" and they need to find a way to recommit to another thing as fast as they can; it's *not* okay to complacently sit in a corner and not do anything to remedy the problem, especially when "people place too high a value on the external rewards of a job, like money, prestige and power" (Korkki, 2010, par. 7).

- **Loss of hope:** If complacency and mediocrity are not enough, the final thing that singles out complacency is a loss of hope in any future opportunities. This is why Iny (2012) considered complacency to be "highly destructive because it's immune to innovation and fails to recognize either new opportunities or potential hazards" (par. 8). We've all lost or sacrificed something so our business could flourish: It could be anything physical, such as sleep or appetite; or it could be money due to a robbery, data loss, or any adverse condition out of your control. But losing hope means you lose the ability to dream big, to explore new avenues; to innovate and to prosper. If you lose hope, you lose any opportunity to grow and embrace the business with your employees. Even if hopelessness is "a diffuse feeling state and consequently too vague and amorphous" for it to be quantified by studies (Beck, Wissman, Lester, & Trexler, 1974, p. 861), you can feel the consequences of lethargy from hopelessness enforced on others. This is arguably the most dangerous *and* challenging sign to tackle—if you lose hope, you lose the opportunity to prosper your business, especially when one in twenty Americans constantly experience these feelings (Shoter, 2014, par. 4).

Table 8: Signs of a Complacent Attitude.

Signs of a complacent attitude
• Smug
• Impatient
• Sensitive to criticism
• Easily disappointed
• Easily frustrated
• Lacks ambition
• Lacks self-awareness
• Stays in the comfort zone
• Thrives in futility
• Plays the victim
• Ceases to find new ways to grow
• Ignorant of opportunities

Note: Adapted from "The psychology of complacency," by M.J. Hurd, 2017, Dr. Hurd, https://drhurd.com/2017/03/25/63474/; "Complacency—how to avoid the silent killer," by L. Quy, 2012, Pick the Brain, https://www.pickthebrain.com/blog/complacency-how-to-avoid-the-silent-killer/; and "Patience and complacency," by M. Schreiner, 2015, Evolution Counseling, https://evolutioncounseling.com/patience-complacency/.

Ambition: Complacency's Polar Opposite

On the other side of complacency lies *ambition*, "the per-sistent and generalized striving for success, attainment, and ac-complishment" that happens when you are passionate and driven towards any goal (Judge & Kammeyer-Mueller, 2012, p. 759). When you're ambitious, you become persistent, and your struggle is unceasing. That's why "ambition is about attaining rather than achieving" (Judge & Kammeyer-Mueller, 2012, p. 759). Unlike complacency, ambitious people don't rest on their laurels and wait until things change; rather, they aim higher within reason and fight for their own goals, no matter the adversities they go through, rendering it much more "specific" and "self-reliant" than other states of mind (Burton, 2014, par. 7).

In a 2012 study, individuals exhibiting greater conscien-tiousness "are more likely to be drawn to success goals" due to their diligence, motivation, and self-direction (Judge & Kammeyer-Mueller, 2012, p. 761). In addition, highly ambitious employees are more proactive and assertive in their careers and the work they execute, and their efforts piggyback off each other through organizational change, work executions, and job context, among other concepts (El Baroudi et al., 2016, p. 88). Also, neurotics, who are already "prone to worry and have doubts," set themselves much more ambitious goals because they feel these targets "will not be met" (p. 761), and the goal of ambition can be twofold: as a self-affirmation of a person's skills and abilities, or as a form of greed that is masked and distorted through ambition (Barsukova, 2015, p. 9). Let me explain: while "good" ambition drives people to develop success through the benefit of their personal merits, "bad" ambition steps on others and damages personal relations for the worse—as a brief description, "the person becomes dependent or aggressive, the person often experiences negative emotions and feeling[s] of disappointment" (p. 11).

But what's the antidote to complacency, you might ask? It's easy: update those error messages and glitches swirling through your head! You no longer need to relive past experiences in order to find a way to protect yourself. You don't need to remember when was the last time a loved one failed you, or the last time you got fired from a job you never liked, just to protect yourself. What you do need to know and embrace are the tools the Inspired Performance Institute provides for you through education, updating, sweeping, and banking your successes in a timely and organized fashion. Experience the relief our special business program provides for people like you, because it's important to remember the many ways you've shown value in your work. Why don't you take the time to explore how you can shake off complacent attitudes and enjoy the value provided by your skills and abilities through the Inspired Performance Program?

Conclusion

Inspired Business Performance – Business Trauma Program

The Inspired Performance Institute can help you if you have ever said any of the following statements;

"Why is my business struggling to get off the ground?"

"Why has my business stopped growing?"

"Why do my businesses hit plateaus?"

"Why am I struggling to get my business to the next level?"

This is something we hear all the time, and from already highly successful people. You see, even high functioning people have the ability for improvement. The Inspired Performance Institute will help you clear the blocks interfering with your peak performance levels.

You have designed a great business plan, thought about everything in great detail. So what's the problem? We don't need to know anything about your business plan to help you fix it. You're probably saying "What!" "That doesn't make any sense." You see, the problem and solution has always been inside of your mind, not ours. All we know is the reason why it's not working and it's a common theme amongst all the people we assist. And that's why our TIPP process is so successful for entrepreneurs and executives. Chances are, you know more about your business than any consultant you can hire. By the time the consultants learn about your business, you may be out of business. Here's what we do know. Your subconscious mind has developed some faulty intelligence throughout your lifetime and your mind has been using these errors in producing thoughts about your business plan. These error messages are below your conscious awareness and that's why you have not seen them and why no one else has been able to help you. Your mind is fine, there's nothing wrong with your mind. You see, your mind has developed some glitches, error messages throughout your lifetime and these are affecting the way your mind operates.

How do we fix that? Simple, we have developed a process that focuses on updating the error messages that have been used in producing your thoughts. Your mind is like a computer and is prone to developing errors. Events and experiences that were threatening, disturbing, or traumatic have an influence on the way your mind produces thoughts. If there are error messages still active in your thought processes it's no wonder the thoughts created ideas with some inherent and invisible flaws. The blocks and belief conflicts need to be updated and cleared to ensure you perform at your highest potential and level.

You see, your subconscious mind records every detail of your life. Disturbing, threatening or traumatic events are recorded as a high-resolution file and the subconscious continues to review these threats. Your subconscious mind will continue to react to these events, even when they are over. It's a glitch in the way our minds have developed. That's what we do, fix the glitch and get your mind cleared and updated. Guess what? Everyone has the same glitch, however, some people's experiences produce a different error message than yours. Perhaps a less complicated error message. Their error message may have a more dramatic effect on their personal life and less on their business life. Their business is flourishing and their personal life is in turmoil. When your mind is centered and present your thought process improves dramatically. Listen on our website to some of the testimonials of the people we have helped. It is not uncommon to see their revenues increase 100% or more after their mind is updated and cleared. You see, when your mind is present, it is focused, and when it is focused it just performs better. It's really that simple. Up until now, you couldn't have done it any other way.

Before you read this you may not have known why you have been struggling. Or, you may have read every self-help book published on the subject of being present and in the moment. The book or seminar presenters speak to you, and it all makes sense. Great material, however, they don't tell you how to get there. Your conscious mind listens to the new ideas presented and when there is any conflict in the subconscious mind the new information will be rejected. Let's say you had picked up an error message when you were a child, for example, one plus one equals three. So now, every time you need to use this formula in something you are doing it won't work and you won't know why. Our programs are designed to update these error messages and improve your thought process. Now I hear you asking, "Is it really that simple"? Here's the short answer, YES!

Here's the "GOOD NEWS"! The Inspired Performance Institute has developed the tools and programs to help. Our programs use the most recent advancements in neuroscience that will clear the blocks and conflicts and get your mind centered and balanced. The error messages are deleted and thoughts become clearer and beneficial. In addition to the clearing, we then set the mind up to use your best resources, successes, and lifetime highlights.

The Inspired Performance Institute focuses on the solution to the problem and not the problem itself. What do you need? Discipline to follow the program. In our experience, you wouldn't be in business if you didn't already have it. So, let's get started!

Here is what you will learn through the TIPP process.

1. The Neuroscience behind how your mind has been working.

2. How to achieve "Alpha" state where the mind is present and highly focused.

3. Techniques that will clear the old error messages.

4. Techniques that will teach your mind to use its best resources.

5. Tools to reinforce and strengthen the process.

6. Pre- and post-assessments to measure progress.

Now that you know the tips and tricks of becoming a successful leader, employee, manager, entrepreneur, or athlete, it's time to put everything you've learned into practice, along with the anchoring techniques you can find in the Inspired Performance Institute. You've learned how to train your mind for success by learning ten things successful people *don't* do—including lying, cheating, garnishing, judging, and so on. And, after reading through each chapter's discussion on topics such as learned helplessness, fear of failure, and the troubles of complacency, you can definitely argue: "Why it's important to highlight what *not* to do if the goal is to become successful?"

Do keep in mind that the subconscious mind can't understand negation. By expressing negation, your subconscious will automatically project the unwanted images in your mind. *Don't* worry—worry. *Don't* conform—conform. *Don't* believe in luck––believe in luck. Through the Inspired Performance Program

(TIPP) you learn to harness the mental tools that will become true in your mind. (*Never* forget about those pink elephants!) So, I propose a solution: instead of *not* worrying, you learn tools to eliminate unnecessary worry in a productive way. Instead of *not* conforming outright, you begin to develop mental tools to make wise choices on whether to comply or not in given circumstances, and the value placed on nonconformity. It doesn't mean that your subconscious won't listen to negation—it won't pay attention to it.

The same holds true for each portion of the extended list that permeated throughout the book. When you *don't* procrastinate, you learn to develop techniques that improve your business efficiency. When you *don't* worry, you're free to use your brain to come up with new, creative ideas to grow your business. When you *don't* blame people, circumstances, and yourself, you learn to take responsibility for your actions, for your successes and failures, to the point where you can be considered a trustworthy leader and a great citizen. In the end, you appreciate how you don't need negative recourses like negation to become successful. The brain is a powerful, healing organ, and has plasticity that allows for new neural pathways to be formed. These new neural pathways will override the old patterns of behavior and lead you down a new path of success.

Think of all the ideas successful people have used and applied in their business and personal lives:

- Procrastination is the wrong way to stave off fear and anxiety. In turn, successful people learn how to, despite their emotions and circumstances, push through their limitations.

- While worry serves as a (misguided) tool for self-protection of any dangers in the future, it's a useless emotion that only serves to diminish the value of your ideas and the direction your business should take, or it creates a mental habit that embraces anxiety as its sole guide.

- Complying in certain circumstances is okay, but conforming out of pressure or a need to please certain benefactors is not. You may have heard that the customer is always right at business school *ad nauseum*, but do the best you can to make customers comfortable and engage them with the core of your brand's identity.

- Blaming others—family, friends, politics, competition and the like—won't do you any favors, at the same time people will treat you and your business projects with unease and immaturity. If there's someone you may need to blame for your predicament, try taking a deep look within yourself-and assume your responsibility for it.

- It's okay to fail. It's not okay to *ignore the lesson* and not learn from failure. In fact, don't treat failures as weaknesses of will or things to be avoided—instead, look at failure as learning experiences that slowly guide you towards success.

- You don't need luck in order to be successful, since what people consider "luck" is only what happens when success and opportunity happen. When you understand that success comes from hard work, you develop a greater appreciation for your skills and abilities, even if others don't take the time and care to appreciate it.

- Straying from your lane isn't necessarily about limiting your own skills and more about *delegating* resources and responsibilities to others. When you delegate, you free time and money to tackle the birth and value of other projects and their respective contributions. If not, you risk suffering burnout or micromanaging your employees and destroying their morale at the same time.

- Asking for help is not only courageous—it's important if you wish to become successful. It's time to shake off your pride and learn to share valuable tips and tricks from others to ensure your success. Also, helping others through corporate social responsibility and mentoring programs will benefit you, as well, by developing your skills and responsibility as a leader who takes care of others.

- It's okay to feel apprehensive when change happens, but it's much better when you embrace any opportunity for change to your business. Change may mean tweaking certain products and services for new crowds, firing and hiring employees with wildly different life experiences and even switching prices if that helps deepen the customer base.

- People feel complacent when they feel excessively satisfied with their accomplishments and don't develop the strength and will to aim for greater accomplishments and successes. At the same time, it's important to gain contentment from what you've accomplished—and a sense of mission for what you will do.

In the end, this book, along with the many techniques that we've provided to you, are essential to create a sense of peace and strength within you. But it's *your* responsibility to steer your company at the helm of success. In the beginning, you may struggle with following your game plan to the letter, and you may need to make some tweaks here or there in order to become successful. But when your hard work pays off, and you and your employees feel satisfied with your efforts towards the company, you will finally appreciate the true value of success with a clear mind and a grateful heart.

References

Abbey-Vital, I. (2014, May 13). *The science of procrastination*. Retrieved August 30, 2017, from The Brain Bank North West: https://thebrainbank.scienceblog.com/2014/05/13/the-science-of-procrastination/

Abeles, N. (2006, January). Psychological projection. *Salem Press Encyclopedia of Health*.

Abramson, L., Seligman, M., & Teasdale, J. (1978). Learned helplessness in humans: Critique and reformulation. *Journal of Abnormal Psychology, 87*(1), 49-74.

Aczel, B., Palfi, P., & Kekecs, Z. (2015, November-December). What is stupid? People's conception of unintelligent behavior. *Intelligence, 53*, 51-58. doi: 10.1016/j.intell.2015.08.010.

Adams, S. (2010, December 16). *How to stop procrastinating*. (Forbes Media, LLC) Retrieved August 24, 2017, from Forbes: https://www.forbes.com/2010/12/16/stop-procrastinating-efficiency-leadership-careers-organization.html

Adams, S. (2013, April 11). *Leadership tip: Hire the quiet neurotic, not the impressive extrovert*. (Forbes Media, LLC) Retrieved October 6, 2017, from Forbes: https://www.forbes.com/sites/susanadams/2013/04/11/leadership-tip-hire-the-quiet-neurotic-not-the-impressive-extrovert/#ba67afc788be

Adler, L., & Gielen, U. (2001). *Cross-cultural topics in psychology*. Westport, Connecticut: Greenwood Publishing Group.

Adriani, F., & Sonderegger, S. (2016). *A theory of esteem based peer pressure*. University of Iowa, Society for the Advancement of Economic Theory. Society for the Advancement of Economic Theory.

Akhavan, P. (2016, November 23). *Men, women, and a new definition of success*. (Oath, Inc.) Retrieved August 19,

2017, from Hufffington Post:
http://www.huffingtonpost.com/payam-akhavan/men-
women-and-a-new-definition-of-
success_b_8619228.html

Akil, B. (2009, September 13). *The theory of social validation.*
(Sussex Publishers, LLC) Retrieved October 7, 2017,
from Psychology Today:
https://www.psychologytoday.com/blog/communication-
central/200909/the-theory-social-validation

Albert, S. (2004, October 4). *The psychology of superstition.*
(WebMD, LLC) Retrieved September 16, 2017, from
WebMD: http://www.webmd.com/mental-
health/features/psychology-of-superstition#1

Alicke, M. (2000). Culpable control and the psychology of
blame. *Psychological Bulletin, 126*(4), 556-574. doi:
10.1037W0033-2909.126.4.556.

Allen, D. (2014, December 8). *Fear of success masquerading as
fear of failure.* (Sussex Publishers, LLC) Retrieved
September 29, 2017, from Psychology Today:
https://www.psychologytoday.com/blog/matter-
personality/201412/fear-success-masquerading-fear-
failure

Allen, S. (2016, July 12). *Cash (flow) really Is king.* (Dotdash)
Retrieved September 9, 2017, from The Balance:
https://www.thebalance.com/cash-flow-really-is-king-
1200759

Allen, T., Eby, L., Poteet, M., Lentz, E., & Lima, L. (2004).
Career benefits associated with mentoring for protégés: A
meta-analysis. *Journal of Applied Psychology, 89*(1),
127-136. doi: 10.1037/0021-9010.89.1.127.

Altman, I. (2017, March 7). *How to overcome the fear of
rejection for sales and careers.* (Forbes Media, LLC)
Retrieved October 16, 2017, from Forbes:
https://www.forbes.com/sites/ianaltman/2017/03/08/how-
to-overcome-the-fear-of-rejection-in-sales-and-
careers/#76b3bef93c67

American Psychological Association. (2007, October 24). *Stress a major health problem in the U.S., warns APA.* Retrieved August 28, 2017, from American Psychological Association: http://www.apa.org/news/press/releases/2007/10/stress.as px

American Psychological Association. (2014, April 23). *Employee distrust is pervasive in U.S. workforce.* (American Psychological Association) Retrieved October 18, 2017, from American Psychological Association: http://www.apa.org/news/press/releases/2014/04/employe e-distrust.aspx

Ames, D. (2004). Inside the mind reader's tool kit: Projection and stereotyping in mental state inference. *Journal of Personality and Social Psychology, 87*(3), 340-353. doi: 10.1037/0022-3514.87.3.340.

Amodeo, J. (2014, April 4). *Deconstructing the fear of rejection.* (Sussex Publishers, LLC) Retrieved October 6, 2017, from Psychology Today: https://www.psychologytoday.com/blog/intimacy-path-toward-spirituality/201404/deconstructing-the-fear-rejection

Andersen, E. (2015, May 27). *How great leaders avoid getting burned out: Two simple secrets.* (Forbes Media, LLC) Retrieved October 14, 2017, from Forbes: https://www.google.com/amp/s/www.forbes.com/sites/eri kaandersen/2015/05/27/how-great-leaders-avoid-getting-burned-out-2-simple-secrets/amp/

Anderson, A. (2013, April 17). *Good employees make mistakes. Great leaders allow them to.* (Forbes Media, LLC) Retrieved July 25, 2017, from Forbes: https://www.forbes.com/sites/amyanderson/2013/04/17/g ood-employees-make-mistakes-great-leaders-allow-them-to/#37094ad9126a

Anderson, A. (2016, January 6). *The fastest way to achieve success is to first help others succeed.* (Forbes Media,

LLC) Retrieved October 14, 2017, from Forbes: https://www.forbes.com/sites/amyanderson/2016/01/06/th e-fastest-way-to-achieve-success-is-to-first-help-others-succeed/#4479190d79f9

Anderson, J. [TEDx Talks]. (2017, July 6). *What is success, really?-Jamie Anderson-TEDxLiège.* Retrieved July 21, 2017, from YouTube: https://www.youtube.com/watch?v=tmc6HohWVCs

Aranda, M. [SciShow]. (2016, May 18). *Why do we procrastinate? [Video file].* Retrieved July 23, 2017, from YouTube: https://www.youtube.com/watch?v=pKyHX0zqynk

Arbesman, S. (2012, November 16). *Luck and skill untangled: The science of success.* (Condé Nast) Retrieved July 26, 2017, from Wired: https://www.wired.com/2012/11/luck-and-skill-untangled-qa-with-michael-mauboussin/

Arkes, H., Faust, D., Guilmette, T., & Hart, K. (1988). Eliminating the hindsight bias. *Journal of Applied Psychology, 73*(2), 305-307.

Arnold, G. (n.d.). *3 giant monsters that are the enemies of success.* Retrieved July 23, 2017, from Business Marketing Engine: https://businessmarketingengine.com/3-giant-monsters-that-are-the-enemies-of-success/

Arruda, W. (2011, February 22). *Conformity vs. consistency.* (Ziff Davis, LLC) Retrieved August 29, 2017, from Toolbox.com: http://hr.toolbox.com/blogs/william-arruda-reach/conformity-vs-consistency-44339

Arruda, W. (2015, May 14). *Why failure is essential to success.* (Forbes Media, LLC) Retrieved July 23, 2017, from Forbes: https://www.forbes.com/sites/williamarruda/2015/05/14/why-failure-is-essential-to-success/#6e3a5ec7923f

Artinger, F., Petersen, M., Gigurenzer, G., & Weibler, J. (2014). Heuristics as adaptive decision strategies in management.

Journal of Organizational Behavior, S33–S52. doi: 10.1002/job.1950.

Ashkenas, R. (2011, July 19). *The dangers of deference.* (Harvard Business Publishing) Retrieved September 2, 2017, from Harvard Business Review: https://hbr.org/2011/07/the-dangers-of-deference.html

Atik, N. (2015, February 23). *How to stop procrastinating—now.* (Telegraph Media Group Limited) Retrieved August 26, 2017, from The Telegraph: http://www.telegraph.co.uk/lifestyle/wellbeing/mood-mind/11422554/How-to-stop-procrastinating-now.html

Baer, D. (2012, August 30). *Success is random, so court serendipity.* (Mansuetto Ventures) Retrieved September 26, 2017, from Fast Company: https://www.fastcompany.com/3000910/success-random-so-court-serendipity

Baer, D. (2014, May 9). *Here's how being neurotic can make you more successful.* (Axel Springer SE) Retrieved September 19, 2017, from Business Insider: http://www.businessinsider.com/neurotic-people-can-be-super-successful-2014-5

Baer, D. (2016, November 11). *How to (kind of) master your neuroticism.* (New York Media, LLC) Retrieved October 17, 2017, from Science of Us: http://nymag.com/scienceofus/2016/11/how-to-deal-with-negative-emotions.html

Baer, J. (2015, August 19). *4 reasons why trying too hard ruins your brand.* (Mansuetto Ventures) Retrieved September 29, 2017, from Inc.: https://www.psychologytoday.com/blog/handy-hints-humans/201510/do-you-try-too-hard

Bakalar, N. (2009, July 18). *A creature of habit: Why mistakes are repeated.* (The New York Times Company) Retrieved July 25, 2017, from The New York Times: http://www.nytimes.com/2009/07/19/sports/baseball/19score.html

Baker, D. (2014, July 27). *What is success?* (Oath, Inc.)
Retrieved July 21, 2017, from Huffington Post:
http://www.huffingtonpost.com/daniel-c-baker/what-is-
success_b_5397752.html

Baker, J., Côte, J., & Hawes, R. (2000). The relationship between
coaching behaviours and sport anxiety in athletes.
Journal of Science and Medicine in Sport, 3(2), 110-119.

Baker, S. (1989). Managing reistance to change. *Library Trends,
37*(1), 53-61.

Bakker, A., Schaufeli, W., Leiter, M., & Taris, T. (2008, July-
September). Work engagement: An emerging concept in
occupaional health psychology. *Work & Stress, 22*(3),
187200-1-4.

Bandura, A. (1994). Self-efficacy. In V. Ramachaudran (Ed.),
Encyclopedia of human behavior (Vol. IV, pp. 71-81).
Academic Press.

Barber, N. (2013, February 14). *On the benefits of failure.*
(Sussex Publishers, LLC) Retrieved October 4, 2017,
from Psychology Today:
https://www.psychologytoday.com/blog/the-human-
beast/201302/the-benefits-failure

Bardwick, J. (2011, May 25). *The high cost of mistrust.* (Oath,
Inc.) Retrieved October 7, 2017, from Huffington Post:
http://www.huffingtonpost.com/judith-m-bardwick/the-
high-cost-of-mistrust_b_526127.html

Barlow, D. (2004). *Anxiety and its disorders: The nature and
treatment of anxiety and panic.* Guildford Press.

Barnes, H. (2015, March 2). *The dangers of complacency.*
(HB.org) Retrieved October 9, 2017, from Harrison
Barnes: https://www.hb.org/the-dangers-of-complacency/

Baron, R. (2006, February 1). Opportunity recognition as pattern
recongition: How entrepeneurs "connect the dots" to
identify new business opportunities. *Academy of
Management Perspectives, 20*(1), 104-119. doi:
10.5465/AMP.2006.19873412.

Barrett, L. (2006). Valence is a basic building block of emotional life. *Journal of Research in Personality, 40*, 35-65. doi: 10.1016/j.jrp.2005.08.006.

Barsukova, O. (2015). Bad ambition. *Journal of Process Management–New Technologies, International, 3*(4), 8-11.

Bar-Tal, D., & Darom, E. (1979). Pupils' attributions of success and failure. *Child Development, 50*, 264-267.

Battis, L. (2015, December). How procrastination is killing you. *Men's Health*, pp. 104-105. Retrieved from Men's Health.

Baumeister, R., & Tice, D. (1990). Anxiety and social exclusion. *Journal of Social and Clinical Psychology, 9*, 165-195.

Baumeister, R., Dale, K., & Sommer, K. (1998, December). Freudian defense mechanisms and empirical findings in modern social psychology: Reaction formation, projection, displacement, undoing, siolation, sublimation, and denial. *Journal of Personality, 66*(6), 1081–1124. doi: 10.1111/1467-6494.00043.

Beaumont, A. (2015, October 9). *Do you try too hard?* (Sussex Publishers, LLC) Retrieved September 29, 2017, from Psychology Today: https://www.psychologytoday.com/blog/handy-hints-humans/201510/do-you-try-too-hard

Beaumont, A. (2016, October 7). *Why you need to be a success at failure.* (Sussex Publishers, LLC) Retrieved July 25, 2017, from Psychology Today: https://www.psychologytoday.com/blog/handy-hints-humans/201610/why-you-need-be-success-failure

Beck, A., Weissman, A., Lester, D., & Trexler, L. (1974). The measurement of pessimissm: The hopelessness scale. *Journal of Consulting and Child Psychology, 42*(6), 861-865.

Belleza, S., Gino, F., & Keinan, A. (2014, March 18). *The surprising benefits of noncomformity.* (Massachusetts Institute of technology) Retrieved July 24, 2017, from MIT Sloan Management Review:

http://sloanreview.mit.edu/article/the-surprising-benefits-of-nonconformity/

Bello, M. (2014, February 24). *Consistency is key to any workplace change*. (Gannett Satellite Information Network, LLC) Retrieved October 7, 2017, from USA Today: https://www.usatoday.com/story/money/business/2014/02/24/nfl-n-word-ban/5784539/

Benabou, R., & Tirole, J. (2003). Intrinsic and extrinsic motivation. *Review of Economic Studies, 70*, 489-520.

Bennet, J. (2017, June 24). *On campus, failure is on the syllabus*. (The New York Times Company) Retrieved October 4, 2017, from The New York Times: https://www.nytimes.com/2017/06/24/fashion/fear-of-failure.html

Berg, S. (2017, May 28). *The strongest leaders are brave enough to admit weakness*. (Oath, Inc.) Retrieved October 16, 2017, from Huffington Post: https://www.huffingtonpost.com/young-entrepreneur-council/the-strongest-leaders-are_b_10166336.html

Berkman, E. (2015, October 8). *Why wait? The psychological origins of procrastination*. (Sussex Publishers, LLC) Retrieved August 24, 2017, from Psychology Today: https://www.psychologytoday.com/blog/the-motivated-brain/201510/why-wait-the-psychological-origins-procrastination

Bet-David, P. [Valuetainment]. (2017, March 21). *12 reasons why smart people fail in business [YouTube video]*. Retrieved July 25, 2017, from YouTube: https://www.youtube.com/watch?v=b4-2K-Sx_Mw

Bieling, P., Israeli, A., & Anthony, M. (2004). Is perfectionism good, bad, or both? Examining models of the perfectionism construct. *Personality and Individual Differences, 36*, 1373-1385. doi: 0.1016/S0191-8869(03)00235-6.

Bingham, S. (2017, January 2). *If employees don't trust you, it's up to you to fix it*. (Harvard Business School Publishing) Retrieved October 18, 2017, from Harvard Busines Review: https://hbr.org/2017/01/if-employees-dont-trust-you-its-up-to-you-to-fix-it

Bivins, T. H. (2006). Chapter 2: Responsibility and accountability. In K. Fitzpatrick, & C. Bronstein, *Ethics in public relations: Responsible advocacy* (pp. 19-38). SAGE Publications.

blame culture. (n.d.). (BusinessDictionary.com) Retrieved September 4, 2017, from BusinessDictionary.com: http://www.businessdictionary.com/definition/blame-culture.html

Block, B. (2012). Chapter IV: The rock of guilt and worry. In *The healing waters: Inspirational problem solving through guided imagery*. BookBaby.

Bloom, L., & Bloom, C. (2015, January 10). *Beware the dangers of FOMO*. (Sussex Publishers, LLC) Retrieved September 2, 2017, from Psychology Today: https://www.psychologytoday.com/blog/stronger-the-broken-places/201501/beware-the-dangers-fomo

Bohns, V., & Flynn, F. (2010, March). "Why didn't you just ask?" Underestimating the discomfort of help-seeking. *Journal of Experimental Social Psychology, 46*(2), 402-409. doi: 10.1016/j.jesp.2009.12.015.

Bond, J. (2008, March/April). The blame culture-an obstacle to improving safety. *Journal of Chemical Health & Safety, 15*(2), 6-9. doi: 10.1016/j.jchas.2007.07.002 .

Booth, J. (2016, July 7). *How I've trained myself to avoid making excuses*. (Mansuetto Ventures, LLC) Retrieved July 25, 2017, from Fast Company: https://www.fastcompany.com/3061587/the-simple-method-ive-used-to-avoid-making-excuses-in-work

Bordens, K., & Horowitz, I. (2012). Chapter 2: The social self. In *Social psychology* (pp. 31-62). Mahwah: Psychology Press.

Borkovec, T. (1994). The nature, functions, and origins of worry. In G. Davey, & F. Tallis (Eds.), *Worry and its psychological disorders: Theory, assessment and treatment.* Sussex, England: Wiley.

Borzykowski, B. (2015, April 2). *Why you can't delegate—and how to fix it.* (British Broadcasting Corporation) Retrieved July 26, 2017, from BBC: http://www.bbc.com/capital/story/20150401-why-you-find-it-hard-to-delegate

Bowerman, M. (2016, October 12). *Survey reveals what Americans fear the most.* (Gannett Satellite Information Network, LLC) Retrieved September 9, 2017, from USA Today: https://www.usatoday.com/story/news/nation-now/2016/10/12/survey-top-10-things-americans-fear-most/91934874/

Brackett, M., Rivers, S., & Salovey, P. (2011). Emotional intelligence: Implications for personal, social, academic, and workplace success. *Social and personality Psychology Compass, 5*(1), 88-103. doi: 0.1111/j.1751-9004.2010.00334.x.

Branson, R. (2016, April 20). *My Metric for Success? Happiness.* Retrieved September 27, 2017, from LinkedIn: https://www.linkedin.com/pulse/my-metric-success-happiness-richard-branson/?trk=mp-reader-card

Brason, R. (2016, April 20). *My metric for success? Happiness.* Retrieved September 14, 2017, from LinkedIn: https://www.linkedin.com/pulse/my-metric-success-happiness-richard-branson/?trk=mp-reader-card

Breazeale, R. (2011, March 25). *Catastrophic thinking.* (Sussex publishers, LLC) Retrieved September 18, 2017, from Psychology Today: https://www.psychologytoday.com/blog/in-the-face-adversity/201103/catastrophic-thinking

Breckler, S., Olson, J., & Wiggins, E. (2006). *Social psychology alive.* Belmont, CA: Thomson Wadsworth.

Bregman, P. (2015, October 21). *The high cost of conformity, and how to avoid it.* (Harvard Business School Publishing) Retrieved September 4, 2017, from Harvard Business Review: https://hbr.org/2015/10/the-high-cost-of-conformity-and-how-to-avoid-it

Bregman, P. (2016, January 11). *The right way to hold people accountable.* (Harvard Business School Publsihing) Retrieved October 2, 2017, from Harvard Business Review: https://hbr.org/2016/01/the-right-way-to-hold-people-accountable

Breines, J. (2017, June 22). *How rejection sensitivity derails relationships.* (Sussex Publishers, LLC) Retrieved October 6, 2017, from Psychology Today: https://www.psychologytoday.com/blog/in-love-and-war/201706/how-rejection-sensitivity-derails-relationships

Brenner, A. (2011, May 6). *The Nature of Change.* (Sussex Publishers, LLC) Retrieved October 31, 2017, from Psychology Today: https://www.psychologytoday.com/blog/in-flux/201105/the-nature-change-0

Brenner, E. (2014, January 30). *Do you mentor mentees or proteges?* (Pilcrow Group, Inc.) Retrieved October 16, 2017, from Copyediting: https://www.copyediting.com/do-you-mentor-mentees-or-proteges/#.WeT25YaDO9Y

Brenner-Roach, T. (2017, April 9). *How to overcome procrastination and the fear of failure: Strategies to excel at anything.* Retrieved August 24, 2017a, from Life, Learn, Grow: https://www.liftlearngrow.com/blog-page/overcome-procrastination

Brenner-Roach, T. (2017, May 18). *Procrastination is the enemy of success—here's how to beat It.* (Observer Media) Retrieved July 23, 2017b, from Observer: observer.com/2017/05/how-to-beat-procrastination-failure-of-success/

Brody, Y. (2013, September 29). *Obedience, consumer culture, and climate change.* (Sussex Publishers, LLC) Retrieved September 2, 2017, from Psychology Today: https://www.psychologytoday.com/blog/limitless/201309 /obedience-consumer-culture-and-climate-change

Brooke Miller [khanacademymedicine]. (2015, April 3). *Conformity and obedience-Behavior-MCAT-Khan Academy [Video file].* Retrieved September 2, 2017, from YouTube: https://www.youtube.com/watch?time_continue=13&v=L oy1zLkbuF0

Brookins, M. (2017). *What causes resistance to change in an organization?* (Hearst Newspapers, LLC) Retrieved October 7, 2017, from Houston Chronicle: http://smallbusiness.chron.com/causes-resistance-change-organization-347.html

Brooks, A. (2014, June). Get excited: Reappraising pre-performance anxiety as excitement. *Journal of Experimental Psychology, 143*(3), 1144-1158. doi: 10.1037/a0035325 .

Brooks, A., & Schweitzer, M. (2011). Can Nervous Nelly negotiate? How anxiety causes negotiators to make low first offers, exit early, and earn less profit. *Organizational Behavior and Human Decision Process, 115*, 43-54. doi: 10.1016/j.obhdp.2011.01.008.

Brooks, C. (2014, February 26). *Dressed for succcess? Harvard researcher says you may be doing it wrong.* (Purch) Retrieved August 29, 2017, from Business News Daily: http://www.businessnewsdaily.com/5979-the-benefits-of-being-nonconforming.html

Bruder, J. (2013, August 21). *The psychological price of entrepreneurship.* (Mansuetto Ventures) Retrieved August 28, 2017, from Inc: https://www.inc.com/magazine/201309/jessica-bruder/psychological-price-of-entrepreneurship.html

Bryner, J. (2010, January 19). *Workplace blame is contagious and detrimental*. (Purch) Retrieved September 23, 2017, from Live Science: https://www.livescience.com/8018-workplace-blame-contagious-detrimental.html

Buehler, R., Griffin, D., & Ross, M. (1994). Explaining the "planning fallacy": Why people underestimate their task completion times. *Journal of Personality and Social Psychology, 67*(3), 366-381.

Burchard, B. (2014, June 14). *How to get our sh** together (The power of personal responsibility) [Video file]*. Retrieved July 27, 2017, from YouTube: https://www.youtube.com/watch?time_continue=53&v=o5n919vsIFg

Burguess, A., & DiPaolo, P. (2015). Chapter 8: Anxiety and perfectionism: Relationships, mechanisms, and conditions. In F. Sirois, & D. Molnar (Eds.), *Perfectionism, health, and well-being* (pp. 177-204). Springer.

Burke, K. (2016, February 19). *Why athletes have such strange superstitions*. (Sporting News Media) Retrieved July 26, 2017, from Sporting News: http://www.sportingnews.com/other-sports/news/superstitions-athletes-coaches-sports-wade-boggs-michael-jordan-serena-williams/8k49ymj6cjhz1w2llfzpbgzym

Burke, R., Davis, R., & Flett, G. (2008, September). Workaholism types, perfectionism and work outcomes. *"İş, Güç" The Journal of Industrial Relations and Human Resources, 10*(4).

Burkeman, O. (2007, October 20). *The "useless emotion"*. (Guardian News and Media Limited) Retrieved September 18, 2017, from The Guardian: https://www.theguardian.com/lifeandstyle/2007/oct/20/healthandwellbeing.features3

Burton, N. (2014, November 16). *The psychology and philosophy of ambition*. (WordPress) Retrieved October

20, 2017, from Outre Monde: https://outre-monde.com/2014/11/16/the-psychology-and-philosophy-of-ambition/

Business Queensland. (2013, December 13). *Pros and cons of business growth.* (The State of Queensland) Retrieved October 3, 2017, from Business Queensland: https://www.business.qld.gov.au/running-business/growing-business/ways-grow/pros-cons

Caan, J. (2015, August 5). *Motivating my staff-how do I ~~do~~ reward them beyond a pay raise?* (Guardian Media Group Limited) Retrieved October 2, 2017, from The Guardian: https://www.theguardian.com/small-business-network/2015/aug/05/motivating-staff-reward-pay-rise-equity

Calonius, E. (2017, April 11). *What lucky people do different.* Retrieved July 26, 2017, from Jonathan Fields: http://www.jonathanfields.com/what-lucky-people-do-differently/

Cannner, N., & Bernstein, E. (2016, August 17). *Why is micromanagement so infectious?* (Harvard Business School Publishing) Retrieved October 14, 2017, from Harvard Business Review: https://hbr.org/2016/08/why-is-micromanagement-so-infectious

Carayon, P., & Zijlstra, F. (1999). Relationship between job control, work pressure, and strain: Studies in the USA and in The Netherlands. *Work & Stress, 13*(1), 32-48.

Cardone, G. (2011, March 22). *Success Is Important!* (Oath, Inc.) Retrieved July 23, 2017, from Huffington Post: http://www.huffingtonpost.com/grant-cardone/importance-of-success_b_837924.html

Carey, B. (2009, January 5). *Some protect the ego by working on their excuses early .* (The New York Times Company) Retrieved September 25, 2017, from The New York Times: http://www.nytimes.com/2009/01/06/health/06mind.html

Carleton, R. (2016, June). Fear of the unknown: One fear to rule them all? *Journal of Anxiety Disorders, 41*, 5-21. doi: 10.1016/j.janxdis.2016.03.011.

Carlston, D. (2010). Chapter 3: Social cognition. In R. Baumeister, & E. Finkel, *Advanced social psychology: The state of the science* (pp. 63-1000). Oxford University Press.

Carnegie, D. (2002). *How to stop worrying and start living.* Pocket Books.

Caron, M., Whitbourne, S., & Halgin, R. (1992). Fraudulent excuse making among college students. *Teaching of Psychology, 19*(2), 90.

Carpenter, J. (2015, August 13). *Toshiba's accounting scandal: How it happened.* (Investopedia, LLC) Retrieved September 2, 2017, from Investopedia: http://www.investopedia.com/articles/investing/081315/t oshibas-accounting-scandal-how-it-happened.asp

Carson, B. (2015, July 1). *There's a dark side to startups, and it haunts 30% of the world's most brilliant people.* (Business Insider, LLC) Retrieved August 28, 2017, from Business Insider: http://www.businessinsider.com/austen-heinzs-suicide-and-depression-in-startups-2015-7

Carter, J., & Peterson, M. (2017). The modal account of luck revisited. *Synthese, 194*, 2175-2184. doi: 10.1007/s11229-016-1047-7.

Carter, N., Gartner, W., Shaver, K., & Gatewood, E. (2003). The career reasons of nascent entrepreneurs. *Journal of Business Venturing, 18*(1), 13-39.

Carter, S. (2013, November 26). *The tell tale signs of burnout...Do you have them?* (Sussex Publishers, LLC) Retrieved October 2, 2017, from Psychology Today: https://www.psychologytoday.com/blog/high-octane-women/201311/the-tell-tale-signs-burnout-do-you-have-them

Chaleff, I. (2015, September 26). *VW's culture of blind obedience: What went wrong and how to fix it.* (NBC

Universal) Retrieved September 2, 2017, from MSNBC: http://www.msnbc.com/msnbc/vws-culture-blind-obedience-what-went-wrong-and-how-fix-it

Chan, J., Fu, K., Schunn, C., Cagan, J., Wood, K., & Kotovsky, K. (2011, August). On the benefits and pitfalls of analogies for innovative design: Ideation performance based on analogical distance, commonness, and modality of examples. *Journal of Mechanical Design, 133*, 081004-1-11.

Chand, S. (2016). *Uplift your mood: Stop ruminating.* (Anxiety and Depression Association of America) Retrieved September 19, 2017, from Anxiety and Depression Association of America: https://adaa.org/blog/uplift-your-mood-stop-ruminating

Chang, L. (2009, April). A study on japanese culture and styles of business negotiation. *Journal of Global Business Management, 5*(1), 1-4.

Cherry, K. (2015, June 25). *What is the norm of reciprocity?* (Dotdash) Retrieved October 5, 2017, from Verywell: https://www.verywell.com/what-is-the-rule-of-reciprocity-2795891

Chu, A., & Choi, J. (2005). Rethinking procrastination: Positive effects of "active" procrastination behavior on attitudes and performance. *The Journal of Social Psychology, 145*(3), 245-264.

Chunn, L. (2016, July 11). *How anxiety became a modern epidemic greater than depression.* (Telegraph Media Group Limited) Retrieved September 13, 2017, from The Telegraph: http://www.telegraph.co.uk/health-fitness/mind/how-anxiety-became-a-modern-epidemic-greater-than-depression/

Cialdini, R. B. (2007). *Influence: The psychology of persuasion.* HarperCollins.

Cialdini, R., & Goldstein, N. (2004). Social influence: Compliance and conformity. *Annual Review of*

Psychology, 55, 591-621. doi: doi: 10.1146/annurev.psych.55.090902.142015.

Cialdini, R., & Guadagno, R. (2001). Chapter 2: Sequential request compliance tactics. In R. Cialdini, *Influence: Science and practice, fourth edition* (4th edition ed.). Allyn & Bacon.

Cialdini, R., Wosinska, W., Barrett, D., Butner, J., & Gornik-Durose, M. (1999, October). Compliance with a request in two cultures: The differential influence of social proof and commitment/consistency on collectivists and individualists. *Personality and Social Psychology Bulletin, 25*(10), 1242-1253. doi: 10.1177/0146167299258006.

Clark, D. (2013, November 5). *How the best leaders embrace change.* (Forbes Media, LLC) Retrieved July 27, 2017, from Forbes: https://www.forbes.com/sites/dorieclark/2013/11/05/how-the-best-leaders-embrace-change/#12cc2a80c1cd

Clear, J. (2017, June 21). *The akrasia effect: Why we don't follow through on what we set out to do and what to do about it.* (Oath, Inc.) Retrieved August 26, 2017, from Huffington Post: http://www.huffingtonpost.com/james-clear/the-akrasia-effect-why-we_b_10576458.html

Clifford, C. (2017, February 28). *Bill Gates and Warren Buffett have the same definition of success—and it has nothing to do with money.* (NBC Universal) Retrieved September 27, 2017, from CNBC: https://www.cnbc.com/2017/02/28/bill-gates-and-warren-buffett-think-success-isnt-about-money.html

Cohen, E. (2011, May 22). *The fear of losing control.* (Sussex Publishers, LLC) Retrieved October 5, 2017, from Psychology Today: https://www.psychologytoday.com/blog/what-would-aristotle-do/201105/the-fear-losing-control

Coker, J. (2016, February 9). *Why people don't like new ideas.* Retrieved September 5, 2017, from LinkedIn:

https://www.linkedin.com/pulse/why-people-dont-like-new-ideas-jared-coker

Collins, S. (2002, November/December). Micromanagement—a costly management style. *Radiology Management, 24*(6), 32-35.

Colombetti, G. (2006). Appraising valence. *Journal of Consciousness Studies, 12*(8-10), 103-26.

Conner, C. (2013, April 14). *Office politics: Must you play? A handbook for survival/success.* (Forbes Media, LLC) Retrieved September 21, 2017, from Forbes: https://www.forbes.com/sites/cherylsnappconner/2013/04/14/office-politics-must-you-play-a-handbook-for-survivalsuccess/#9fe99c74e308

Connors, C. (2016, July 21). *The first step towrad success is defining success for yourself.* (Medium) Retrieved July 21, 2017, from The Mission: https://medium.com/the-mission/the-first-step-toward-success-is-defining-success-for-yourself-92dcfc3dd61c

Conroy, D., & Elliot, A. (2004, September). Fear of failure of achievement goals in sport: Addressing the issue of the chicken and the egg. *Anxiety, Stress, and Coping, 17*(3), 271-285. doi: 10.1080/1061580042000191642.

Conroy, D., Kaye, M., & Fifer, A. (2007, December). Cognitive links between fear of failure and perfectionism. *Journal of Rational-Emotive & Cognitive-Behavior Therapy, 25*(4), 237–253. doi: 10.1007/s10942-007-0052-7.

Constable, S., Shuler, Z., Klaber, L., & Raskauskas, M. (1999, May 1). *Conformity, compliance, and obedience.* (Miami University) Retrieved August 29, 2017, from Living a Social Word: https://www.units.miamioh.edu/psybersite/cults/cco.shtml

Corcuera, L. (2014, September 10). *Become a better leader by asking for help.* (Mansuetto Ventures) Retrieved July 26, 2017, from Inc.: https://www.inc.com/lorie-corcuera/become-a-better-leader-by-asking-for-help.html

Cordes, C., & Dougherty, T. (1999). A review and an integration of research on job burnout. *Academy of Management Review, 18*(4), 621-656.

Coxen, M. (2011, January). The problem with rumination. *The Psychologist, 24*(1), 70-71.

Crampton, S., Hodge, J., & Mishra, J. (1998). The informal communication network: Factors influencing grapevine activity. *Public Personnel Management, 27*(4), 569-584.

Crawford, A. (2013, February). *Why the best success stories often begin with failure.* (Smithsonian Institution) Retrieved July 25, 2017, from Smithsonian Magazine: http://www.smithsonianmag.com/innovation/why-the-best-success-stories-often-begin-with-failure-3851517/

Cruddas, S. (2016, March 26). *The hidden psychology of failure.* (British Broadcasting Corporation) Retrieved July 25, 2017, from BBC: http://www.bbc.com/capital/story/20160316-the-hidden-psychology-of-failure

Dabbah, M. (2017, August 19). *Is your personal branding at risk thanks to your lack of self-awareness?* Retrieved October 20, 2017, from Red Shoe Movement: https://redshoemovement.com/is-your-personal-branding-at-risk/

Dahl, M. (2014, December 27). *Worrying about stuff is a sign of intelligence.* (Oath, Inc.) Retrieved September 16, 2017, from Huffington Post: http://www.huffingtonpost.com/2014/12/26/worrying-intelligence_n_6369370.html?ncid=fcbklnkushpmg00000063

Daily Mail Reporters. (2011, November 9). *How was bubble wrap invented? The unlikely stories of the brainwaves we all take for granted.* (Associated Newspapers Ltd) Retrieved October 26, 2017, from The Daily Mail: http://www.dailymail.co.uk/news/article-2059678/How-bubble-wrap-invented-unlikely-stories-brainwaves-granted.html#ixzz4weR6pAB1 dallasnews Administrator. (2014, August). *The dangers in taking on too much responsibility.* (The Dallas Morning News) Retrieved July 25, 2017, from Dallas News: https://www.dallasnews.com/opinion/commentary/2014/0 8/22/the-dangers-in-taking-on-too-much-responsibility

Dame, J., & Gedmin, J. (2013, October 2). *Three tips for overcoming your blind spots.* (Harvard Business School Publishing) Retrieved October 11, 2017, from Harvard Business Review: https://hbr.org/2013/10/three-tips-for-overcoming-your-blind-spots

Damisch, L., Stoberock, B., & Mussweiler, T. (2010). Keep your fingers crossed! How superstition improves performance. *Psychological Science, 21*(7), 1014-1020. doi: 10.1177/0956797610372631.

Davey, G. (2013, May 21). *What do we worry about?* (Sussex Publishers, LLC) Retrieved September 9, 2017, from Psychology Today: https://www.psychologytoday.com/blog/why-we-worry/201305/what-do-we-worry-about

Day, M. (2008, July 19). *Hi-tech is turning us all into time-wasters.* (Guardian News and Media Limited) Retrieved August 26, 2017, from The Guardian: https://www.theguardian.com/science/2008/jul/20/psycho logy.mobilephones

de Botton, A. [The School of Life]. (2015, July 22). *What is "success"? [Video file].* Retrieved July 21, 2017, from YouTube: https://www.youtube.com/watch?v=P8b4mZvrui4&featur e=youtu.be

de Botton, A. (2016, September 19). *The dangers of being dutiful [Video file].* Retrieved July 25, 2017, from YouTube: https://www.youtube.com/watch?v=FTBEb-W6Xgo

de Botton, A.; Morris, A. [The School of Life]. (2017, November 14). *Procratination [Video file].* Retrieved July 25, 2017, from YouTube: https://www.youtube.com/watch?v=3QetfnYgjRE

Dean, J. (2009, June 8). *Why group norms kill creativity*. Retrieved September 5, 2017, from Psyblog: http://www.spring.org.uk/2009/06/why-group-norms-kill-creativity.php

Dean, J. (2011, December 7). *Why people secretly fear creative ideas*. Retrieved September 6, 2017, from Psyblog: http://www.spring.org.uk/2011/12/why-people-secretly-fear-creative-ideas.php

Dean, J. (2012, June 6). *The hindsight bias: I knew it all along!* Retrieved October 11, 2017, from Psyblog: http://www.spring.org.uk/2012/06/the-hindsight-bias-i-knew-it-all-along.php

DeCaro, M., Thomas, R., Albert, N., & Beilock, S. (2011). Choking under pressure: Multiple routes to skill failure. *Journal of Experimental Psychology: General, 140*(3), 390-406. doi: 10.1037/a0023466.

Delacroix, E., & Guillard, V. (2008). Understanding, defining and measuring the trait of superstition. *Selected Proceedings of the IARPEP/SABE 2008 Conference at LUISS in Rome.* Rome: IAREP/SABE World Meeting.

DeMers, J. (2015, February 19). *The importance of social validation in online marketing*. (Forbes Media, LLC) Retrieved October 7, 2017, from Forbes: https://www.forbes.com/sites/jaysondemers/2015/02/19/the-importance-of-social-validation-in-online-marketing/#4bd69f58364d

deNoyelles, A., Hornik, S., & Johnson, R. (2014, June). Exploring the dimensions of self-efficacy in virtual world learning: Environment, task, and content. *MERLOT Journal of Online Learning and Teaching, 10*(2), 255-271.

DePaulo, B., & Fisher, J. (1980). The costs of asking for help. *Basic and Applied Social Psychology, 1*(1), 23-55.

Deutsch, M., & Gerard, H. (1955). A study of normative and informational social influences upon individual judgment.

The Journal of Abnormal and Social Psychology, 51(3), 629-636. doi: 10.1037/h0046408.

Diaconis, P. (1983). *Theories of data analysis from magical thinking through classical statistics.* Stanford University, Department of Statistics. Stanford University.

Dias, A., & Teixiera, A. (2014). The anatomy of a business failure: A qualitative account of its implications for future business success [Research work in progress]. *FEP Working Papers*(550).

Diener, C., & Dweck, C. (1980). An analysis of learned helplesness: II. The processing of success. *Journal of Personality and Social Psychology, 39*(5), 940-952.

Dimidijan, S., Martell, C., & Christensen, A. (2008). Chapter 3: Integrative behavioral couple therapy. In A. Gurman (Ed.), *Clinical handbook of couple therapy* (4th Edition ed., pp. 73-106). Guilford Press.

Ditto, P., & Lopez, D. (1992). Motivated skepticism: Use of differential decision criteria for preferred and non preferred conclusions. *Journal of Personality and Social Psychology, 63*(4), 568-584.

Divorced Moms. (2017, January 8). *Stay in your lane to keep negative thoughts & people away!* (The Good Men Project) Retrieved October 13, 2017, from The Good Men Project: https://goodmenproject.com/guy-talk/stay-in-your-lane-to-keep-negative-thoughts-people-away-dg/

Dix, A., Ormerod, T., Twidale, M., Sas, C., Gomesa da Silva, P., & McKnight, L. (2006, March). Why bad ideas are a good idea. *Proceedings of HCIEd.*

Dizik, A. (2016, November 17). *The strange psychology of stress and burnout.* (British Broadcasting Corporation) Retrieved October 2, 2017, from British Broadcasting Corporation: http://www.bbc.com/capital/story/20161116-stress-is-good-for-you-until-it-isnt The strange psychologicy of stress and burnout

Dominguez, T. [. (2016, September 3). *Why being a failure is a good thing [Video file].* Retrieved July 25, 2017, from YouTube: https://www.youtube.com/watch?v=kEQNA13yVIM

Dorison, A. (2015, September 22). *The one thing successful people don't make... excuses.* (Oath, Inc.) Retrieved July 25, 2017, from Huffington Post: http://www.huffingtonpost.com/adrienne-dorison/the-one-thing-successful-_b_8177924.html

Downey, G., & Feldman, S. (1996). Implications of rejection sensitivity for intimate relationships. *Journal of Personality and Social Psychology, 70*(6), 1327-1343.

Drexler, P. (2016, June 13). *Managing up: When your boss is an obsessive micromanager.* (Forbes Media, LLC) Retrieved October 14, 2017, from Forbes: https://www.forbes.com/sites/peggydrexler/2013/06/13/managing-up-when-your-boss-is-an-obsessive-micromanager/#74fb004b332a

Duckworth, A., Peterosn, C., Matthews, M., & Kellyy, D. (2007). Grit: Perseverance and passion from long-term goals. *Journal of Personality and Social Psychology, 92*(6), 1087-1101. doi: 10.1037/0022-3514.92.6.1087.

Dumb Little Man. (2011, May 20). *How to become wildly successful at anything.* (Business Insider, Inc.) Retrieved August 17, 2017, from Business Insider: http://www.businessinsider.com/how-to-become-wildly-successful-at-anything-2011-5

Dunn, P. (2017, February 13). *Remedies for worrying about money can lead to more worries.* (Gannett Satellite Information Network, LLC) Retrieved September 9, 2017, from USA Today: https://www.usatoday.com/story/money/personalfinance/2017/02/04/remedies-worrying-money-can-lead-more-worries/96945682/

Dunning, D., Johnson, K., Ehrlinger, J., & Kruger, J. (2003). Why people fail to recognize their own icnompetence.

Current Directions in Psychological Science, 12(83), 605-632. doi: 10.1111/1467-8721.01235.

Dweck, C. (1975). The role of expectations and attributions in the alleviation of learned helplessness. *Journal of Personality and Social Psychology, 31*(4), 674-685.

Dyke, L., & Murphy, S. (2006). How we define success: A qualitative study of what matters most to women and men. *Sex Roles, 55*, 357-371. doi: 10.1007/s11199-006-9091-2.

Dzombak, D. (2014, August 25). *What is success?* (http://www.dandzombak.com/what-is-success/) Retrieved July 21, 2017, from http://www.dandzombak.com/what-is-success/

Eakin, S. (2016, September 21). *Making excuses hurts your business more than taxes and politicians.* (Entrepeneur Media, Inc.) Retrieved July 25, 2017, from Entrepeneur: https://www.entrepreneur.com/article/281689

Ejova, A., Navarro, D., & Delfabbros, P. (2013, July). Success-slope effects on the illusion of control and on remembered. *Judgment and Decision Making, 8*(4), 498-511.

El Baroudi, S., Fleisher, C., Khaphova, S., Jansen, P., & Richardson, J. (2017). Ambition at work and career satisfaction: The mediating role of taking charge behavior and teh moderating role of pay. *Career Development International, 22*(1), 87-10210.1108/CDI-07-2016-0124.

Elejalde-Ruiz, A. (2016, October 17). *Study finds your micromanaging boss could be killing you.* (Tronc, Inc.) Retrieved October 14, 2017, from Chicago Tribune: http://www.chicagotribune.com/business/ct-workplace-flexibility-death-indiana-study-1018-biz-20161017-story.html

Ellard, J. (2017, February 18). *The most needed, and least taught, job skill: Awareness.* (Oath, Inc.) Retrieved October 2, 2017, from Huffington Post: http://www.huffingtonpost.com/jae-ellard/the-most-

needed-and-least-taught-job-skill-
awareness_b_9258436.html

Elliot, A., & Thrash, T. (2004, August 8). The intergenerational transmission of fear of failure. *Personality and Social Psychology Bulletin, 30*(8), 957-971. doi: 10.1177/0146167203262024.

Elliott, E., & Dweck, C. (1988). Goals: An approach to motivation and achievement. *Journal of Personality and Social Psychology, 54*(1), 5-12. doi: 10.1037/0022-3514.54.1.5.

Eltringham, M. (n.d.). *Gulf in levels of employee engagement between US and Europe.* (Insight Publishing) Retrieved October 20, 2017, from Workplace Insight: http://workplaceinsight.net/gulf-levels-employee-engagement-us-europe/

E-Myth. (2009, October 27). *The many hats of the business owner.* Retrieved October 13, 2017, from E-Myth: http://www.e-myth.com/cs/user/print/post/the-many-hats-of-the-business-owner

Enderwick, P. (2017). *A dictionary of business and management in India.* Oxford: Oxford University Press.

Endler, N., & Kocovski, N. (2011, May-June). State and trait anxiety revisited. *Journal of Anxiety Disorders, 15*(3), 231-245. doi: 10.1016/S0887-6185(01)00060-3.

Epley, N., & Gilovich, T. (1999). Just going along: Nonconscious priming and confomrity to social pressures. *Journal of Experimental Social Psychology*, 578-589.

Erlich, L., & Hansford, B. (1999). Mentoring: Pros and cons for HRM. *Asia Pacific Journal of Human Resources, 37*(3), 92-107.

Estrem, P. (2016, August 25). *Why failure is good for success.* (SUCCESS Magazine) Retrieved July 25, 2017, from Success: http://www.success.com/article/why-failure-is-good-for-success

Eurich, T. (2017, May 3). *The evil twin of introspection.* (Medium) Retrieved September 19, 2017, from Thrive Global: https://journal.thriveglobal.com/why-rumination-is-the-enemy-of-insight-15bea5bab139

Everett, F. (2010, 24 May). *Are you ruled by superstition? It seems the modern world is driving us mad with irrational fears and OCD on the rise.* (Asosciated Newspapers Ltd.) Retrieved October 11, 2017, from Daily Mail: http://www.dailymail.co.uk/femail/article-1280741/Are-YOU-ruled-superstition-It-modern-world-driving-mad-irrational-fears-OCD-rise.html

Ewing, J. (2017, August 1). *European bank cuts funds to VW because of emissions fraud.* (The New York Times Company) Retrieved September 2, 2017, from The New York Times: https://www.nytimes.com/2017/08/01/business/volkswagen-loans-diesel-emissions.html?mcubz=0

Eyal, N. (2014, February 18). *Why do fads fade? The inevitable death of Flappy Bird.* (Medium) Retrieved October 19, 2017, from Psychology of Stuff: https://medium.com/behavior-design/why-do-fads-fade-5421ece2d598

Eysenck, M., Derakshan, N., Santos, R., & Calvo, M. (2007). Anxiety and cognitive performance: Attentional control theory. *Emotion, 7*(2), 336-353. doi: 10.1037/1528-3542.7.2.336.

Fallon, N. (2014, December 3). *Is your team missing this important business skill?* Retrieved October 20, 2017, from Business News Daily: http://www.businessnewsdaily.com/7532-critical-thinking-in-business.html

Fast, N. (2010, May 13). *How to stop the blame game.* (Harvard Business School Publishing) Retrieved July 25, 2017, from Harvard Business Review: https://hbr.org/2010/05/how-to-stop-the-blame-game

Fast, N., & Tiedens, L. (2010). Blame contagion: The automatic transmission of self-serving attributions. *Journal of Experimental Social Psychology, 46*, 97-106. doi: 10.1016/j.jesp.2009.10.007.

Federer, D. (2013, November 13). *Humble or arrogant: What's your company culture?* Retrieved October 6, 2017, from Federer Performance Management Group, LLC: https://federerperformance.com/2013/11/13/humble-arrogant-whats-company-culture/

Feldman, D., Hosea, J., Ponce, J., Wall, M., & Banker, L. (2015). *Cause, influence & the next generation workfoce: The 2015 millenial impact report.* The Case Foundation, Achieve. Washington: The Case Foundation.

Feldman, R. S. (2011). *Understanding psychology, tenth edition* (10th edition ed.). McGraw Hill.

Fell, D. (2016, January 19). *Business plans gone bad: Five ways to fix your focus.* Retrieved October 3, 2017, from Chief Outsiders: https://www.chiefoutsiders.com/blog/business-plan

Ferrari, J. (1992). Procrastination in the workplace: Attributions for failure among individuals with similar behavioral tendencies. *Personality and Individual Differences, 13*(3), 315-319.

Ferrari, J. (1994, November). Dysfunctional procrastination and its relationship with self-esteem, interpersonal dependency, and self-defeating behaviors. *Personality and Individual Differences, 17*(5), 673-679. doi: 10.1016/0191-8869(94)90140-6 .

Ferrari, J., & Díaz-Morales, J. (2014). Procrastination and mental health coping: A brief report related to students. *Individual Differences Research, 12*(1), 8-11.

Ferrari, J., Johnson, J., & McCown, W. (1995). Chapter 2: Procrastination research. In *Procrastination and task avoidance: Theory, research, and treatment* (The Springer Series in Social Clinical Psychology ed., pp. 21-46). Springer.

Field, P. (2014). *The chi of <u>chang</u>: How hypnotherapy can help you heal and turn your life around—regardless of your past.* John Hunt Publishing.

Fisher, R., & Wakefield, K. (1998, January). Factors leading to group identification: A field study of winners and losers. *Psychology & Marketing, 15*(1), 23–40.

Fisman, R. (2008, May 15). *Like there's no tomorrow.* (The Slate Group) Retrieved August 26, 2017, from Slate: http://www.slate.com/articles/life/procrastination/2008/05/like_theres_no_tomorrow.html

Flaxingon, B. (2013, May 25). *Help-my boss is incompetent!* (Sussex Publishers, LLC) Retrieved October 3, 2017, from Psychology Today: https://www.psychologytoday.com/blog/understand-other-people/201305/help-my-boss-is-incompetent

Fleming, S., Thomas, C., & Dolan, R. (2010). Overcoming status quo bias in the human brain. *Proceedings of the National Academy of Sciences, 107*, 6005-6009. <u>doi:.</u>

Fletcher, M. (2012). Chapter 10: Complacency in leadership (The curse of success). In *Leadership becomes you: <u>Understnading</u> the psychology of leadership and you* (pp. 97-106). Bloomington, Indiana: AuthorHouse.

Flynn, F. B. (2008). If you need help, just ask: Underestimating compliance with direct requests for help. *Journal of Personality and Social Psychology, 95*(1), 128-143. doi: 10.1037/0022-3514.95.1.128.

Fontaine Ortiz, E., Gorita, I., & Vistykh, V. (2004). *Delegation of authority and accountability, part II: Series on managing for results in the United Nations system.* United Nations, Joint Inspection Unit. Geneva: United Nations.

Forbis, A. (2004, Spring). *Is personal accountability in your job description? [PDF document].* Retrieved October 2, 2017, from Division of Personnel Solutions: http://www.compuhigh.com/demo/work_exp/Solutionsspg3-4.pdf

Foster, K., & Kokko, H. (2009). The evolution of superstitious and superstition-like behaviour. *Proceedings of the Royal Society B: Biological Sciences, 276*, 31-37. doi: 10.1098/rspb.2008.0981.

Fotopulos, D. (2010, April 21). *Top 10 reasons business fail: Lack of experience*. (DF Consulting, Inc.) Retrieved September 30, 2017, from Hidden Profit Prophet: https://hiddenprofitprophet.com/2010/04/top-ten-reasons-businesses-fail-reason-one/

Frank, R. (2016, May). *Why luck matters more than you might think*. (Atlantic Media) Retrieved July 26, 2017, from The Atlantic: https://www.theatlantic.com/magazine/archive/2016/05/why-luck-matters-more-than-you-might-think/476394/

Frankel, A., Leonard, M., & Denham, C. (2006, August). Fair and just culture, team behavior, and leadership engagement: The tools to achieve high reliability. *Health Research and Educational Trust, 41*(4), 1690–1709. doi: 10.1111/j.1475-6773.2006.00572.x.

Franklin Templeton Investments. (2012, October 6). *Investors should beware the role of "availability bias"*. (Business Insider, Inc.) Retrieved October 11, 2017, from Business Insider: http://www.businessinsider.com/the-availability-bias-is-driving-investor-decisions-2012-10

Frost, A. (n.d.). *3 better ways to define success in your life (Because it's not about the money)*. (Daily Muse, Inc.) Retrieved July 23, 2017, from The Muse: https://www.themuse.com/advice/3-better-ways-to-define-success-in-your-life-because-its-not-always-about-the-money

Furnham, A. (2017, February 28). *The military and management incompetence*. (Sussex Publishers, LLC) Retrieved October 3, 2017, from Psychology Today: https://www.psychologytoday.com/blog/sideways-view/201702/the-military-and-management-incompetence

Galef, J. (2016). *A day late and a dollar short: The planning fallacy explained.* (The Big Think, Inc.) Retrieved August 24, 2017, from Big Think: http://bigthink.com/in-their-own-words/why-you-cant-plan

Gallegos, C. (2017, February 19). *What is success?* (Youngry) Retrieved August 17, 2017, from Youngry: https://youngry.com/what-is-success/

Garnett, L. (2014, December 18). *How do you define success?* (Mansuetto Ventures) Retrieved July 21, 2017, from Inc.: https://www.inc.com/laura-garnett/how-do-you-define-success.html

Gaspard, T. (2014, November 3). *How being too self-reliant can destroy your relationship.* (Oath, Inc.) Retrieved October 6, 2017, from Huffington Post: https://www.huffingtonpost.com/terry-gaspard-msw-licsw/how-self-reliance-can-destroy-a-relationship_b_6071906.html

Gee, C. (2014, October 10). *Stop blaming other people and pick up a mirror.* (Oath, Inc.) Retrieved July 25, 2017, from Hufington Post: http://www.huffingtonpost.ca/collette-gee/blaming-others_b_5962174.html

Geiger, E. (2016, December 7). *Stay in your lane, or own the whole?* (LifeWay Christian Resources) Retrieved October 13, 2017, from LifeWay Leadership: http://www.lifeway.com/leadership/2016/12/07/stay-in-your-lane-or-own-the-whole/

Gigerenzer, G., & Gaissmaier, W. (2011). Heuristic decision making. *Annual Review of Psychology, 62*, 451-482. doi: 10.1146/annurev-psych-120709-145346.

Gilbert, E. [TED]. (2014, April 25). *Success, failure, and the drive to keep creating—Elizabeth Gilbert [Video file].* Retrieved July 25, 2017, from YouTube: https://www.youtube.com/watch?v=_waBFUg_oT8

Gino, F. (2016, October). *Let your workers rebel.* (Harvard Business School Publishing) Retrieved July 23, 2017, from Harvard Business Review: https://hbr.org/cover-story/2016/10/let-your-workers-rebel

Gino, F., Kouchaki, M., & Galinsky, A. (2015). The moral virtue of authenticity: How inauthenticity produces feelings of immorality and impurity. *Psychological Sicence, 26*(7), 983-996. doi: 10.1177/0956797615575277.

Gitlin, A. (2016, June 2). *Etymoogy of success.* Retrieved August 17, 2017, from LinkedIn: https://www.linkedin.com/pulse/etymology-success-alex-gitlin

Goldberg, C. (2009, March 2). *When perfectionism becomes a problem.* (Boston.com) Retrieved September 18, 2017, from Boston.com: http://archive.boston.com/news/health/articles/2009/03/02/when_perfectionism_becomes_a_problem/?page=full

Goleman, D. (1984, June 12). *A bias puts self at center of everything.* (The New York Times Company) Retrieved October 16, 2017, from The New York Times: http://www.nytimes.com/1984/06/12/science/a-bias-puts-self-at-center-of-everything.html?pagewanted=all

Goleman, D. (1984, March 6). *Excuses: New theory defines their role in life.* (The New York Times Company) Retrieved September 25, 2017, from The New York Times: http://www.nytimes.com/1984/03/06/science/excuses-new-theory-defines-their-role-in-life.html?pagewanted=all&mcubz=1

Golpour, R., Mohammad Amini, Z., Kasraie, S., & Senobar, L. (2015, December). The role of self-compassion components on prediction procrastination and depression in students. *Journal of Educational and Management Studies, 5*(4), 204-210.

Goltz, J. (2011, March/April). *What causes some small businesses to fail? [PDF document].* Retrieved September 29, 2017, from Consumer Credit Counseling Service of the Black Hills:

http://www.cccsbh.com/pdf/CCCSBH%20Newsletter%2
0Mar_April_2011_Elec.pdf

Gorvin, L., & Brown, D. (2012). The psychology of feeling like a burden: A review of the literature. *Social Psychology Review, 14*(1), 28-41.

Gots, J. (2011, August 5). *Failure is not an option. It's a necessity.* (The Big Think, Inc.) Retrieved September 29, 2017, from Big Think: http://bigthink.com/think-tank/failure-is-not-an-option-its-a-necessity

Gourguechon, P. (2015, September 25). *The cause of your worst mistakes? A psychological gremlin you've never heard of.* (Forbes Media, LLC) Retrieved October 4, 2017, from Forbes: https://www.forbes.com/sites/prudygourguechon/2017/09/25/the-cause-of-your-worst-mistakes-a-psychological-gremlin-you-never-heard-of/#3984a76b94a9

Govorun, O., Fuegen, K., & Payne, B. (2006). Stereotypes focus defensive projection. *Personality and Social Psychology Bulletin, 32*(6), 781-793. doi: 10.1177/0146167205285556.

Graham, C., & Meeten, D. (2016). The perseverative worry ?bout: A review of cognitive, affective and motivational factors that contribute to worry perseveration. *Biological Psychology, 121*, 233-243. doi: 10.1016/j.biopsycho.2016.04.003.

Grant, A. (2013, February 1). *A road map for turning epic failures into future successes.* (Brazen Technologies) Retrieved July 24, 2017, from Brazen Blog: https://www.brazen.com/blog/archive/career-growth/a-road-map-for-turning-epic-failures-into-future-success/

Grant, A. (2016, January 16). *Why I taught myself to procrastinate.* (The New York Times Company) Retrieved July 23, 2017, from The New York Times: https://www.nytimes.com/2016/01/17/opinion/sunday/why-i-taught-myself-to-procrastinate.html

Gratton, L. (2014, June 6). *Can altriusm be good for business?* (Guardian News Media Limited) Retrieved October 14, 2017, from The Guardian: https://www.theguardian.com/sustainable-business/altruism-good-business-community

Great-West Life Centre for Mental Health in the Workplace. (2016, February 18). *Why blame and shame don't work [PDF document]*. (Great-West Life Centre for Mental Health in the Workplace) Retrieved September 21, 2017, from Workplace Strategies for Mental Health: https://www.workplacestrategiesformentalhealth.com/pdf/Blame_and_shame.pdf

Greczyn, R. (n.d.). *Where the buck stops: Personal responsibility in a "not-me" society*. (Appalachian State University) Retrieved July 25, 2017, from Walker College of Business: https://business.appstate.edu/events/boyles-ceo-lecture-series/where-buck-stops-personal-responsibility-not-me-society

Green, A. (2017, February 27). *Is business and investment success due to skill... or luck?* (The Oxford Club) Retrieved July 26, 2017, from Investment U: http://www.investmentu.com/article/detail/53717/business-investment-success-skill-luck

Green, C. [TEDx Talks]. (2014, June 20). *Programming your mind for success-Carrie Green-TEDxManchester [Video file]*. Retrieved July 21, 2017, from YouTube: https://www.youtube.com/watch?v=MmfikLimeQ8&feature=youtu.be

Greenstreet, K. (n.d.). *Why small businesses fail (or fail to thrive and grow)*. (Passion For Business LLC, Small Business Coaching and Consulting) Retrieved October 31, 2017, from Passion for Business: http://www.passionforbusiness.com/articles/why-businesses-fail.htm

Grenny, J. (2017, April 20). *What to do about mediocrity on your team*. (Harvard Business School Publishing) Retrieved

October 20, 2017, from Harvard Business Review: https://hbr.org/2017/04/what-to-do-about-mediocrity-on-your-team

Griffith, E. (2014, September 25). *Why startups fail, according to their founders.* (Time Inc.) Retrieved September 30, 2017, from Fortune: http://fortune.com/2014/09/25/why-startups-fail-according-to-their-founders/

Griffiths, A. (2010). *101 secrets to building a winning business.* ReadHowYouWant.com.

Griffiths, S. (2015). *Self-efficacy in sport and exercise: Determining effort, persistence and performance.* Retrieved October 7, 2017, from BelievePerform: http://believeperform.com/performance/self-efficacy-sport-exercise-determining-effort-persistence-performance/

Grimshaw, J., Baron, G., Mike, B., & Edwards, N. (2006). How to combat a culture of excuses and promote accountability. *Strategy & Leadership, 34*(5), 11-18. doi: 10.1108/10878570610684793.

Grinnell, R. (2016, July 17). *Just-world hypothesis.* (Psych Central) Retrieved July 17, 2017, from Psych Central: https://psychcentral.com/encyclopedia/just-world-hypothesis/

Häfner, A., Obserst, V., & Stock, A. (2014, March 21). Avoiding procrastination through time management: An experimental interventuion study. *Educational Studies, 40*(3), 352-360. doi: 10.1080/03055698.2014.899487.

Haanaes, K. [. (2016, August 22). *Two reasons companies fail—and how to avoid them—Knut Haaanaes [YouTube video].* Retrieved July 25, 2017, from YouTube: https://www.youtube.com/watch?v=XVXmYD0UPRQ

Haislip, A. (2012, December 4). *Can you succeed through serendipity?* (Forbes Media, LLC) Retrieved September 26, 2017, from Forbes: https://www.forbes.com/sites/alexanderhaislip/2012/12/04/can-you-succeed-through-serendipity/#297654e66c14

Hale, E. (2012, June 18). *How your locus of control impacts business success*. (Mansuetto Ventures) Retrieved September 25, 2017, from Fast Company: https://www.fastcompany.com/1840496/how-your-locus-control-impacts-business-success

Hales, S. (2016). Why every theory of luck is wrong. *NOÛS, 50*(3), 490-508. doi: 10.1111/nous.12076.

Hales, S., & Johnson, J. (2014). Luck attributions and cognitive bias. *Metaphilosophy, 45*(4-5), 509–528. doi: 10.1111/meta.12098.

Halford, S. (2016, July 12). *The illusion of control: Letting go of anxiety when we have a choice*. (Oath, Inc.) Retrieved October 11, 2017, from Huffington Post: https://www.huffingtonpost.com/scott-halford/the-illusion-of-control-l_b_7781908.html

Hambrick, D. (2016, February 26). *The psychology of the breathtakingly stupid mistake*. (Nature America, Inc.) Retrieved October 4, 2017, from Scientific American: https://www.scientificamerican.com/article/the-psychology-of-the-breathtakingly-stupid-mistake/

Hamel, G. (2014, November 4). *Bureaucracy must die*. (Harvard Business Publishing) Retrieved September 21, 2017, from Harvard Business Review: https://hbr.org/2014/11/bureaucracy-must-die

Hamilton, B. (2014, August 10). *Watch out for the five hazards of growing too quickly*. (Forbes Media, LLC) Retrieved October 3, 2017, from Forbes: https://www.forbes.com/sites/sageworks/2014/08/10/five-hazards-of-growing-a-business-quickly/#173ae7c49804

Hand, D. (2016, September 6). *How to foster a no-blame culture*. (CEO Magazine) Retrieved July 25, 2017, from The CEO Magazine: http://www.theceomagazine.com/business/foster-no-blame-culture/

Hand, D. (2017, January 12). *The deceptions of luck*. (NautilusThink Inc.) Retrieved October 2, 2017, from

Nautilus: http://nautil.us/issue/44/luck/the-deceptions-of-luck

Hanin, Y. (2007). Chapter 2: Emotions in sport: Current issues and perspectives. In G. Tenenbaum, & R. Eklund, *Handbook of sport psychology* (pp. 31-57). John Wiley & Sons.

Hanson, J. [. (2017, March 17). *What is luck? [YouTube video].* Retrieved July 26, 2017, from YouTube: https://www.youtube.com/watch?v=JNBXaHT2ebE

Harke, B. (2014, April 7). *Failure is not an option.* (Oath, Inc.) Retrieved September 29, 2017, from Huffington Post: http://www.huffingtonpost.com/brian-harke/failure-is-not-an-option_1_b_4725169.html

Harper, D. (2017). *Procrastination.* Retrieved August 26, 2016, from Online Etymology Dictionary: http://www.etymonline.com/index.php?term=procrastination

Harper, D. (2017). *ruminate.* Retrieved September 19, 2017, from Online Etymology Dictionary: www.etymonline.com/index.php?term=ruminate

Harper, D. (n.d.). *Success.* Retrieved August 17, 2017, from Online Etymology Dictionary: http://www.etymonline.com/index.php?term=success

Harris, B. (2015, September 9). *The status of critical thinking in the workplace.* (Pearson) Retrieved October 20, 2017, from Pearson Education: https://www.pearsoned.com/the-status-of-critical-thinking-in-the-workplace/

Haselhuhn, M., Wong, E., & Ormiston, M. (2017). With great power comes shared responsibility: Psychological power and the delegation of authority. *Personality and Individual Differences, 108*, 1-4. doi: 10.1016/j.paid.2016.11.052.

Hassel, D. (2014, October 27). *Failure it's not an option. It's required.* (Entrepreneur Media, Inc.) Retrieved September 29, 2017, from Entrepreneur: https://www.entrepreneur.com/article/238925

Hatfield, R. (2017, August 13). *Difference between state and trait anxiety*. Retrieved September 14, 2017, from Livestrong Foundation: http://www.livestrong.com/article/98672-differences-between-state-anxiety-/

Heathfiled, S. (2017, July 7). *Top principles of employee empowerment*. (Dotdash) Retrieved October 14, 2017, from The Balance: https://www.thebalance.com/top-principles-of-employee-empowerment-1918658

Henderson, R. (2016, September 29). *How powerful is status quo bias?* (Sussex Publishers, LLC) Retrieved September 4, 2017, from Psychology Today: https://www.psychologytoday.com/blog/after-service/201609/how-powerful-is-status-quo-bias

Hendrikson, E. (2016, April 1). *How to ask for help*. (Macmillan Holdings) Retrieved October 5, 2017, from QuickAndDirtyTips.com: http://www.quickanddirtytips.com/health-fitness/mental-health/how-to-ask-for-help

Henry, J. [TEDx Talks]. (2015, May 4). *The theory of success-Jesse Hendry-TEDxFSU [Video file]*. Retrieved July 21, 2017, from YouTube: https://www.youtube.com/watch?v=hSnzeODH3lE&feature=youtu.be

Herbert, W. (2010, June 11). *How lucky checks really work*. Retrieved October 12, 2017, from Association for Psychological Science: https://www.psychologicalscience.org/news/were-only-human/how-lucky-charms-really-work.html

Herbert, W. (2013, December 18). *No fate! Or fate. What's your choice?* Retrieved October 10, 2017, from Association for Psychological Science: https://www.psychologicalscience.org/news/were-only-human/no-fate-or-fate-whats-your-choice.html

Hermanowickz, J. (2013). The culture of mediocrity. *Minerva, 51*, 363-367. doi: 10.1007/s11024-013-9231-0.

Herriott, J. (n.d.). *The true meaning of success.* Retrieved August 17, 2017, from Unity Worldwide Ministries: http://www.unity.org/resources/articles/true-meaning-success

Hess, M. (2013, March 6). *Think for yourself: The danger of blind obedience.* (CBS Interactive Inc.) Retrieved September 2, 2017, from Moneywatch: https://www.cbsnews.com/news/think-for-yourself-the-danger-of-blind-obedience/

Hewlett, S. (2009, July 7). *The altruistic Gen Y employee.* (Forbes Media, LLC) Retrieved October 14, 2017, from Forbes: https://www.forbes.com/2009/07/07/gen-y-volunteer-mentor-forbes-woman-leadership-community.html

Hoberecht, S. (2011, October 25). *Sharing the responsibility of leading: Employee engagement & shared leadership.* (Saybrook University) Retrieved October 2, 2017, from Saybrook University: https://www.saybrook.edu/blog/2011/10/25/sharing-responsibility-leading-employee-engagement-shared-leadership/

Hogan, M. (2016, March 15). *How leaders can encourage even the businest employees to take intiiative.* (Forbes Media, LLC) Retrieved October 20, 2017, from Forbes: https://www.forbes.com/sites/yec/2016/03/15/how-leaders-can-encourage-even-the-busiest-employees-to-take-initiative/#188d32394f38

Holland, C. (2008, August 4). *The staggering cost of procrastination.* (CBS News) Retrieved August 26, 2017, from Moneywatch: https://www.cbsnews.com/news/the-staggering-cost-of-procrastination/

Hotten, R. (2015, December 10). *Volkswagen: The scandal explained.* (British Broadcasting Corporation) Retrieved September 2, 2017, from BBC News: http://www.bbc.com/news/business-34324772

Hough, X. (2014, December 8). *Is learned helplessness killing your company?* Retrieved September 27, 2017, from LinkedIn: https://www.linkedin.com/pulse/20141208152748-42650741-is-learned-helplessness-killing-your-company

Huebsch, R. (n.d.). *Cash flow problems in a business.* (Hearst Newspapers, LLC) Retrieved October 3, 2017, from Houston Chronicle: http://smallbusiness.chron.com/cash-flow-problems-business-4916.html

Hugos, M. (2009, March 4). *Hard times bring malicious obedience [When we really need bsuiness agility].* (IDG Communications, Inc.) Retrieved September 2, 2017, from CIO: https://www.cio.com/article/2373073/it-organization/hard-times-bring-malicious-obedience--when-we-really-need-business-agility-.html

Hurd, M. (2014, October 11). *What really causes success?* (Michael J. Hurd) Retrieved July 21, 2017, from Dr. Hurd: https://drhurd.com/2014/10/11/49081/

Hurd, M. (2017, March 25). *The psychology of complacency.* Retrieved October 7, 2017, from DrHurd.com: https://drhurd.com/2017/03/25/63474/

Hutson, M. (2012, April 6). *In defense of superstition.* (The New York Times Company) Retrieved October 12, 2017, from The New York Times: https://mobile.nytimes.com/2012/04/08/opinion/sunday/in-defense-of-superstition.html

Indiana University. (2010, October 6). *Algortihms and heuristics.* (The Trustees of Indiana University) Retrieved October 11, 2017, from Indiana University: http://www.indiana.edu/~p1013447/dictionary/alg_heur.htm

International Civil Aviation Organization. (2006). *Directors general of civil avaiation conference on a global strategy for aviation safety [Working paper].* International Civil Aviation Organization. Montréal: International Civil Aviation Organization.

Iny, D. (2016, November 8). *What science says about going outside your comfort zone.* (Mansuetto Ventures) Retrieved July 27, 2017, from Inc.: https://www.inc.com/danny-iny/what-science-says-about-going-outside-your-comfort-zone.html

Iqbal, J. (2007, July-December). Why managers don't delegate and how to get them to do so? *The Journal of Managerial Sicences, 1*(2), 57-73.

IU Bloomington Newsroom. (2016, October 17). *Worked to death? IU study says lack of control over high-stress jobs can lead to early grave.* (The Trustees of Indiana University) Retrieved October 2, 2017, from IU Bloomington Newsroom: http://archive.news.indiana.edu/releases/iu/2016/10/worked-to-death-job-control-mortality.shtml

Ivtzan, I., Lomas, T., Hefferon, K., & Worth, P. (2015). Chapter 8: The hero's journey. In *Second wave positive psychology: Embracing the dark side of life* (pp. 175-196). New York, New York: Routledge.

J., D. (2008, July 1). *Improve your mind-reading: Focus on the big picture you.* Retrieved October 5, 2017, from Psyblog: http://www.spring.org.uk/2008/07/improve-your-mind-reading-focus-on-big.php

Jackson, S., & Csikszentmihalyi, M. (1999). Chapter 3: Finding your skills balance. In *Flow in sports* (pp. 35-62). Human Kinetics.

Jacobs, T. (2014, February 12). *Belief in fate: A way to avoid making tough decisions?* (The Social Justice Foundation) Retrieved October 10, 2017, from Pacific Standard: https://psmag.com/social-justice/belief-fate-way-avoid-tough-decisions-74566

Jaffe, E. (2013, March 29). *Why wait? The science behind procrastination.* (Association for Psychological Science) Retrieved July 23, 2017, from Association for Psychological Science:

http://www.psychologicalscience.org/observer/why-wait-the-science-behind-procrastination

Jenkin, M. (2014, December 19). *Do entrepreneurs make their own luck?* (Guardian News and Media Limited) Retrieved July 26, 2017, from The Guardian: https://www.theguardian.com/small-business-network/2014/dec/19/success-business-down-to-chance

Jenkins, A., Brundin, E., & Wiklund, J. (2010). Grief or relief? Emotional responses to firm failure. *Frontiers of Entrepreneurial Research*, 1-15.

Johnston, K. (n.d.). *Personal responsibility in business.* (Hearst Newspapers, LLC) Retrieved July 25, 2017, from Houston Chronicle: http://smallbusiness.chron.com/personal-responsibility-business-62169.html

Jolly, C. (2016, October 1). *Complacency and mediocrity.* Retrieved October 7, 2017, from The Sun: http://sundominica.com/articles/complacency-and-mediocrity-3837/

Jones, R., & Jones, E. (1964). Optimum conformity as an ingratiation tactic. *Journal of Personality, 32*(3), 436–458.

Joseph, C. (n.d.). *What are positive impacts of change in business?* (Hearst Newspapers, LLC) Retrieved October 18, 2017, from Houston Chronicle: http://smallbusiness.chron.com/positive-impacts-change-business-559.html

Jost, J. (2015). Resistance to change: A social psychological perspective [In press]. *Social Research: An International Quarterly*.

Judge, T., & Kammeyer-Mueller, J. (2012). On the value of aiming high: The causes and consequences of ambition. *Journal of Applied Psychology, 97*(4), 758-775. doi: 10.1037/a0028084.

Judge, T., Higgins, C., Thoresen, C., & Barrick, M. (1999). The big five personality traits, general mental ability, and career success <u>accross</u> the life span. *Personnel Psychology, 52*(3), 621-652. doi: 10.1111/j.1744-6570.1999.tb00174.x.

Jun, P. (2017, May 15). *The real meaning of success.* Retrieved August 17, 2017, from Lifehacker: http://www.lifehack.org/articles/work/the-true-meaning-of-success.html

Junn, J. (2016, August 19). *Failed but not finished: Dealing with the social stigma of entrepreneurial failure.* Retrieved October 3, 2017, from Idealog: http://idealog.co.nz/venture/2016/08/failed-not-finished-dealing-social-stogma-entreprenuerial-failure

Kahneman, D., & Tversky, A. (1973, July). On the psychology of prediction. *Psychological review, 80*(4), 237-351.

Kalis, A., Mojzisch, A., Schweizer, T., & Kaiser, S. (2008). Weakness of will, akrasia, and the neuropsychiatry of decision making: An interdisciplinary perspective. *Cognitive, Affective, & Behavioral Neuroscience, 8*(4), 402-417. doi: 10.3758/CABN.8.4.402.

Kamenetz, A. (2012, December 11). *How a culture of fear can damage your organization.* (Mansuetto Ventures) Retrieved September 21, 2017, from Fast Company: https://www.fastcompany.com/3023313/how-a-culture-of-fear-can-damage-your-organization

Kapur, M. (2014). Productive failure in learning math. *Cognitive Science, 38*, 1008-1022. doi: 10.1111/cogs.12107.

Karbasfrooshan, A. (2006, February 1). *5 ways to avoid complacency.* Retrieved October 19, 2017, from Askmen: https://www.askmen.com/money/professional_60/80_professional_life.html

Karlen, N. (2013, June 14). *What to do about a workplace culture of blame.* (TechWell Corp.) Retrieved September 21, 2017, from Techwell: https://www.techwell.com/techwell-insights/2013/06/what-do-about-workplace-culture-blame

Karmin, A. (2015). *Good enough: Do you take excessive responsibility?* (Psych Central) Retrieved September 26, 2017, from Psych Central: https://blogs.psychcentral.com/anger/2014/02/good-enough-do-you-take-excessive-responsibility/

Kaya, Ç., Uğur, E., Sar, H., & Ercengiz, M. (2017, May). Self-handicapping and irrational beliefs about approval in a sample of teacher candidates. *Castamonu Education Journal, 25*(3), 869-880.

Kelman, H. (1958). Compliance, identification, and internalization: Three processes of attitude change. *Journal of Conflict Resolution*, 51-60.

Kennon, J. (2016, June 3). *What is opportunity cost?* Retrieved October 3, 2017, from The Balance: https://www.thebalance.com/what-is-opportunity-cost-357200

Kerr, B., Godfrey-Smith, P., & Feldman, M. (2004, March). What is altruism? *Trends in Ecology and Evolution, 19*(3), 135–140. doi: 10.1016/j.tree.2003.10.004.

Khazan, O. [. (2016, October 6). *The cognitive science behind repeating mistakes [Video file].* Retrieved July 25, 2017, from YouTube: https://www.youtube.com/watch?v=y4Uejjv_iBQ

Khodarahimi, S., & Pole, N. (2009). Cognitive behavior therapy and worry reduction in an outpatient with generalized anxiety disorder. *Clinical Case Studies, 9*(53), 53-62. doi: 10.1177/1534650109351306.

Kiesel, L. (2015, February 9). *Men and women define success differently—and not everyone bases it on money.* (Business Insider, Inc.) Retrieved August 19, 2017, from Business Insider: http://www.businessinsider.com/men-and-women-define-success-differently-and-not-everyone-bases-it-on-money-2015-2

Kiisel, T. (2013, July 12). *Preparation + opportunity = success.* Retrieved July 26, 2017, from Lendio:

https://www.lendio.com/blog/preparation-opportunity-success/

Kilburn, E., & Whitlock, J. (n.d.). *Coping: Literature review [PDF document]*. Retrieved from Self-injury and recovery research and resources.

Kilduff, G., Elfenbein, H., & Staw, B. (2010). The psychology of rivalry: A relationally dependent analysis of competition. *Academy of Management Journal, 53*(5), 943-969.

King, M. (2016, July 25). *Time*. (Time, Inc.) Retrieved September 21, 2017, from 5 signs you're not playing the political game at work: http://time.com/money/4421661/playing-office-politics/

Kingston, R. (2013, October). Why do people worry and ruminate? Investigating factors that maintain repetitive negative thought.

Knaus, W. (2017, January 30). *How fear of failure feeds procrastination*. Retrieved August 28, 2017, from New Harbinger Publications: https://www.newharbinger.com/blog/how-fear-failure-feeds-procrastination

Knight, R. (2015, August 2). *How to overcome burnout and stay motivated*. (Harvard Business School Publishing) Retrieved October 2, 2017, from Harvard Business Review: https://hbr.org/2015/04/how-to-overcome-burnout-and-stay-motivated

Koestenbaum, P. (2001). Looking back and looking to the future: The growing role of personal responsibility. *Journal for Quality and Participation, 24*(4), 6-11.

Kohut, A., Wise, R., Horowitz, J., Poushter, J., & Barker, C. (2011). *The American-Western European values gap*. Pew Research Project, Pew Global Attitudes Project. Washington: Pew Charitable Trusts.

Konatham, S. (2017, March 24). *The importance of personal development in life*. (Hyderabad Media House Limited/The Hans India) Retrieved OCTOBER 20, 2017, from The Hans India:

http://www.thehansindia.com/posts/index/Education-&-Careers/2017-03-24/The-importance-of-personal-development-in-life-/288677

Konnikova, M. (2012, February 26). *Why are we so afraid of creativity.* (Nature America, Inc.) Retrieved September 6, 2017, from Scientific American: https://blogs.scientificamerican.com/literally-psyched/why-are-we-so-afraid-of-creativity/

Konnikova, M. (2014, July 22). *Getting over procrastination.* (Condé Nast) Retrieved August 26, 2017, from The New Yorker: https://www.newyorker.com/science/maria-konnikova/a-procrastination-gene

Konovsky, M., & Jaster, F. J. (1989). "Blaming the victim" and other ways business men and women account for questionable behavior. *Journal of Business Ethics, 8*(5), 391–398.

Korkkijuly, P. (2010, July 17). *The true calling that wasn't.* (The New York Times Company) Retrieved October 20, 2017, from The New York Times: http://www.nytimes.com/2010/07/18/jobs/18search.html

Kotter, J., & Schesinger, L. (2008, July-August). *Choosing strategies for change.* (Harvard Business School Publishing) Retrieved October 7, 2017, from Harvard Business Review: https://hbr.org/2008/07/choosing-strategies-for-change

Koval, C., Fitzsimons, G., vanDellen, M., & Ranby, K. (2015). The burden of responsibility: Interpersonal costs of high self-control. *Journal of Personality and Social Psychology, 108*(5), 750-766. doi: 10.1037/pspi0000015.

Krishnen, S. (2016, November 4). *Why entreprenenurs need mentors and how to find them.* (Entrepreneur Media, LLC) Retrieved October 6, 2017, from Entrepreneur: https://www.entrepreneur.com/article/250625

Kruger, J. (2016, September 18). *Self-enhancement in a small world.* (Sussex Publishers, LLC) Retrieved October 13, 2017, from Psychology Today:

https://www.psychologytoday.com/blog/one-among-many/201609/self-enhancement-in-small-world

Kulaga, J. (2015, December 24). *Why ruminating hurts success and how to handle those thoughts.* (Forbes Meida, LLC) Retrieved August 28, 2017, from Forbes: https://www.forbes.com/sites/womensmedia/2015/12/24/why-ruminating-hurts-success-and-how-to-hurdle-those-thoughts/#4603f51112b1

Kumar, A., & Kaushal, S. (2017, June). Procratination among government and private secondary school teachers. *International Journal of Information Research and Review, 4*(6), 4222-4224.

La Vertu, C. (2017). *Giraffenecksoup.* Claude La Vertu Media.

LaBier, D. (2012, May 2). *Why today's workplace creates emotional conflicts: The dark side of success.* (Oath, Inc.) Retrieved August 17, 2017, from Huffington Post.

Lai, C., Altavilla, D., Ronconi, A., & Aceto, P. (2016). Fear of missing out (FOMO) is associated with activation of the right middle temporal gyrus during inclusion social cue. *Computers in Human Behavior, 61*, 516-521. doi: 10.1016/j.chb.2016.03.072.

Lair, D., Sullivan, K., & Cheney, G. (2005, February). Marketization and the recasting of the professional self: The rhetoric and ethics of personal branding. *Management Communication Quarterly, 18*(3), 307-343. doi: 10.1177/0893318904270744.

Lam, B. (2015, May 22). *Being a go-getter is no fun.* (Atlantic Media) Retrieved July 25, 2017, from The Atlantic: https://www.theatlantic.com/business/archive/2015/05/being-a-go-getter-is-no-fun/393863/

Landry, M. (2012, December). The fine art of delegation. *PM Network*, 54-59.

Langens, T., & Schüler, J. (2005). Written emotional expression and emotional well-being: The moderating role of fear of rejection . *Society for Personality and Social Psychology, 31*(6), 818-830. doi: 10.1177/0146167204271556.

Langer, E. (1975). The illusion of control. *Journal of Personality and Social Pyschology, 32*(2), 311-328.

Lanthier, T. (2016). The role of self-assessment in your personal success. *Access, 30*(2), 14-15.

Lau, R. (2009). The contemporary culture of blame and the fetishization of the modernist mentality [Working paper]. *Current Sociology, 57*(5), 661-663.

Lauer, C. (2005, July). The allure of toxic leaders by Jean Lipman-Blumen. *Speed Reviews of New and Noteworthy Books for Business Executives.*

Lay, C. (1986). At last, my research on procrastination. *Journal of Research in Personality, 20,* 474-495.

Leahy, R. (2009, March 30). *Sixth week: How to use your emotions rather than worry about them.* (Sussex Publishers, LLC) Retrieved September 18, 2017, from Psychology Today: https://www.psychologytoday.com/blog/anxiety-files/200903/sixth-week-how-use-your-emotions-rather-worry-about-them

Leahy, R. (2010). Chapter 7: "Yeah, but what if:" Generalized anxiety disorder. In *Anxiety free: Unravel your fears before they unravel you, second edition* (2nd edition ed., pp. 234-283). Hay House.

Leal, P., Goes, T., Ferreira, L., & Teixeira-Silva, F. (2017, August 14). Trait vs. state anxiety in different threatening situations. *Trends in Psychiatry and Psychotherapy,* https://dx.doi.org/10.1590/2237-6089-2016-0044.

Lebowitz, S. (2017, March 22). *12 rich, powerful people share their surprising definitions of success.* (Business Insider, Inc) Retrieved July 21, 2017, from Business Insider: http://www.businessinsider.com/how-successful-people-define-success-2017-3#xxri=4

Lee, C., Lumpkin, G., & Bangar, R. (2015). The impact of stigma of failure on social entrepreneurship entry decisions: A cross-country analysis. *Frontiers of Entrepreneurship Research, 15*(1), 358-363.

Lehmann, J. (2015, December 7). *What is the meaning of success?* (Forbes Media, LLC) Retrieved August 17, 2017, from Forbes: https://www.forbes.com/sites/jplehmann/2015/12/07/what-is-the-meaning-of-success/#2754af214205

Levett-Jones, T., & Lathlean, J. (2009). "Don't rock the boat:" Nursing students' experiences of conformity and compliance. *Nurse Education Today, 29*, 342-349. doi: 10.1016/j.nedt.2008.10.009.

Levy, N. (2012, February 6). *Explainer: Does luck exist?* (The Conversation US, Inc.) Retrieved October 10, 2017, from The Conversation: http://theconversation.com/explainer-does-luck-exist-5139

Lewis, S., Holton, A., & & Coddington, M. (2017). 10: From participation to reciprocity in the journalist-audience relationship. In C. Peters, & M. Broersma, *Rethinking journalism again: Societal role and public relevance in a digital age* (pp. 161-175). New York: Routledge.

Leyboun, E. (2016, January 14). *#noprojects–Outcomes: The value of change.* (C4Media Inc.) Retrieved July 27, 2017, from Infoq: https://www.infoq.com/articles/noprojects3-value-change

Lilly, F. (2017, February 6). *The road to success after failure.* Retrieved July 25, 2017, from LinkedIn: https://www.linkedin.com/pulse/road-success-after-failure-friday-lilly

Lindner, J. (1998, June). Understanding employee motivation. *Journal of Extension, 36*(3).

Linley, P., & Maltby, J. (2009). Personal responsibility. In S. Lopez (Ed.), *The encyclopedia of positive psychology.* John Wiley & Sons.

Lipshitz, R., & Strauss, O. (1997, February). Coping with uncertainty: A naturalistic decision-making analysis. *Organizatonal Behavior and Human Decision Processes, 69*(2), 149-163.

Livni, E. (2016, October 30). *The career benefits of being a noncomformist*. (Atlantic Media) Retrieved July 24, 2017, from Quartz: https://qz.com/820111/to-jumpstart-your-career-dont-exceed-expectations-rebel-against-them/

Llopis, G. (2011, January 17). *How distrust, indifference and lack of integrity will destroy our business*. (Forbes Media, LLC) Retrieved October 18, 2017, from Forbes: https://www.forbes.com/sites/glennllopis/2011/01/17/how-distrust-indifference-and-lack-of-integrity-will-destroy-your-business/amp/

Llopis, G. (2013, July 8). *10 signs your employees are growing complacent in their careers*. (Forbes Media, LLC) Retrieved July 28, 2017, from Forbes: https://www.forbes.com/sites/glennllopis/2013/07/08/10-signs-your-employees-are-growing-complacent-in-their-careers/amp/

Llopis, G. (2016, October 20). *Leaders that grow complacent leave chaos in their wake*. (Fox News Network, LLC) Retrieved October 9, 2017, from Fox News: http://www.foxnews.com/us/2016/10/20/leaders-that-grow-complacent-leave-chaos-in-their-wake.html

Llopis, G. (2016, August 29). *Three strategies to break free from complacency*. (Forbes Media, LLC) Retrieved July 28, 2017, from Forbes: https://www.forbes.com/sites/glennllopis/2016/08/29/three-strategies-to-break-free-from-complacency/#2125c6453d13

Lloyd, S. (n.d.). *Managers must delegate effectively to develop employees*. Retrieved July 26, 2017, from Society for Human Resource Management: https://www.shrm.org/resourcesandtools/hr-topics/organizational-and-employee-development/pages/delegateeffectively.aspx

Loehr, J. (2008). Three: Old stories. In *The power of story: Change your story, change your Destiny in business and in life* (pp. 68-85). Simon and Schuster.

Lohr, S. (2007, December 20). *Is information overload a $650 billion drag on the economy*. (The New York Times Company) Retrieved August 26, 2017, from The New York Times: https://bits.blogs.nytimes.com/2007/12/20/is-information-overload-a-650-billion-drag-on-the-economy/?ref=technology

Lord, K., Lee, M., & Choong, P. (2001). Differences in normative and informational social influence. *NA-Advances in Consumer Research, 28*, 280-285.

Loveless, P. (2015, November 17). *Employee engagement: Are your happy workers disengaged*. (DVV Media international) Retrieved October 20, 2017, from Personnel Today: http://www.personneltoday.com/hr/employee-engagement-are-your-happy-workers-disengaged/

Lucas, S. (2011, August 15). *Scientific proof that micro-management is bad for your company (and how to fix it)*. (CBS Interactive, Inc.) Retrieved October 14, 2017, from MoneyWatch: https://www.cbsnews.com/news/scientific-proof-that-micro-management-is-bad-for-your-company-and-how-to-fix-it/

Lunenburg, F. (2011). Self-efficacy in the workplace: Implications for motivation and performance. *International Journal of Management, Business, and Administration, 14*(1), 1-6.

Lush, M. [. (2016, January 29). *How to achieve a blame-free culture [YouTube]*. Retrieved July 25, 2017, from YouTube: https://www.youtube.com/watch?v=z6XjwraVFiU

Lyubomirsky, S., King, L., & Diener, E. (2005). The benefits of frequent positive affect: Does happiness lead to success? *Psychological Bulletin, 131*(6), 803-855. doi: 10.1037/0033-2909.131.6.803.

Lyubomirsky, S., Tucker, K., Caldwell, N., & Berg, K. (1999). Why ruminators are poor problem solvers: Clues from the phenomenology of dysphoric rumination. *Journal of Personality and Social Psychology, 77*(5), 1041-1060.

Macaro, A., & Baggini, J. (2013, October 25). *The shrink & the sage: How important is luck?* (The Financial Times Ltd.) Retrieved September 26, 2017, from Finanical Times: https://www.ft.com/content/d30e4dfc-373a-11e3-9603-00144feab7de

MacDonald, A. (1970). Revised scale for ambiguity tolerance: Reliability and validity. *Psychological Reports, 26*, 791-796.

MacDonald, L. (n.d.). *Examples of enlightened self-interest in business*. (Hearst Newspapers, LLC) Retrieved October 17, 2017, from Houston Chronicle: http://smallbusiness.chron.com/examples-enlightened-selfinterest-business-22880.html

Mack, S. (n.d.). *How to handle an employee who doesn't take intiiative*. (Hearst Newspapers, LLC) Retrieved October 20, 2017, from Houston Chronicle: http://smallbusiness.chron.com/handle-employee-doesnt-initiative-23809.html

Madon, S., Willard, J., Guyll, M., & Scherr, K. (2011). Self-fulfilling prophecies: Mechanisms, power, and links to social problems. *Social and Personality Psychology Compass, 5*(8), 578-590. doi: 10.1111/j.1751-9004.2011.00375.x.

Madrigal, A. (2011, September 27). *Why WD-40 is called WD-40*. (The Atlantic Monthly Group) Retrieved October 26, 2017, from The Atlantic: https://www.theatlantic.com/technology/archive/2011/09/why-wd-40-is-called-wd-40/245734/

Magazine. (2011, April 6). *Why do we believe in luck?* (British Broadcasting Corporation) Retrieved July 26, 2017, from BBC: http://www.bbc.com/news/magazine-12934253

Maltby, J., Day, L., Gill, P., Colley, A., & Wood, A. (2008). Beliefs around luck: Confirming the empirical conceptualization of beliefs around luck and the development of the Darke and Freedman beliefs around luck scale. *Personality and Individual Differences, 65,* 655–660. doi: doi:10.1016/j.paid.2008.07.010.

Marconi, F. (2016, July 12). *Success is not a matter of luck—it's an algorithm.* (NBC Universal) Retrieved October 11, 2017, from CNBC: https://www.cnbc.com/2016/07/12/success-is-not-a-matter-of-luck-its-an-algorithm-commentary.html

Markman, A. (2017, February 22). *"Poor communication" is often a symptom of a different problem.* (Harvard Business Publishing) Retrieved September 21, 2017, from Harvard Business Review: https://hbr.org/2017/02/poor-communication-is-often-a-symptom-of-a-different-problem

Marlin, L. (2010, August 23). *You CAN stop worrying: How to train your brain to kick the habit.* (Associated Newspapers Ltd) Retrieved September 18, 2017, from The Daily Mail: http://www.dailymail.co.uk/femail/article-1305297/You-CAN-stop-worrying-How-train-brain-kick-habit.html#ixzz4t36vksyK

Martini, F. (2013). *The influence of active procrastination and passive procrastination on university students' education and success in college.* Glassboro, NJ: Rowan University.

Martins, P., Rosado, A., Ferreira, V., & Biscaia, R. (2017, June 22). Personal and social responsibility among athletes: The role of self-determination, achievement goals and engagement. *Journal of Human Kinetics, 57,* 39-50. doi: 10.1515/hukin-2017-0045.

Mask, C. (2014, November 4). *The 4 reasons why people start their own businesses.* (American City Business Journals) Retrieved September 29, 2017, from The Business Journals: https://www.bizjournals.com/bizjournals/how-to/growth-strategies/2014/11/4-reasons-why-people-start-their-own-businesses.html

Maslach, C. (2003). Job burnout. *New Directions in Research and Intervention, 12*(5), 189-192.

Mastroianni, K., & Storberg-Walker, J. (2014). Do work relationships matter? Characteristics of workplace interactions that enhance or detract from employee perceptions of well-being and health behaviors. *Health Psychology and Behavioural Medicine, 2*(1), 798-819. doi: 10.1080/21642850.2014.933343.

McCrea, S. (2008). Self-handicapping, excuse making, and counterfactual thinking: consequences for self-esteem and future motivation. *Journal of Personality and Social Psychology, 2*, 274-292. doi: 10.1037/0022-3514.95.2.274.

McKay, B., & McKay, K. (2010, February 23). *Leadership: The importance of knowing how to delegate.* Retrieved October 2, 2017, from The Art of Manliness: http://www.artofmanliness.com/2010/02/23/leadership-the-importance-of-knowing-how-to-delegate/

McKenna, E. (2001). Human information processing. In *Business psychology and organisational behaviour: A student's handbook, third edition* (3rd Edition ed., pp. 212-245). New York: Psychology Press.

McKinniss, C., & Natella, A. (1994). Chapter 4: First impressions. In *Business in Mexico: Managerial behavior, protocol, and etiquette* (pp. 57-68). Binghamton, NY: The Haworth Press.

McLain, D., Kefallonitis, E., & Armani, K. (2015). Ambiguity tolerance in organizations: Definitional clarification and perspectives on future research . *Frontiers in Psychology, 6*(344), doi: 10.3389/fpsyg.2015.00344.

McLaughlin, K., Menin, D., & Farach, F. (2007). The contributory role of worry in emotion generation and dysregulation in generalized anxiety disorder. *Behaviour Research and Therapy, 45*, 1735-1752. doi: 10.1016/j.brat.2006.12.004.

McLeod, L. (2011, July 22). *Self-enhancing bias: Why so many people won't acknowledge external factors in their success*. (Oath, Inc.) Retrieved October 13, 2017, from Huffington Post: https://www.huffingtonpost.com/lisa-earle-mcleod/self-enhancing-bias_b_856686.html

McLeod, S. (2008). *Asch experiment*. Retrieved August 29, 2017, from Simply Psychology: https://www.simplypsychology.org/asch-conformity.html

McLeod, S. (2012). *Attribution theory*. Retrieved October 9, 2017, from Simply Psychology: https://www.simplypsychology.org/attribution-theory.html

McLeod, S. (2016). *What is conformity?* Retrieved July 23, 2017, from Simply Psychology: https://www.simplypsychology.org/conformity.html

McPherson, C., Wilson, K., Lobchuk, M., & Brajtman, S. (2007). Self-perceived burden to others: Patient and, family caregiver correlates. *Journal of Palliative Care, 23*(3), 135-142.

Medvec, V., Madey, S., & Gilovich, T. (1995, October). When less is more: Counterfactual thinking and satisfaction among Olympic medalists. *Journal of Personality and Social Psychology, 69*(4), 603–610.

Meinert, D. (2015, December 1). *How to change a culture of fear*. (Society for Human Resource Management) Retrieved September 22, 2017, from Society for Human Resource Management: https://www.shrm.org/hr-today/news/hr-magazine/pages/0116-execbrief.aspx

Mello, T. (2017, March 2). *Managing your anxiety throughout the rollercoaster of entrepreneurship*. (Forbes Media, LLC) Retrieved September 14, 2017, from Forbes: https://www.forbes.com/sites/theyec/2017/03/02/managing-your-anxiety-throughout-the-rollercoaster-of-entrepreneurship/#1c9877a82cb5

Mellorate. (2015, February 11). *Killed by a corporate culture of complacency*. Retrieved October 7, 2017, from

torbenrick.eu:
https://www.torbenrick.eu/blog/culture/killed-by-a-
corporate-culture-of-complacency/

Menges, L. (2017, January). The emotion account of blame. *Philosophical Studies, 174*(1), 257-273. doi: 10.1007/s11098-016-0680-9.

Meninger, K. (2016, November 8). *Are you too self-reliant at work?* (Executive Career Success, LLC) Retrieved October 6, 2017, from Executive Career Success: http://executivecareersuccess.com/self-reliant-work/

Menon, S. (2001). Employee empowerment: An integrative psychological approach. *Applied Psychology: An international review, 50*(1), 153-180. doi: 10.1111/1464-0597.00052.

Metcalfe, J., & Dunlosky, J. (2008). Metamemory. In H. Roediger (Ed.), *Learning and memory: A comprehensive reference* (pp. 349-362). Oxford: Elsevier.

Meyer, J., Becker, T., & Vandenberghe, C. (2004). Employee commitment and motivation: A conceptual analysis and integrative model. *Journal of Applied Psychology, 89*(6), 991-1007. doi: 10.1037/0021-9010.89.6.991.

Meyer, S. (2014, July 3). *A poker champion explains why you make bad business decisions*. (Forbes Media, LLC) Retrieved October 26, 2017, from Forbes: https://www.forbes.com/sites/stevemeyer/2014/06/03/a-poker-champion-explains-why-you-make-bad-business-decisions/

Michael, A. (2006). *Mentoring and coaching: Topic gateway series no. 50 [PDF document].* Association of International Certified Professional Accountants, The Chartered Institute of Management Accountants. London: The Chartered Institute of Management Accountants.

Michel, A. (2015, February). *Burnout and the brain.* Retrieved October 14, 2017, from Association for Psychological Science:

https://www.psychologicalscience.org/observer/burnout-and-the-brain

Milgram, S. (1963). Behavioral study of obedience. *Journal of Abnormal and Social Psychology, 67*(4), 371-378.

Miller, B. [. (2014, October 14). *Locus of control, learned helplessness, and the tyranny of choice-Khan Academy [Video file].* Retrieved July 25, 2017, from YouTube: https://www.youtube.com/watch?v=Vx1dnPMPhl0

Molinaro, V. (2016, September 8). *Gut check: Are you doing way too much in your leadership role?* Retrieved July 25, 2017, from Vince Molinaro: http://theleadershipcontract.com/2016/09/08/gut-check-are-you-doing-way-too-much-in-your-leadership-role/

Molinsky, A. (2016, June 29). *If you're not outside your comfort zone, you won't learn anything.* (Harvard Business School Publishing) Retrieved July 27, 2017, from Harvard Business Review: https://hbr.org/2016/07/if-youre-not-outside-your-comfort-zone-you-wont-learn-anything

Molm, L., Schaefer, D., & Collett, J. (2007). The value of reciprocity. *Social Psychology Quaterly, 70*(2), 199-217.

Mooney, L. (n.d.). *Benefits from change in the workplace.* (Hearst Newspapers, LLC) Retrieved October 18, 2017, from Houston Chronicle: http://smallbusiness.chron.com/benefits-change-workplace-13255.html

Moore, D., & Loewenstein, G. (2004, June). Self-interest, automaticity, and the psychology of conflict of interest. *Social Justice Research, 17*(2), 189-202.

Morin, A. (2014, July 18). *The 8 myths about emotions that are holding us back.* (Forbes Media, LLC) Retrieved October 6, 2017, from Forbes: https://www.forbes.com/sites/amymorin/2014/07/18/the-8-myths-about-emotions-that-are-holding-us-back/#7004dd3e4eb4

Moss, S. (2016, July 5). *Engagement at work.* Retrieved September 4, 2017, from Sicotests: http://www.sicotests.com/psyarticle.asp?id=345

Moss, S. (2016, July 7). *The planning fallacy.* Retrieved August 26, 2017, from Sicotests: http://www.sicotests.com/psyarticle.asp?id=385

Mueller, B., & Shepherd, D. (2016). Making the most of failure experiences: Exploring the relationship between business failure and the identification of business opporutnities. *Entrepeneurship Theory & Practice, 40*(3), 457–487. doi: 10.1111/etap.12116.

Mueller, D. [Veritasium]. (2010, October 12). *Learned helplessness [Video file].* Retrieved July 25, 2017, from YouTube: https://www.youtube.com/watch?v=z6XjwraVFiU

Mueller, J., Melwani, S., & Goncalo, J. (2012). The bias against creativity: Why people desire but reject creative ideas. *Psychological Science, 23*(1), 13-17. doi: 10.1177/0956797611421018.

Mueller, S. (2017, March 30). *The meaning of success and how to define success in life.* Retrieved July 21, 2017, from Planet of Success: http://www.planetofsuccess.com/blog/2010/accomplishm ent-the-meaning-of-success-and-how-to-define-success-in-life/

Munyikwa, Z. (2013, April 30). *An in-depth look at fads.* (Duke University) Retrieved October 19, 2017, from Surprise Endings: Social Science and Literature ISIS/ENG 390-S taught by Professors Dan Ariely and Cathy Davidson: https://sites.duke.edu/english390-5_01_s2013/2013/04/30/an-in-depth-look-at-fads/

Murphy, M. (2017, March 12). *The secret fear that causes bosses to micromanage.* (Forbes Media, LLC) Retrieved October 2, 2017, from Forbes: https://www.forbes.com/sites/markmurphy/2017/03/12/th e-secret-fear-that-causes-bosses-to-micromanage/

Murray Law, B. (2005, November). *Probing the depression-rumination cycle.* Retrieved September 19, 2017, from American Psychological Association: http://www.apa.org/monitor/nov05/cycle.aspx

Myers, C. (2016, February 6). *An entrepreneur's guide to managing anxiety.* (Forbes Media, LLC) Retrieved July 24, 2017, from Forbes: https://www.forbes.com/sites/chrismyers/2016/02/08/an-entrepreneurs-guide-to-managing-anxiety/#60c7a1e74b9b

Myers, D. G. (2011). *Psychology, ninth edition.* New York, NY: Worth Publishers.

Narvacan, N., Atienza-Bulaqueña, E., & Evangelista, L. (2014, April). Effects of visualization on academic performance of college students. *International Journal of Information and Education Technology, 4*(2), 156-160. doi: 10.7763/IJIET.2014.V4.389.

Nelson, B. (n.d.). *How to involve employees and encouraging initiative.* (John Wiley & Sons) Retrieved October 20, 2017, from Dummies: http://www.dummies.com/business/human-resources/employee-relations/how-to-involve-employees-and-encouraging-initiative/

Nemaenzhe, P. (2011). Retrospective analysis of failure causes in South African small businesses.

Nevid, J. (2017, March 3). *Worry and guilt: The useless emotions.* (Sussex Publishers, LLC) Retrieved July 24, 2017, from Psychology Today: https://www.psychologytoday.com/blog/the-minute-therapist/201703/worry-and-guilt-the-useless-emotions

Newark, D. (2013, December). *Need someone's help? Ask the person who just turned you down.* (Harvard Business School Publishing) Retrieved October 14, 2017, from Harvard Business Review: https://hbr.org/2013/12/need-someones-help-ask-the-person-who-just-turned-you-down

Newman, M., Llera, S., Erickson, T., Przeworski, A., & Castonguay, L. (2013). Worry and generalized anxiety disorder: A review and theoretical synthesis of evidence on nature, etiology, mechanisms, and treatment. *Annual Review of Clinical Psychology, 9*, 275-297. doi: 10.1146/annurev-clinpsy-050212-185544 .

Ngah, R., & Salleh, Z. (2015). Emotional intelligence and entrepeneur's innovativeness toward entrepeneurial success: A preliminary study. *American Journal of Economics, 5*(2), 285-290. doi: 10.5923/c.economics.201501.37.

Niemand, T. (n.d.). 7 deadly sins of business owners: Flying solo for too long. *Finweek*, 53.

Nolen-Hoeksema, S. (2000). The role of rumination in depressive disorders and mixed anxiety/depressive symptoms. *Journal of Abnormal Psychology, 109*(3), 504-511.

Nolen-Hoeksema, S., & Larson, J. (1999). Chapter 3: Coping and personality. In S. Nolen-Hoeksema, & J. Larson, *Coping with Loss* (pp. 61-83). Mahwah, New Jersey: Lawrence Erlbaum Associates Publishers.

Nolen-Hoeksema, S., Wisco, B., & Lyubimorsky, S. (2008). Rethinking rumination. *Perspectives on Psychological Science, 3*, 400-424. doi: 10.1111/j.1745-6924.2008.00088.x.

Norbutus, D. (2007, July). Exploring the expereince of organizational transformation: Contrasting episodic change with continuous change [Dissertation]. *Regent University.*

Norman, A. (2013). Psychological projection. In *Psychology and mental health (Salem Press encyclopedia of health)* (Online ed.). Salem Press.

O'Donoghue, T., & Rabin, M. (2000). *Choice & procrastination.* University of California, Berkeley, Department of Economics. California Digital Library. Retrieved from

http://iamdawnielwinningham.com/2017/02/procrastinati
on-killing-success/

Ogilvie, B. (1968). The unconscious fear of success. *Quest,
10*(1), 35-39.

Oksman, O. (2016, July 25). *The psychology of luck: How
superstition can help you win*. (Guardian News Media
Limited) Retrieved September 26, 2017, from The
Guardian:
https://www.theguardian.com/lifeandstyle/2016/jul/25/ps
ychology-donald-trump-win-luck-superstition

Ongari, H. (2009, January). Managing behind the scenes: A view
point on employee empowerment. *African Journal of
Business Management, 3*(1), 009-015.

Oppong, T. (2016, December 5). *Why nonconformity is a
precondition for innovation*. (Mansuetto Ventures)
Retrieved September 5, 2017, from Inc:
https://www.inc.com/thomas-oppong/why-
nonconformity-is-a-basic-precondition-for-
innovation.html

Orellana-Damacela, L., Tindale, R., & Suarez-Balcazar, Y.
(2000). The impact of self-descrepancies on people's
tendency to procrastinate. *Journal of Personality and
Social Behavior, 15*, 225-238.

Orr, L., & Orr, D. (2014). Chapter 8: Business operations. In L.
Orr, & D. Orr, *Eliminating waste in business: Run lean,
boost profitability* (pp. 263-302). New York City, New
York: Apress.

Ossola, A. (2015, March 17). *The science of luck*. (Bonnier
Corporation) Retrieved October 10, 2017, from Popular
Science: https://www.popsci.com/luck-real

Pachur, T., Hertwig, R., & Steinmann. (2012). How do people
judge risks: Availability heuristic, affect heuristic, or
both? *Journal of Experimental Psychology: Applied,
18*(3), 314-330. doi: 10.1037/a0028279.

Pajaron, T. (2012, November 15). *There's a difference between
good and bad procrastination*. (Business Insider)

Retrieved August 30, 2017, from Business Insider: http://www.businessinsider.com/could-procrastination-actually-be-good-for-your-career-2012-11

Palmer, S., & Raftery, J. (1999, June 5). Opportunity cost. *The BMJ, 318*(7197), 1551-1552.

Pandey, J., & Rastogi, R. (1979). Machiavedllianism and ingratiation. *The Journal of Social Pschology, 108*, 221-226.

Pappas, S. (2015, June 4). *Oxytocin: Facts About the 'Cuddle Hormone'*. (Purch) Retrieved September 28, 2017, from Livescience: https://www.livescience.com/42198-what-is-oxytocin.html

Passione, V. (2014, August 21). *5 trends in the post-recession economy*. (Mansuetto Ventures) Retrieved September 29, 2017, from Inc.: https://www.inc.com/vince-passione/five-trends-in-the-post-recession-economy.html

Patel, S. (2014, December 26). *How asking for help can lead to business growth*. (Forbes Media, LLC) Retrieved July 26, 2017, from Forbes: https://www.forbes.com/sites/sujanpatel/2014/12/26/how-asking-for-help-can-lead-to-business-growth/#2518b29430b3

Pater, R. (2013, October 1). *Overcoming "soft" complacency*. (1105 Media, Inc.) Retrieved October 20, 2017, from Occupational Health and Safety: https://ohsonline.com/articles/2013/10/01/overcoming-soft-complacency.aspx

Paul, A. (2012, April 25). *Why floundering is good*. (Time, Inc.) Retrieved October 4, 2017, from Time: http://ideas.time.com/2012/04/25/why-floundering-is-good/

Pech, R. (2001). Reflections: Termites, group behaviour, and the loss of innovation: Conformity rules! *Journal of Managerial Psychology, 16*(7), 559-574.

Penn, J. (2014, March 1). *What is your definition of success? How do you measure it?* (The Creative Penn) Retrieved

August 17, 2017, from The Creative Penn:
https://www.thecreativepenn.com/2014/03/01/definition-of-success/

Penney, A., Miedema, V., & Mazmanian, D. (2015, February). Intelligence and emotional disorders: Is the worrying and ruminating mind a more intelligent mind? *Personality and Individual Differe ces, 74*, 90-93. doi: 10.1016/j.paid.2014.10.005.

Pepe, J., & Cataldo, P. (2011, July-August). Manage risk, build a just culture. *Health Progress, 92*(4), 56-60.

Perry, M. (n.d.). *Fear of the unknown: How can I overcome it?* (HealthGuidance.org) Retrieved October 17, 2017, from HealthGuidance:
http://www.healthguidance.org/entry/14229/1/Fear-of-the-Unknown-How-Can-I-Overcome-It.html

Peterson, C. (2000, January). The future of optimism. *American Psychologist, 55*(1), 44-55.

Petryshyn, I. (2017). *The etymology of the words success, erfolg, and uspix [PDF document].* (Academia) Retrieved August 17, 2017, from Academia:
http://www.academia.edu/6737326/THE_ETYMOLOGY_OF_THE_WORDS_SUCCESS_ERFOLG_AND_USPIX_

Pfeffer, J. (1999, November 1). *The knowing-doing gap.* Retrieved October 31, 2017, from Stanford Graduate School of Business:
https://www.gsb.stanford.edu/insights/knowing-doing-gap

Pickard, H. (2013, October). Irrational blame. *Analysis, 73*(4), 613-626. doi:10.1093/analys/ant075.

Pink, D. (2003, June 30). *How to make your own luck.* (Mansuetto Ventures) Retrieved September 26, 2017, from Fast Company:
https://www.fastcompany.com/3000910/success-random-so-court-serendipity

Pittman, N., & Pittman, T. (1979). Effects of amount of helplessness training and internal-external locus of control on mood and performance. *Journal of Personality and Social Personality, 37*(1), 39-47.

Pomlett, M. (2016, August 16). *You're not alone: Top things people worry most about.* Retrieved September 9, 2017, from Psychological Health Care: https://www.psychologicalhealthcare.com.au/blog/youre-not-alone-top-things-people-worry-most-about/

Poon, C., Koehler, D., & Buehler, R. (2014, May). On the psychology of self-prediction: Consideration of situational barriers to intended. *Judgment and Decision Making, 9*(3), 207-225.

Pozin, I. (2014, January 22). *Should you be a perfectionist when building your business?* (Forbes Media, LLC) Retrieved September 18, 2017, from Forbes: https://www.forbes.com/sites/ilyapozin/2014/01/22/should-you-be-a-perfectionist-when-building-your-business/#139169e25e36

Praveen. (2017, April 30). *Don't try to define success.* (Medium) Retrieved July 23, 2017, from Thrive Global: https://journal.thriveglobal.com/dont-try-to-define-success-15ffd1471b9e

Premier Quantitative Consulting, Inc. (2015). *Research on undercapitalization as a contributor to business failure for women entrepreneurs.* Orlando: Premier Quantitative Consulting, Inc.

Princic, L. (n.d.). *You don't need luck, you have way more to offer.* Retrieved July 26, 2017, from Lisa Princic: https://lisaprincic.com/you-dont-need-a-luck-you-have-way-more-to-offer/

Pritchard, D., & Smith, M. (2004, April). The psychology and philosophy of luck. *New Ideas in Psychology, 22*(1), 1-28. doi: 10.1016/j.newideapsych.2004.03.001.

Procrastinate. (n.d.). (Houghton Mifflin Harcourt) Retrieved August 19, 2017, from The American Heritage

Dictionary of the English Language:
https://ahdictionary.com/word/search.html?q=procrastinat
ion

Przybylski, A., Murayama, K., DeHaan, C., & Gladwell, V.
(2013). Motivational, emotional, and behavioral
correlates of fear of missing out. *Computers in Human
Behavior, 29*, 1841-1848. doi:
10.1016/j.chb.2013.02.014.

Psychology Student #-55. (2012, June 4). *What are the
similarities and differences between conformity,
compliance, and obedience?* Retrieved August 29, 2017,
from Pavlov's Couch:
https://onpavlovscouch.wordpress.com/2012/06/04/what-
are-the-similarities-and-differences-between-conformity-
compliance-and-obedience/

Quan. (2015, May 7). *10 uncommon mental exercises to change
your bad emotional habits*. Retrieved August 24, 2017,
from The Quintessential Mind:
https://thequintessentialmind.com/10-uncommon-mental-
exercises-to-change-your-bad-emotional-habits/

Quast, L. (2012, November 26). *Overcome the 5 main reasons
people resist change*. (Forbes Media, LLC) Retrieved
October 7, 2017, from Forbes:
https://www.forbes.com/sites/lisaquast/2012/11/26/overc
ome-the-5-main-reasons-people-resist-
change/#5273ab983efd

Quy, L. (2012, December 15). *Complacency—how to avoid the
silent killer*. Retrieved October 7, 2017, from Pick the
Brain: https://www.pickthebrain.com/blog/complacency-
how-to-avoid-the-silent-killer/

Raedeke, W. (n.d.). *Awareness on the job*.
(SafetyToolboxTopics) Retrieved October 2, 2017, from
SafetyToolboxTopics:
http://safetytoolboxtopics.com/General/wally.html

Raes, F. (2010). Rumination and worry as mediators of the
relationship between self-compassion and depression and

anxiety. *Personality and Individual Differences, 48*, 757-761.

Ragins, B., & Scandura, T. (1999). Burden or blessing? Expected costs and benefits of being a mentor. *Journal of Organizational Behavior, 20*, 493-509.

Ragunathan, R., & Pham, M. (1999). All negative moods are not equal: Motivational influences of anxiety and sandess on decision making. *Organizational Behavior and Human Decision Processes, 79*(1), 56-77.

Rampell, C. (2011, November 23). *Fatalism and the American Dream.* (The New York Times Company) Retrieved October 10, 2017, from The New York Times: https://economix.blogs.nytimes.com/2011/11/23/fatalism-and-the-american-dream/

Rampton, J. (2016, June 13). *10 steps to recovering after a business failure.* (Mansuetto Ventures) Retrieved July 25, 2017, from Inc.: https://www.inc.com/john-rampton/multi-millionaire-to-broke-10-steps-to-recover-from-failure-and-achieve-greater-.html

Rao, H., Greve, H., & Davis, G. (2001, September). Fool's gold: Social proof in the initiation and abandonment of coverage by wall street analysts. *Administrative Science Quarterly, 46*(3), 502-526.

Rapp, S. (n.d.). *Why success always starts with failure.* (Adobe) Retrieved July 25, 2017, from 99u: http://99u.com/articles/7072/why-success-always-starts-with-failure

Rappaport, A. (2011, October 25). *Doing the right thing and self-interest.* (Harvard Business School publishing) Retrieved October 17, 2017, from Harvard Business Review: https://hbr.org/2011/10/doing-the-right-thing-and-self

Rayfield, C. (2011, December 15). *Employee engagement–a manager's burden?* Retrieved October 13, 2017, from Juice, Inc.: https://www.juiceinc.com/blog/show/employee-engagement-a-managers-burden

Read, K. (2016, October 20). *Getting out of your comfort zone is good for you*. Retrieved July 27, 2017, from Star Tribune: http://m.startribune.com/getting-out-of-your-comfort-zone-is-good-for-you/397509611/

Reb, J., Jayanth, N., & Ho, Z. (2015). Mindfulness at work: Antecedents and consequences of employee awareness and absent-mindedness. *Mindfulness, 6*(1), 111-122.

Reeves, R., Venator, J., & Howard, K. (2014). *The character factor: Measures and impact of drive and prudence.* Brookings Institute, Center on Children & Families at Brookings. Washington: Brookings Institute.

Reiss, S., Peterson, R., Gursky, D., & McNally, R. (1986). Anxiety sensitivity, anxiety frequency and the prediction of fearfulness. *Behaviour Research and Therapy, 24*(1), 1-8.

Reyes, S. (2017, February 22). *Fundamentals, shortcuts, and complacency*. (WordPress) Retrieved October 20, 2017, from Scott Reyes: http://www.scottreyes.com/fundamentals-shortcuts-complacency/

Rinnell, R. (2016, July 17). *Just-world hypothesis*. (Psych Central) Retrieved September 4, 2017, from Psych Central: https://psychcentral.com/encyclopedia/just-world-hypothesis/

Rionda, Z., Baird, V., Kramer, C., & Wofford, D. (2012). *What is corporate social responsibility? 8 questions and answers.* CATALYST Consortium. Washington: CATALYST Consortium.

Risen, J., & Nussbaum, A. (2013, October 4). *Sense and superstition*. (The New York Times Company) Retrieved September 17, 2017, from The New York Times: http://www.nytimes.com/2013/10/06/opinion/sunday/sense-and-superstition.html

Roach, S. (2017, August 23). *Why can't you stay in your lane?* Retrieved October 13, 2017, from Sean Roach: http://seanroach.com/why-cant-you-stay-in-your-lane/

Roberts, K. (2016, October 5). *The psychology of victim-blaming*. (Atlantic Media) Retrieved July 25, 2017, from The Atlantic: https://www.theatlantic.com/science/archive/2016/10/the-psychology-of-victim-blaming/502661/

Robinson, R. (2016, September 7). *10 reasons why perfectionism is an entrepeneur's worst enemy*. (Dotdash) Retrieved September 18, 2017, from The Balance: https://www.thebalance.com/why-perfectionism-is-an-entrepreneurs-enemy-3986767

Robinson, T. (2017, June 13). *The fear of being complacent*. (Oddysey M3edia Group) Retrieved October 9, 2017, from Oddisey: https://www.theodysseyonline.com/the-fear-of-being-complacent

Robison, J. (2010, June 9). *The business case for wellbeing*. Retrieved August 28, 2017, from Gallup: http://www.gallup.com/businessjournal/139373/business-case-wellbeing.aspx

Roese, N., & Vohs, K. (2012, December 17). *Did you know it all along?: The psychology of hindsight bias?* (Oath, Inc.) Retrieved October 11, 2017, from Huffington Post: https://www.huffingtonpost.com/neal-roese/did-you-know-it-all-along_b_1973985.html

Romm, C. (2017, March 2). *Stop worrying that you worry too much*. (New York Media LLC) Retrieved September 14, 2017, from Science of Us: http://nymag.com/scienceofus/2017/04/heres-why-worrying-can-actually-be-good-for-you.html

Rooks, G., Tazelaar, F., & Snijders, C. (2011). Gossip and reputation in business networks. *European Sociological Review, 27*(1), 90-106. doi: 10.1093/esr/jcp06.

Ropeik, D. (2011, August 29). *Why futurism has a bright future*. (The New York Times Company) Retrieved October 11, 2017, from The New York Times: https://www.nytimes.com/roomfordebate/2010/12/27/wh

y-do-we-need-to-predict-the-future/why-futurism-has-a-bright-future

Rose, R., Kumar, N., & Yen, L. (2006). The dynamics of entrepreneurs' success factors in influencing venture growth. *Journal of Asia Entrepreneurship and Sustainability, 2*(3).

Rosenfeld, J. (2017, May 22). *Psychologists have great news for people who worry a lot.* (Atlantic Media) Retrieved September 18, 2017, from Quartz: https://qz.com/988711/psychologists-have-good-news-for-people-who-worry-a-lot/

Rothbard, N. (2001). Enriching or depleting? The dynamics of engagement in work and family roles. *Administrative Science Quaterly, 46*, 655-684.

Roudledge, C. (2014, May 8). *Why we believe in a fate, sometimes.* (Sussex Publishers, LLC) Retrieved October 10, 2017, from Psychology Today: https://www.psychologytoday.com/blog/more-mortal/201405/why-we-believe-in-fate-sometimes

Rowling, J. (2008, June). *The fringe benefits of failure, and the importance of imagination [PDF document].* Retrieved October 4, 2017, from Harvard University Commencement Address: http://www.margiehartley.com/home/wp-content/uploads/file/The_Fringe_Benefits_of_Failure.pdf

Rozental, A., & Carlbring, P. (2014, September). Understanding and treating procrastination: A review of a common self-regulatory failure. *Psychology, 5*, 1488-1502. doi: 10.4236/psych.2014.513160.

Ruark, B. (2017, February). Breaking mediocrity and complacency in bureaucratic service cultures: How to close the performnce gap by transforming expectations. *Performance Improvement, 56*(2), 22-30. doi: 10.1002/pfi.21688.

Rue, L. (1987, March). Breaking the delegation barrier. *Laboratory Medicine, 18*(3), 173-175.

Ryan, L. (2016, October 19). *Ten unmistakable signs of a toxic culture*. (Forbes Media, LLC) Retrieved September 21, 2017, from Forbes: https://www.forbes.com/sites/lizryan/2016/10/19/ten-unmistakable-signs-of-a-toxic-culture/#3f92541c115f

Ryan, R., & Deci, E. (2000). Intrinsic and extrinsic motivations: Classic definitions and new directions. *Contemporary Educational Psychology, 25*, 54–67. doi: doi:10.1006/ceps.1999.1020.

Sackett, T. (2015, January 20). *Want a smooth running operation? Then stay in your lane.* (ERE MEdia) Retrieved October 2, 2017, from TLNT: https://www.tlnt.com/want-a-smooth-running-organization-then-stay-in-your-lane/

Sagar, S., & Stoeber, J. (2009). Perfectionism, fear of failure, and affective responses to success and failure: The central role of fear of experiencing shame and embarassment. *Journal of Sport and Exercise Psychlogy, 31*, 602-627.

Sagie, A., & Koslowsky, M. (2000). Chapter 6: Employee empowerment. In *Participation and empowerment in organizations* (pp. 81-98). Thousand Oaks, California: SAGE Publications.

Sagone, E., & De Caroli, M. (2014, August 22). Locus of control and beliefs about superstition and luck in adolescents: What's their relationship? *Procedia—Social and Behavioral Sciences, 140*, 318-323. doi: 10.1016/j.sbspro.2014.04.427.

Saks, A. (2006). Antecedents and consequences of employee engagement. *Journal of Managerial Psychology, 21*(7), 600-619. doi: 10.1080/02678370802393649.

Salesby, C. (1907). Chapter XXI: Worry as a matter of religions. In *Worry: The disease of teh age* (pp. 257-277). Stokes.

Saltzman, J. (2014, October 28). *Why competition is good.* (Entrepreneur Media) Retrieved October 3, 2017, from Entrepreneur: https://www.entrepreneur.com/article/239043

Sandfefer, J. (2012, May 17). *The one key trait for successful entrepreneurs: A tolerance for ambiguity.* (Forbes Media, LLC) Retrieved October 7, 2017, from Forbes: https://www.forbes.com/sites/acton/2012/05/17/the-one-key-trait-for-successful-entrepreneurs-a-tolerance-for-ambiguity/#31905dd37604

Santor, D., Messervey, D., & Kusumakar, V. (2000). Measuring peer pressure, popularity, and conformity in adolescent boys and girls: Predicting school performance, sexual attitudes, and substance abuse. *Journal of Youth and Adolescence, 29*(2), 163-182.

Sassaroli, S., & Ruggiero, G. (2005). The role of stress in the association between low self-esteem, perfectionism, and worry, and eating disorders. *International Journal of Eating Disorders, 37*(2), 135-141.

Schaufeli, W., Salanova, M., González-Roma, V., & Bakker, A. (2002). The measurement of engagement and burnout: A two sample confirmatory factor analytic approach. *Journal of Happiness Studies, 3*, 71-92.

Schlenker, B., Pontari, B., & Christopher, A. (2001). Excuses and character: Personal and social implications of excluses. *Personality and Social Psychology Review, 5*(1), 15-32.

Schlitzer, V. (n.d.). *Are men really better suited for success than women?* Retrieved August 19, 2017, from Bentley University: http://www.bentley.edu/impact/articles/are-men-really-better-suited-success-women

Schreiner, M. (2015, January 15). *Patiency and complacency.* Retrieved October 7, 2017, from Evolution Counseling: https://evolutioncounseling.com/patience-complacency/

Schulman, V. (2016, February 3). *The one skill you need: Ambiguity tolerance.* (Yale University) Retrieved October 17, 2017, from Career Network for Student Scientists and Postdocs at Yale: https://campuspress.yale.edu/cnspy/2016/02/03/the-one-skill-you-need-ambiguity-tolerance/

Schultz, D., & Schultz, S. (2009). Chapter 5: Henry Murray: Personality. In D. Schultz, & S. Schultz, *Theories of personality, ninth edition* (pp. 181-204). Boston: Wadsworth Cengage Learning.

Schuman, V., Sander, D., & Scherer, K. (2013, May). Levels of valence. *Frontiers in Psychology, 4*, 1-17.

Schuster, B., Fösterlung, F., & Weiner, B. (1989, June). Perceiving the causes of success and failure: A cross-cultural examination of attributional concepts. *Journal of Cross-Cultural Psychology, 20*(2), 191-213.

Schwartz, M. (2011, May 25). *What is a mistake?* (Sussex Publishers, LLC) Retrieved October 4, 2017, from Psychology Today: https://www.psychologytoday.com/blog/shift-mind/201105/what-is-mistake

Schwartz, T. (2012, August 1). *Our unhealthy obsession with winning.* (Harvard Business School Publishing) Retrieved September 29, 2017, from Harvard Business Review: https://hbr.org/2012/08/our-unhealthy-obsession-with-winning.html

Scott, G. (2017). *Avoiding the responsbility trap.* (American Management Association) Retrieved September 26, 2017, from American Management Association: http://www.amanet.org/training/articles/the-responsibility-trap.aspx

Scott, L. (2017). *The four major reasons for new business failure.* (Hearst Newspapers, LLC) Retrieved September 30, 2017, from Houston Chronicle: http://smallbusiness.chron.com/four-major-reasons-new-business-failure-51924.html

Seaton, J. (2017, July 12). *Millenials are attending events in droves because fear of missing out.* Retrieved September 2, 2017, from Skift: https://skift.com/2017/07/12/millennials-are-attending-events-in-droves-because-of-fear-of-missing-out/

Seaton, M., Marsh, H., & Craven, R. (2009). Earning its place as a pan-human theory: Universality of the big-fish-little-pond effect accross 41 culturally and economically diverse countries. *Jorunal of Educational Psychology, 101*(2), 403-419. doi: 10.1037/a0013838.

Seibert, S., Kraimer, M., & Crant, J. (2001, December). What do proactive people do? A longitudinal model linking proactive personality and career success. *Personnel Psychology, 54*, 845–874. doi:10.1111/j.1744-6570.2001.tb00234.x.

Selinger, E., & Frischmann, B. (2016, December 10). *Why it's dangerous to outsource our critical thinking to computers.* (Guardian News and Media Limited) Retrieved October 20, 2017, from The Guardian: https://www.theguardian.com/technology/2016/dec/10/google-facebook-critical-thinking-computers

Seltzer, L. (2015, May 15). *Anxiety and self-doubt: Perfect recipe for underachievement.* Retrieved August 28, 2017, from Psychology Today: https://www.psychologytoday.com/blog/evolution-the-self/201505/anxiety-and-self-doubt-perfect-recipe-underachievement

Serrat, O. (2010, February). Embracing failure [PDF document]. *Knowedge Soclutions, 75*, pp. 1-3.

Sexton, D., & Bowman, N. (1985). The entrepeneur: A capable executive and more. *Journal of Business Venturing, 1*(1), 129-140.

Shane, S. (2012, January 12). *Why small business failure rates are declining.* (Entrepreneur Media, Inc.) Retrieved September 29, 2017, from Entrepreneur: https://www.entrepreneur.com/article/254871

Shanmugam, M. (2015, July 25). *Dangers of the culture of obedience.* (Star Media Group Berhad) Retrieved September 2, 2017, from The Star: http://www.thestar.com.my/business/business-news/2015/07/25/dangers-of-the-culture-of-obedience/

Shepherd, D. (2003). Learning from business failure: Propositions of grief recovery for the self-employed. *The Academy of Management Review, 28*(2), 318-328.

Shepherd, D., Wiklund, J., & Haynie, J. (2009). Moving forward: Balancing the financial and emotional costs of business failure. *Journal of Business Venturing, 24*, 134-148. doi: 10.1016/j.jbusvent.2007.10.002 .

Shermer, M. (2006, April 1). *As luck would have it.* (Nature America, Inc.) Retrieved July 26, 2017, from Scientific America: https://www.scientificamerican.com/article/as-luck-would-have-it/

Shoter, E. (2014, June 21). *Sad, worthless, hopeless?* (Sussex Publishers, LLC) Retrieved October 20, 2017, from Psychology Today: https://www.psychologytoday.com/blog/how-everyone-became-depressed/201406/sad-worthless-hopeless

Silver, F. (n.d.). *The effects of lack of planning in an organization.* Retrieved October 3, 2017, from AzCentral: http://yourbusiness.azcentral.com/effects-lack-planning-organization-11394.html

Simmons, T. (2002, February). Behavioral integrity: The perceived alignment between managers' words and deeds as a research focus. *Organization Science, 13*(1), 18-35.

Single, J. (2017, April 12). *The just-world fallacy could explain some of the reactions to the United Airlines incident.* (New York Media, LLC) Retrieved September 25, 2017, from Science of Us: http://nymag.com/scienceofus/2017/04/the-just-world-fallacy-could-explain-victim-blaming.html

Sirois, F. (2014). Procrastination and stress: Exploring the role of self-compassion. *Self and Identity, 13*, 128-145. doi: 10.1080/15298868.2013.763404.

Sirois, F., & Pychyl, T. (2016). *Procrastination, health, and well-being* (1st edition, ed.). Elsevier, Academic Press.

Sisson, M. (2016, October 6). *6 reasons why mistakes are important for success.* Retrieved July 23, 2017, from

Mark's Daily Apple: http://www.marksdailyapple.com/6-reasons-why-mistakes-are-important-for-success/

Sisson, M. (2016, October 6). *6 reasons why mistakes are important for success*. Retrieved July 21, 2017, from Mark's Daily Apple: http://www.marksdailyapple.com/6-reasons-why-mistakes-are-important-for-success/

Sitkin, S. (1992). Learning through failure: The strategy of small losses. *Research in Organizational Behavior, 14*, 231-236.

Smelser, N., & Baltes, P. (2001). Automaticity of action, psychology of. In *International encyclopedia of the social & behavioral studies, first edition* (1st edition ed., pp. 991-993). Elsevier Science Ltd.

Smith, J. (2014, October 3). *This is how Americans define success*. (Business Insider, Inc.) Retrieved August 18, 2017, from Business Insider: http://www.businessinsider.com/how-americans-now-define-success-2014-10

Smith, N. (2012, May 29). *Good luck in business is hard work.* (Purch) Retrieved July 26, 2017, from Business News Daily: http://www.businessnewsdaily.com/2592-luck-role-business-success.html

Sofield, D. (2015, June 20). *Worry—The useless emotion.* Retrieved September 18, 2017, from Deb Sofield: http://debsofield.com/worry-the-useless-emotion/

Son, S. (2015, July 13). *The pittfalls of a competitive organizational culture.* Retrieved September 29, 2017, from TINYpulse: https://www.tinypulse.com/blog/sk-the-pitfalls-of-a-competitive-organizational-culture

St. John, R. [TEDx Talks]. (2013, April 5). *8 traits of successful people-Richard St. John [Video file].* Retrieved July 21, 2017, from YouTube: https://www.youtube.com/watch?v=NOl0v54DaXo&feature=youtu.be

Stöeber, J., & Joorman, J. (2001). Worry, procrastination, and perfectionism: Differentiating amount of worry,

888

pathological worry, anxiety, and depression. *Cognitive Therapy and Research, 25*(1), 49-60.

Stöeber, J., Otto, K., Pescheck, E., Becker, C., & Stoll, O. (2003, April). Perfectionism and competitive anxiety in ahtletes: DIfferentiating striving for perfection and negative reactions to imperfection. *Personality and Individual Differences, 42*(6), 959-969. doi: 959-969.

Staff Report. (1999, December 20). *Trend vs. fad is a marketing question.* (American City Business Journals) Retrieved October 19, 2017, from Buffalo Business First: https://www.bizjournals.com/buffalo/stories/1999/12/20/smallb2.html

Stahl, A. (2016, June 26). *5 key traits of successful people.* (Forbes Media, LLC) Retrieved July 21, 2017, from Forbes: https://www.forbes.com/sites/ashleystahl/2017/06/26/5-key-traits-of-the-successful-people/#e57eda93fd45

Stahl, A. (2016, April 28). *A millenial manifesto: Why Gen Y will change the world.* (Forbes Media, LLC) Retrieved October 14, 2017, from Forbes: https://www.forbes.com/sites/ashleystahl/2016/04/28/a-millennial-manifesto/#6046e75e2616

Stallard, M. (2014, January 30). *When "failure is not an option".* (FOX News Network, LLC) Retrieved September 29, 2017, from Fox Business: http://www.foxbusiness.com/features/2014/01/30/when-failure-is-not-option.html

Steel, P. (2007). The nature of procrastination: A meta-analytic and theorteical review of quintessential self-regulatory failure. *Psychological Bulletin, 133*(1), 65-94.

Steel, P. (2010, December 10). *The true meaning of procrastination.* (Sussex Publishers, LLC) Retrieved July 23, 2017, from Psychology Today: https://www.psychologytoday.com/blog/the-procrastination-equation/201012/the-true-meaning-procrastination

Steel, P. (2016, April 8). *The original myth.* (Sussex Publishers, LLC) Retrieved July 23, 2017, from Psychology Today: https://www.psychologytoday.com/blog/the-procrastination-equation/201012/the-true-meaning-procrastination

Stewart, J., & Harrison, T. (2016, Fall). Top 3 advantages of mentorship in the workplace. *Armed Forces Comptroller*, 14-16.

Stibel, J. (2014, December 10). *The science behind failure: How it actually makes you smarter.* Retrieved September 12, 2017, from LinkedIn: https://www.linkedin.com/pulse/20141210171908-461078-the-science-behind-failure-how-it-actually-makes-you-smarter

Stroebe, M., & Schut, H. (2010). The dual process model of coping with bereavement: A decade on. *Omega, 61*(4), 273-289. doi: 10.2190/OM.61.4.b.

Stultz, P., & Michels, B. (2012, May 8). *The comfort zone.* (Sussex Publishers, LLC) Retrieved October 9, 2017, from Psychology Today: https://www.psychologytoday.com/blog/the-tools/201205/the-comfort-zone

Suárez, J. (1993). *Managing fear in the workplace.* Office of the Under Secretary of the Navy, Total Quality Leadership Office. Department of the Navy.

Sudler, E. (2014). *Academic procrastination as mediated by executive functioning, perfectionism, and frustration intolerance in college students.* Jamaica, NY: St. John's University.

Sundheim, D. (2013, August 15). *Good leaders get emotional.* (Harvard Business School Publishing) Retrieved October 6, 2017, from Harvard Business Review: https://hbr.org/2013/08/good-leaders-get-emotional

Surowiecki, J. (2010, October 11). *Later.* (Condé Nast) Retrieved August 26, 2017, from The New Yorker: http://www.newyorker.com/magazine/2010/10/11/later

Sutton, R. (2010, March 27). *Blame is contagious, except when people have high self-worth.* (Sussex Publishers, LLC) Retrieved September 4, 2017, from Psychology Today: https://www.psychologytoday.com/blog/work-matters/201003/blame-is-contagious-except-when-people-have-high-self-worth

Swan, R. (2017, March 2). *Feeling stressed can make you forgetful: Long-term anxiety causes inflammation in the brain that leads to memory loss.* (Associated Newspapers Ltd) Retrieved September 14, 2017, from The Daily Mail: http://www.dailymail.co.uk/sciencetech/article-3471386/Feeling-stressed-make-forgetful-Long-term-anxiety-causes-inflammation-brain-leads-memory-loss.html

Swanson, A. (2016, April 27). *The real reasons you procrastinate—and how to stop.* Retrieved July 23, 2017, from The Washington Post: https://www.washingtonpost.com/news/wonk/wp/2016/04/27/why-you-cant-help-read-this-article-about-procrastination-instead-of-doing-your-job/?utm_term=.290e9297d9ca

Sweeny, K., & Dooley, M. (2017). The surprising upsides of worry. *Social and Personality Psychology Compass, 11*(4), 1-10. doi: 10.1111/spc3.12311.

Szalavitz, M. (2012, June 8). *Q&A: Why superstition and "magical thinking" have real benefits.* (Time, Inc.) Retrieved October 12, 2017, from Time: http://healthland.time.com/2012/06/08/qa-why-superstition-and-magical-thinking-have-real-benefits/

Szymanski, J. (2011, October 3). *Perfectionism: Healthy or hurtful?* (Harvard Business Publishing) Retrieved September 18, 2017, from Harvard Business Review: https://hbr.org/2011/10/is-perfectionism-helping-or-hu

Taber, C., & Lodge, M. (2006, July). Motivated skepticism in the evaluation of political beliefs. *Association Journal of Political Science, 50*(3), 755-769.

Taffer, J. [. (2015, April 14). *Jon Taffer: The biggest reason businesses fail—Inc. Magazine [YouTube video].* Retrieved July 25, 2017, from YouTube: https://www.youtube.com/watch?v=E3UNTyMAamo

Tang, S., Shepherd, S., & Kay, A. (2014, February). Do difficult decisions motivate belief in fate? A test in the context of the 2012 U.S. presidential election. *Psychological Science, 25*(4), 1046-1048. doi: 10.1177/0956797613519448.

Tartakovsky, M. (2011, January 20). *Why ruminating is unhealthy and how to stop.* Retrieved August 28, 2017, from Psych Central: https://psychcentral.com/blog/archives/2011/01/20/why-ruminating-is-unhealthy-and-how-to-stop/

Tauer, J., & Harackiewicz, J. (1999). Winning isn't everything: Competition, achievement orientation, and intrinsic motivation. *Journal of Experimental Social Psychology, 35*, 209-238. doi: 10.1006/jesp.1999.1383.

Taylor, K. (2010, June 11). *Psychological vs. biological altruism.* (PhilosophyTalk.org) Retrieved October 14, 2017, from Philosophy Talk: https://www.philosophytalk.org/blog/psychological-vs-biological-altruism

Tefula, M. (2014, April 28). *Student life: Combat the four Ps of procrastination.* (Telegraph Media Group Limited) Retrieved August 19, 2017, from The Telegraph: http://www.telegraph.co.uk/education/educationadvice/10788257/Student-life-combat-the-four-Ps-of-procrastination.html

Tepper, T. (2014, November 3). *Why you're better off with a hard-working child than a smart one.* (Time, Inc.) Retrieved July 21, 2017, from Money: time.com/money/3551606/hardworking-child-versus-smart/

The American Heritage Dictionary of the English Language. (n.d.). *Procrastinate.* (Houghton Mifflin Harcourt)

Retrieved August 19, 2017, from The American Heritage Dictionary of the English Language: https://ahdictionary.com/word/search.html?q=procrastinat ion

Thompson, D. (2014, August 26). *The procrastination doom loop—and how to break it*. (Atlantic Media) Retrieved July 23, 2017, from The Atlantic: https://www.theatlantic.com/business/archive/2014/08/th e-procrastination-loop-and-how-to-break-it/379142/

Thoms, P., Dose, J., & Scott, K. (2002, Fall). Relationships between accountability, job satisfaction, and trust. *Human Resource Development Quarterly, 13*(3), 307-323. doi: 10.1002/hrdq.1033.

Thorne, B. (2015, July 1). *Why you should always write down your bad ideas*. Retrieved August 29, 2017, from I Done This Blog: http://blog.idonethis.com/bad-ideas/

Tice, D., & Baumeister, R. (1999, November). Longitudinal study of procrastination, performance, stress, and health: The costs and benefits of dawdling. *Psychological Science, 8*(6), 454-458.

Time, F. (n.d.). *Advertising & compliance techniques*. (Hearst Newspapers, LLC) Retrieved September 1, 2017, from Houston Chronicle: http://smallbusiness.chron.com/advertising-compliance-techniques-34342.html

Titus, S. (2009). *Key reasons why small businesses fail [White paper]*. Institute of Independent Business, IIB-Business Support Americas. Institute of Independent Business.

Tjan, A. (2011, July 6). *Why some people have all the luck*. (Harvard Business School Publishing) Retrieved July 26, 2017, from Harvard Business Review: https://hbr.org/2011/07/why-some-people-have-all-the-l

Tognazzini, N., & Coates, D. (2014, May 1). *Blame*. (The Metaphysics Research Lab) Retrieved September 23, 2017, from The Stanford Encyclopedia of Philosophy: https://plato.stanford.edu/archives/spr2016/entries/blame/

Torres, L. (2009). Latino definitions of success: A cultural model of intercultural competence. *Hispnaic Journal of Behavioral Sciences, 31*(4), 576-593. doi: 10.1177/0739986309349186.

Tracy, J. (2013, November 7). *Psych 305A: Lecture 20: Cognitive approach wrap up [PDF document].* (University of British Columbia Department of psychology) Retrieved September 25, 2017, from UBC Emotion & Self Lab: http://ubc-emotionlab.ca/wp-content/uploads/2013/08/Lecture-20-Cognition-wrap-up-Begin-Emotions.pdf

Tracy, J., & Robbins, R. (2007). The psychological structure of pride: A tale of two facet. *Journal of Personality and Social Psychology, 92*(3), 506-525. doi: 10.1037/0022-3514.92.3.506.

Treynor, W., Gonzalez, R., & Nolen-Hoeksema, S. (2003, June). Rumination reconsidered: A psychometric analysis. *Cognitive Therapy and Research, 27*(3), 247-259.

Tugeno, A. (2007, July 7). *Why is asking for help so difficult?* (The New York Times Company) Retrieved October 5, 2017, from The New York Times: http://www.nytimes.com/2007/07/07/business/07shortcuts.html

Twenge, J. (2014, October 2). *Why so many people are stressed and depressed.* (Sussex Publishers, LLC) Retrieved September 13, 2017, from Psychology Today: https://www.psychologytoday.com/blog/our-changing-culture/201410/why-so-many-people-are-stressed-and-depressed

U.S. Bureau of Labor Statistics. (2016, April 28). *Business employment dynamics.* (Department of Labor) Retrieved September 29, 2017, from U.S. Bureau of Labor Statistics: https://www.bls.gov/bdm/entrepreneurship/entrepreneurship.htm

Ucbasaran, D., Shepherd, D., Lockett, A., & Lyon, S. (2013). Life after business failure: The process and consequences of business failure for entrepeneurs. *Journal of Management, 39*(1), 163-202. doi: 10.1177/0149206312457823.

Ucbasaran, D., Westhead, P., Wright, M., & Flores, M. (2010). The nature of entrepeneurial experience, business failure and comparative optimism. *Journal of Business Venturing, 25*, 541-555. doi: 10.1016/j.jbusvent.2009.04.001 .

ULifeline. (n.d.). *Good stress, bad stress.* (The Jed Foundation) Retrieved October 25, 2017, from ULifeline: http://www.ulifeline.org/articles/450-good-stress-bad-stress

Urban, T. (2016, February). *Inside the mind of a master procrastinator.* (TED Conferences, LLC) Retrieved July 23, 2017, from TED: https://www.ted.com/talks/tim_urban_inside_the_mind_o f_a_master_procrastinator?language=en

UT McCombs School of Business. (2013, August 18). *Obedience to authority [Video file].* Retrieved September 2, 2017, from YouTube: https://www.youtube.com/watch?v=Xw-L-ljrzbo

Vaden, R. (2012, March 19). *Is procrastination killing you and your company? Author offers proven distraction busters.* (CNBC, LLC) Retrieved August 26, 2017, from CNBC: https://www.cnbc.com/id/46750183

Valdesolo, P. (2010, October 19). *Why "magical thinking" works for some people.* (Nature America, Inc.) Retrieved July 26, 2017, from Scientific American: https://www.scientificamerican.com/article/superstitions-can-make-you/

Vallerand, R., & Verner-Filion, J. (2013). Making people's life most worth living: On the importance of passion for positive psychology. *Terapia Psicológica, 31*(1), 35-48.

Van Eerde, W. (2009). Procrastination: self-regulation in initiating aversive goals. *Applied Psychology: An International review, 49*(3), 372-389.

Varghese, S. (2009, December 30). *Harnessing the power of hte self-fulfilling prophecy.* (Forbes Media, LLC) Retrieved October 12, 2017, from Forbes: https://www.forbes.com/2009/12/30/self-fulfilling-prophecy-leadership-managing-varghese.html

Vermunt, S. (n.d.). *Success vs. Happiness: Don't be fooled into thinking they're the same.* (Entrepeneur Media, Inc.) Retrieved July 21, 2017, from Entrepeneur: https://www.entrepreneur.com/article/243605

Villareal, R. (2016, February 16). *Why personal responsibility is important for life success.* (Livestrong Foundation) Retrieved July 25, 2017, from Livestrong: http://www.livestrong.com/article/14698-accepting-personal-responsibility/

Vlaskovits, P. (2011, August 25). *Henry Ford, innovation, and that "faster horse" quote.* (Harvard Business School Publishing) Retrieved October 26, 2017, from Harvard Bussiness Review: https://hbr.org/2011/08/henry-ford-never-said-the-fast

Voigt, J. (2014, September 22). *I'll do that tomorrow: The high cost of procrastination on personal finance.* Retrieved August 26, 2017, from Nerdwallet: https://www.nerdwallet.com/blog/finance/budgeting/cost-procrastination-personal-finance/

Wakeman, C. (2010, October 12). *Why learned helplessness is the fast track to disaster.* (Forbes Media, LLC) Retrieved July 25, 2017, from Forbes: https://www.forbes.com/sites/cywakeman/2010/10/12/why-learned-helplessness-is-the-fast-track-to-disaster/#71d707801af8

Walsh, G., & Cunningham, J. (2016). Business failure and entrepreneurship: Emergence, evolution and future research. *Foundations and Trends in Entrepeneurship, 12*(3), 163-285. doi: 10.1561/0300000063.

Wand, T. (2017). Considering the culture of blame in mental health care and service delivery. *International Journal of Mental Health Nursing, 26*, 3-4. doi: 10.1111/inm.12258.

Wang, J. (2009, February 11). *Turn superstition into marketing gold.* (Entrepeneur Media, Inc.) Retrieved July 26, 2017, from Entrepeneur: https://www.entrepreneur.com/article/200024

Ward, D. (2014, January 11). *Why we help others instead of ourselves.* (Sussex Publishers, LLC) Retrieved October 14, 2017, from Psychologty Today: https://www.thebalance.com/top-principles-of-employee-empowerment-1918658

Warr, P. (1990, September). The measurement of well-being and other aspects of mental health. *Journal of Occupational and Organizational Psychology, 63*(3), 193–210. doi: 10.1111/j.2044-8325.1990.tb00521.x.

Warrell, M. (2013, March 25). *Why you procrastinate, and how to stop it. Now.* (Forbes Media, LLC) Retrieved August 28, 2017, from Forbes: https://www.forbes.com/sites/margiewarrell/2013/03/25/why-you-procrastinate-and-how-to-stop-it-now/#561fc5b41837

Watkins, E. (2008, March). Constructive and unconstructive repetitive thought. *Psychological Bulletin, 134*(2), 163-206. doi: 10.1037/0033-2909.134.2.163.

Watzlawick, P. (2010). 32. Self-fulfilling prophecies. In J. O'Brien (Ed.), *The production of reality: Essays and readings on social interaction* (pp. 392-403). Thousand Oaks, California: Pine Forge Press.

Waude, A. (2017, January 19). *Ingratiation as a persuasive strategy: How likability affects compliance.* Retrieved September 5, 2017, from Psychologist World: https://www.psychologistworld.com/behavior/compliance/strategies/ingratiation-persuasion

Webb, C. (2016, July 29). *How to beat procrastination.* (Harvard Business School Publishing) Retrieved July 23, 2017, from Harvard Business Review: https://hbr.org/2016/07/how-to-beat-procrastination

Webber, R. (2010, May 1). *Make your own luck.* (Sussex Publishers, LLC) Retrieved September 26, 2017, from Psychology Today: https://www.psychologytoday.com/articles/201005/make-your-own-luck

Wegner, D. (2009). How to think, say, or do precisely the worst thing for any occasion. *Science, 325,* 48-50. doi: 10.1126/science.1167346.

Weick, K., & Quinn, R. (1999). Organizational change and development. *Annual Reviews of Psychology, 50,* 361-386.

Werber, C. (2017, July 12). *East and West have opposing views of personal success, according to psychologists.* (Atlantic Media) Retrieved July 23, 2017, from Quartz: https://qz.com/1025291/east-and-west-have-opposite-views-of-personal-success-according-to-psychologists/

Westby, E., & Dawson, V. (1995). Creativity: Asset or burden in the classroom? *Creativity Research Journal, 8*(1), 1-10. doi: 10.1207/s15326934crj0801_1.

Wheatley, T., & Wegner, D. (2001). Automaticity of action, Psychology of. In N. Smelser, & P. Baltes (Eds.), *International encyclopedia of the social & behavioral sciences* (pp. 991-993). Elsevier Science Ltd.

White, A. (2017, May 27). *How do you define success?* (Emerson Colelge) Retrieved 21 2017, July, from HowlRound: http://howlround.com/how-do-you-define-success

White, G. (2016, March 14). *What motivates companies to do good—altriusm, or guilt?* (The Atlantic Monthly Group) Retrieved October 14, 2017, from The Atlantic: https://www.theatlantic.com/business/archive/2016/03/what-motivates-companies-to-do-good/473511/

White, M. (2017, June 21). *Defining success for yourself.* (Sussex Publishers, LLC) Retrieved July 21, 2017, from Psychology Today: https://www.psychologytoday.com/blog/maybe-its-just-me/201706/defining-success-yourself

White, R. (2010). The micromanagement disease: Symptoms, diagnosis, and cure. *Public Personnel Management, 3*(1), 71-76.

Whiteley, G. (2013). How trait and state anxiety influence athletic performance (Electronic thesis or dissertation).

Whitney, B. (n.d.). *Habits of highly successful men.* Retrieved August 17, 2017, from Askmen: http://www.askmen.com/money/successful_60/83_succes s.html

Wilkins, M. (2014, November 11). *Signs that you're a micromanager.* (Harvard Business School Publishing) Retrieved October 2, 2017, from Harvard Business Review: https://hbr.org/2014/11/signs-that-youre-a-micromanager

Wilkinson College. (2016, October 11). *America's top fears 2016.* Retrieved September 9, 2017, from Chapman University: https://blogs.chapman.edu/wilkinson/2016/10/11/america s-top-fears-2016/

Williams, C. (2015, July 8). *How important is success to you?* Retrieved July 21, 2017, from LinkedIn: https://www.linkedin.com/pulse/how-important-success-you-chloe-williams

Williams, D. (2017, September 26). *Lost your passion for work? It's your fault (and how to get out of your rut).* (Forbes Media, LLC) Retrieved October 20, 2017, from Forbes: https://www.forbes.com/sites/davidkwilliams/2016/09/26 /lost-your-passion-for-work-its-your-fault-and-how-to-get-out-of-your-rut/#8ca4caa4fb3b

Williams, R. (2016, August 9). *America's obsession with winners and losers.* (Sussex Publishers, LLC) Retrieved

September 29, 2017, from Psychology Today:
https://www.psychologytoday.com/blog/wired-success/201608/americas-obsession-winners-and-losers

Wilson, J. (2012, March 26). *Six benefits of taking personal responsibility.* (AICPA.org) Retrieved July 25, 2017, from American Insitute of Certified Public Accountants:
https://www.aicpastore.com/Content/media/PRODUCER_CONTENT/Newsletters/Articles_2012/CPA/Mar/Perso nalResponsibility.jsp

Wilson, J., & Elman, N. (1990, April). Organizational benefits of mentoring. *Academy of Management Perspectives, 4*(4), 88-94. doi: 10.5465/AME.1990.4277215.

Winterman, D. (2013, October 17). *Rumination: the danger of dwelling.* (British Broadcasting Corporation) Retrieved August 28, 2017, from BBC News:
http://www.bbc.com/news/magazine-24444431

Wiseman, R. (2003, May/June). The luck factor [PDF document]. *Skeptical Inquirer*, pp. 1-5. Retrieved from Skeptical Inquirer:
http://richardwiseman.com/resources/The_Luck_Factor.pdf

Wiseman, R. (2009, February 16). *Why some people have all the luck.* (Bennett, Coleman, & Co. Ltd.) Retrieved July 26, 2017, from Times of India:
http://timesofindia.indiatimes.com/Why-some-people-have-all-the-luck/articleshow/3896391.cms

Witt, D. (2011, April 25). *Is employee performance a shared responsibility in your organization?* Retrieved October 2, 2017, from Blanchard LeaderChat:
https://leaderchat.org/2011/04/25/is-employee-performance-a-shared-responsibility-in-your-organization/

Wohl, M., Pychyl, T., & Bennett, S. (2010). I forgive myself, now I can study: How self-forgiveness for procrastinating can reduce future procrastination. *Personality and*

Individual Differences, 48, 803-808. doi:
doi:10.1016/j.paid.2010.01.029.

Wooden, J. (2001, January). *The difference between winning and succeeding.* (TED Conferences, LLC) Retrieved August 16, 2017, from TED:
https://www.ted.com/talks/john_wooden_on_the_differen
ce_between_winning_and_success/transcript

Wright, J. (2017, February 23). *Why bad ideas are sometimes good.* (Grey Fox Business Ventures, LLC) Retrieved August 29, 2017, from Intentionally Inspirational:
http://intentionallyinspirational.com/2017/02/23/why-
bad-ideas-are-sometimes-good/

Yaeger, D. (2017, January 11). *What Nick Saban taught me about greatness and its worst nemesis: Complacency.* (Forbes Media, LLC) Retrieved October 9, 2017, from Forbes:
https://www.forbes.com/sites/donyaeger/2017/01/11/what
-nick-saban-taught-me-about-greatness-and-its-worst-
nemesis-complacency/#25ae0bd83986

Yanko, K. (2016, October 7). *How to stop making the same mistakes over and over again.* (Mansuetto <u>Venutres</u>, Inc.) Retrieved July 25, 2017, from <u>Entrepeneur</u>:
https://www.entrepreneur.com/article/236543

Yates, B. (n.d.). *The mind doesn't hear negatives...?* Retrieved August 24, 2017, from Selfgrowth.com:
http://m.selfgrowth.com/?url=http%3A%2F%2Fwww.sel
fgrowth.com%2Farticles%2Fthe_mind_doesn_t_hear_ne
gatives&utm_referrer=#2732

Yon, L. (2014, November 16). *How a punitive culture will punish you.* Retrieved September 21, 2017, from LinkedIn:
https://www.linkedin.com/pulse/20141116155230-
46662976-how-a-punitive-culture-will-punish-you

Zenger, J. (2015, July 16). *Taking responsibility is the highest mark of great leaders.* (Forbes Media, LLC) Retrieved September 26, 2017, from Forbes:

https://www.forbes.com/sites/jackzenger/2015/07/16/taking-responsibility-is-the-highest-mark-of-great-leaders/#24fb16ae48f2

Zhang, X., & Bartol, K. (2010). Linking empowering leadership and employee creativity: The influence of psycholgoical empowerment, instrinsic motivation, and creative process engagement. *Academy of Management Journal, 53*(1), 107-128.

Zur, O. (2008, October 15). Rethinking "don't blame the victim": The psychology of victimhood. *Journal of Couple Therapy, 4*(3/4), 15-36. doi: 10.1300/J036v04n03_03.

Index

A

Abbey-Vital, I., 27
accountability, 53, 76, 81, 88, 89, 140, 143
active engagement, 173, 187
Adams, S., 168
Adler, L.L. & Guelen, U.P., 113
Adriani, F. & Sonderegger, S., 52
Akhavan, P., 15
Albert, S., 43, 124
algorithm, 118, 122, 123
alignment, 82
Allen, D.M., 98
Allen, T.D., Eby, L.T., Poteet, M.L., Lentz, E., & Lima, L., 162
Altman, I., 156
ambiguity tolerance, 41, 170
ambition, 194, 195
    bad, 195
    good, 195
    lack of, 194
    unrestrained, 7
American Psychological Association, 41, 139, 172
Amodeo, J., 156
Anderson, A.R., 108
anxiety, 37, 42
    and depression, 34
    and valence, 39
    and worry, 43
    conceptualization, 37
    correlated with, 28
    damages of, 42
    definition, 40
    embracing, 198
    expectancy, 38
    generalized, 44
    living with, 40
    sensitivity, 38
    social, 57
    state, 39

    success, 25
    trait, 40
    trigger, 87
Aranda, M., 27
Artinger, F., Petersen, M., Gigurenzer, G., & Weibler, J., 120
Ashkenas, R., 60
atmospheric conditions, 36, 52, 89, 95, 111, 114, 116, 119, 122, 136, 139, 147, 161, 164, 165
authority, 55
    conscious, 176
    deference to, 60
    delegating. See delegation
    experiments on, 58
    hierarchical, 137
    obedience to, 58
    submission to, 61
    temporary, 132
    unconscious, 176
automaticity, 140, 176
awareness, 155, 176
    brand, 159
    public, 183
    self-, 190

B

Baby Boomers, 167
bad ideas, 68, 69, 70
    benefits of, 69
    fear of, 68
Baer, D., 51, 95, 144, 168
Baker, D.C., 3, 155
Baker, J. Côte, J. & Hawes, R., 40
Baker, S.L., 157, 171
Bakker, A.B., Schaufeli, W.B., Leiter, M.P., & Taris, T.W., 82
bankruptcy, 101, 106
Bardwick, J.M., 173
Barlow, D.H., 44
Barrett, L.F., 39
Barsukova, O.V., 195
Beaumont, A., 95

371

psychological safety, 82

R

Raedeke, W., 139
Ragins, B.R. & Scandura, T.A., 161
Ragunathan, R. & Pham, M.T., 39
Rampell, C., 115
Rao, H. Greve, H.R., & Davis, G.F., 173
Rappaport, A., 172
Read, K., 177
reciprocity, 56, 154
    communicative. *See* reciprocity, symbolic
    definition, 54
    instrumental, 154, 155
    symbolic, 154, 155
Reiss, Peterson, Gursky, & McNally, R.N., 38
response styles theory, 50
restoration orientation, 105
Reyes, S., 191
Risen, J.L., 125
Roach, S., 135
Robinson, J., 48
Roese, N. & Vohs, K., 119
Romm, C., 43
Rooks, G., Tazelaar, F., & Snijders, C., 79
Ropeik, D., 117
Rowling, J.K., 106
Ruark, B.E., 186
Rue, L.W., 138
rumination, 43, 48, 49, 50, 96, 168
    and depression, 50
    definition, 49
    two-factor model for, 49
    worry and, 49
Ryan & Deci, 31
Ryan, L., 77

S

Sackett, T., 132

Sagar, S.S. & Stoeber, J., 107
Sagie, A. & Koslowski, M., 132
Sagone, E. & De Caroli, M.E., 124, 127
Saks, A.M., 82
Salesby, C.W., 125
Saltzman, J., 103
Sandfeler, J., 170
Santor, D.A., Messervey, D., & Kusumakar, V., 52, 53
Sassaroli, S. & Ruggiero, G.M., 47
scarcity, 54
Schlenker, B.R., Pontari, B.A., & Christopher, A.N., 84
Schlitzer, V., 14
Schreiner, M., 185
Schulman, V., 170
Schultz, D.P. & Schultz, S.E., 107
Schuman, V., Sander, D., & Scherer, K.R., 39
Schuster, B., 8
Scott, G.G., 89
Seaton, J., 9, 57
Seibert, Kraimer, & Crant, 13
self-compassion, 33, 50
self-control, 13
self-defeating behavior, 28
self-enhancement, 136
self-fulfilling prophecy, 96, 121, 127
    definition, 121
self-handicapping, 84, 85
    form of, 85
    graphical description of, 86
self-interest, 150, 171, 172
    enlightened, 172
    parochial, 172
self-interests, 171
self-perceived burden, 153
self-reliance, 157
Selinger, E. & Frischmann, B., 188
Serrat, O., 106, 107
Shane, S., 98
Shepherd, D.A., 99, 105
Ucbasaran, D., 105
Shorter, E., 193
Silver, F., 102
Single, J., 85

Successful People Don't...

380

Made in the USA
Las Vegas, NV
17 November 2021

34651806R00216